Wind Power
and Power Politics

Routledge Studies in Science, Technology and Society

Wind Power
and Power Politics

International Perspectives

**Edited by Peter A. Strachan,
David Toke & David Lal**

Routledge
Taylor & Francis Group

LONDON AND NEW YORK

First published 2010
by Routledge
2 Park Square, Milton Park, Abingdon, Oxon OX14 4RN
52 Vanderbilt Avenue, New York, NY 10017

Routledge is an imprint of the Taylor & Francis Group, an informa business

First published in paperback 2012

Typeset in Sabon by IBT Global.

Library of Congress Cataloging-in-Publication Data
Wind power and power politics : international perspectives / edited by Peter Strachan, David Lal & David Toke.
    p. cm. — (Routledge studies in science, technology, and society ; 9)
    Includes bibliographical references and index.
    1. Wind power—Government policy—Case studies. 2. Power resources—Government policy—Case studeis. I. Strachan, Peter A. II. Lal, David. III. Toke, David.
    TJ820.W5765 2009
    333.9'2—dc22
    2008030927

ISBN13: 978-0-415-65325-1 (pbk)
ISBN13: 978-0-415-96130-1 (hbk)

For Jennie, Lewis, Alexander and Jenna

Contents

Figures

Tables

Appendices

Foreword

The global energy system is a rapidly changing environment. Twin concerns of sustainability and security are driving energy policies toward low-carbon technologies. What the characteristics of a future sustainable energy system will be is unclear, given all the unknowns and variables of achieving a sustainable future. However, we do know that transforming from one energy system to another requires all the system components to be addressed: not only economics and technology issues, but also institutional, governance, social and cultural, and planning issues. Moreover, this transformation is required urgently. The globe does not have the luxury of a slow, 'perfect' transformation—'we' have to get on with it. This is not only the responsibility of national governments—it is everyone's responsibility. Of course, to a large extent, it is the responsibility of central governments to establish environments conducive to innovation and change. They will have to implement the mechanisms and necessary institutional alterations to enable the transformation. However, individuals, academics, financiers, local government, companies, and others will all have to play a role in this move.

This volume will be of invaluable assistance to all of these groups in this task. It provides in-depth, evidence-based analysis of the issues involved in delivering wind energy, a key technology in meeting the challenge of climate change. Moreover, it does this from the perspective of many different countries. It is true that a great deal has been written about wind energy, but this volume is different in that it brings together up-to-date empirical information while at the same time trying to bring together the necessary chapters to both explain the barriers in place and to put forward concrete recommendations for change.

It is also timely given the recent publications and target announcement. For example, the IPCCs 4th Assessment Report warned of the dangers of climate change, the need for urgency in combating it, and its assessment that renewable energy will be the number one tool in mitigating it up to 2100. All countries have their aspirations. But take the European Commission: its target of 20 per cent of final energy consumption being supplied by renewable energy in 2020 is just one example of the major expectations for renewable energy. Wind energy, because of its particular characteristics—its modularity, its range of sizes, its geographic reach, and its technological maturity—is expected to be at the forefront of this revolution. While many countries have implemented sustainable and wind-energy policies, many have not. Moreover, most countries could improve the policies they have in place.

As an optimist, I have to believe that we, as a globe, can meet the challenge of climate change. This volume is a good, complementary, aid to that endeavour.

Catherine Mitchell
Professor of Energy Policy, University of Exeter

1 Assessing National Patterns of Wind Ownership

Peter A. Strachan, David Toke, and David Lal

INTRODUCTION

Renewable energy sources including biomass, wave, tidal, solar, and wind power are near the top of European agendas for sustainable development. Cowell and Strachan (2007) note that renewable energy sources—wind power in particular—have an exalted position that is owed to a combination of factors. Concerns over 'peak' oil and security of energy, the economics and market for 'green technologies', and further climate change have all fuelled demands for renewable energy to make an ever-increasing contribution to the energy mix (Meyers 2007; Strachan et al. 2006).

In setting the international policy context for this book, one of the main motivations for the interest in renewable energy is that it offers countries a way of meeting their 2010 Kyoto obligations for reducing greenhouse gas emissions. Blok (2006) also notes the prospect of even more dramatic reductions in the years and decades to come. In Europe, the interest in renewable energies started back in 1996 with the publication of the Green Paper, *Energy for the Future* (CEC 1996), and in more recent years, European Union (EU) member-states have set ambitious targets for renewable energy. The EU has committed itself to increasing the contribution of renewable energy sources from the current 6 per cent to 12 per cent by 2010 (CEC 2001). Further, on 9 March 2007, European leaders committed the EU to generating some 20 per cent of its energy from renewable sources by 2020, with wind power having an elevated position (Cowell and Strachan 2007). The interest in wind power stems from the fact that it is currently the most technically and economically feasible option for supplying clean energy, as well as providing a strong basis for more sustainable or greener growth (Strachan and Lal, 2004).

If the market and environmental concerns propelling wind power are reasonably clear, what requires further explanation is the uneven progress of wind power deployment across and beyond the member states of the EU. This unevenness makes it an interesting laboratory for public policy and social science research. Further, in attracting social conflict and heightening debate about low-carbon alternatives, wind power raises important theoretical and policy-related concerns about target setting, instrument choice or support mechanisms, social acceptability, and, consequently, environmental governance. However, rigorous cross-national and theory-building renewable energy research is still in its infancy, with this book aiming to spark a more critical investigation of the factors affecting wind-power development, and to deepen possible policy and management lessons for future study. Such factors include financing and support mechanisms, and wind power and 'the planning problem' (Cowell 2007).

The financing and support mechanisms established to support wind power are widely identified as important factors influencing wind-power deployment. The key concern here is the extent to which governments offer subsidies to foster the growth of wind power, including importantly stable and favourable systems with long-term contracts. However, much of the energy—wind power in particular—literature has often been dominated by simplistic debates of the merits of feed-in tariffs which are deemed to be responsible for the expansion of wind power in Denmark, Germany, and Spain, and criticisms of renewable portfolio standards or quota systems that are commonly used in countries such as the United Kingdom.

A number of the chapters in this book, including Breukers (Chapter 3), Agterbosch (Chapter 4) and Ó Gallachóir et al. (Chapter 6), aim to move beyond such technical descriptions of the characteristics of policy instruments and support mechanisms and their respective claimed performance, and importantly investigate how a range of important factors influence the deployment of wind power in practice. The aforementioned contributors deal with a range of important factors, including the levels of political support and institutional arrangements; the market, planning, and regulatory environment; and social conditions, including the enthusiasm of key actors (e.g., corporate electricity companies and utilities, independent entrepreneurs, cooperatives, and local communities). On this latter point, Agterbosch (Chapter 4, this volume) states:

> Not economic, but ideological arguments were decisive in the origin of the Dutch wind cooperatives. There were no national incentives in place when these organisations were set up. On the contrary, national social and institutional conditions. . . . were very much to their disadvantage. Despite these negative national conditions and despite limited organisational resources, such as finances and expertise, most cooperatives managed to implement one or a couple of wind turbines. This relative success depended on their own decisiveness and enthusiasm, combined with regional and local institutional regulatory and social conditions, such as the willingness at the side of the regional energy distributor to pay a proper compensation per kWh. Local social relations and short communication lines added to the implementation capacity of particular cooperatives.

Social resistance to wind-energy development is another factor that is widely identified as influencing deployment, leading many commentators,

such as Breukers (Chapter 3, this volume) and Warren et al. (2005), to identify the planning system as a barrier that needs to be overcome. However,
the planning process plays somewhat of a contradictory role in wind-power
deployment. It also aims to resolve public and other social resistance to wind-
power projects; balance the interests of key corporate, public, and other
stakeholder groups; and minimize adverse environmental and other impacts
where necessary. In illustrating these points, Breukers (Chapter 3, this volume) states:

> In the early nineties, it became clear that municipalities in North Rhine
> Westphalia had difficulties in planning for wind power e.g. in balanc-
> ing different interests, dealing with nature and landscape impact is-
> sues, and in aligning their plans with regional plans.

There has been significant opposition and, at times, organized resistance
in various parts of the EU. Strachan and Lal (2004), for example, outline
the position in the United Kingdom and, in particular, Scotland and identify the landscape and other sensory impacts of wind turbines, which have
resulted in significant opposition. In Scotland and England, as well as a
number of other EU member-states, such as The Netherlands and Germany,
such opposition has led both governments and the business community to
express concern about delays in the consents process and other barriers to
the realization of wind-power projects (Toke 2005). Breukers (Chapter 3,
this volume) further illustrates this point by stating: "Wind project developers in various (German) states were complaining about local permitting
procedures, which they regarded as lengthy, inconsistent and complex."

However, many of the chapters presented in this volume further reveal
that member-states have used national energy policies and institutional
planning structures to find a fairer or more acceptable distribution of locations. In some situations, central governments have funnelled national targets into preferred areas, or or left it to local government to identify the most
acceptable locations for this technology. The Netherlands and later North
Rhine–Westphalia (NRW) in Germany have adopted the former approach,
but at times have met considerable resistance in doing so. Cowell (2007)
also highlights a similarly emerging picture in the national context of Wales.
However, Agterbosch and Breukers (Chapters 3 and 4 in this volume) also
highlight a more bottom-up approach which seemed to work very effectively
in Germany during the 1970s and 1980s, at least, and in doing so, a range of
wider benefits have been realized. Breukers (Chapter 4) states that:

> In North Rhine Westphalia, early wind energy policies—and not
> planning institutions—supported a practice of locally based project
> planning. A project development approach in which part of the local
> community was involved helped to garner local social acceptance and
> prevented the early rise of local opposition against wind projects.

While recognizing the importance of these factors, the key theme of this book centres around the issue of 'wind ownership' and how we conceptualize different ownership arrangements—by individuals, cooperatives, municipalities, and corporations—and the performance (including benefits and limitations) attached to different ownership arrangements. However, it would be inappropriate, as outlined above, to attempt to discuss ownership issues without fully considering financial and support mechanisms and the planning problem, as they are intricately intertwined. Hence, our broader interest in examining the political, corporate, and social dimensions of wind-power deployment more generally.

Commentators often portray a continuum from corporate ownership through to local ownership, where an important axiom of comparative policy commentary has been that smaller-scale, community, or locally owned wind turbines or farms provide a more effective means for expansion when compared to corporate ownership. This argument has been extrapolated from the experience of countries such as Denmark and Germany, where local ownership has been a critical feature of expansion, but this raises an interesting question: How far are the policies and strategies—and the social worlds which produced widespread local ownership in Denmark and Germany—replicable elsewhere?

The opposite view of ownership is one of a corporate-led wind-power industry which dominates in countries such as the United Kingdom, Spain, and the United States of America, with large corporations providing the finance and know-how to most effectively—or so it is argued—mainstream renewable sources into the energy mix. However, the issue of local ownership schemes and other community benefits has recently become of interest to both policy-makers and corporate interests in such countries, where wind-power expansion has been slower due to a combination of siting and planning issues and social acceptability problems.

The Department of Trade and Industry (DTI) Report, *Community Benefits from Wind Power* (2005), for example, recently identified that, in the absence of local ownership, other sorts of community benefits might accelerate the deployment of wind power. The DTI (2005: 6) states that such community benefits might include community fund contributions, community compensation, pre-approval contribution, local taxes, jobs, individual investments, and cooperative investments.

While ownership does appear to be an important issue, the following question, however, does arise in countries such as Ireland, the United Kingdom, and the United States: To what extent is 'ownership' actually central to the issues of public opposition and social acceptability to wind-farm developments?

THIS BOOK'S AIMS

It is against this backdrop that the threefold principal aims of this book are made manifest. The first is concerned with investigating and documenting examples of wind-farm ownership developments in different countries, particularly European countries where there has been significant growth in wind-power generating capacity in recent years. In particular, this book presents national case studies from Germany, Ireland, The Netherlands, Spain, and the United Kingdom. We have also commissioned a further chapter—on the United States—to provide a flavour for developments beyond Europe. Linked to the question of performance highlighted earlier, we attempt to address the following question: How can you account for national variations in wind-power deployment?

The second aim of this book is concerned with conceptualizing and documenting different types of ownership structures and then assessing the importance of other associated factors including support schemes, regulatory and planning structures, social and cultural conditions, and other factors, under which wind power is deployed. These key integrating factors will run through the presentation of the national cases and, in doing so, the prevalence, political and policy consequences, and advantages and disadvantages of corporate and local ownership will be examined. During the course of this book, a further research question which we attempt to address is: What impact do governmental support schemes, planning and regulatory structures, social and cultural conditions, and other factors have on wind-power deployment?

The final aim of this book is concerned with ascertaining what, if any, community benefits arise from corporate and local ownership schemes, the impact that ownership has on the rate of wind-power deployment in these countries, and whether the level or type of benefit might make a difference in planning consents and community acceptance, which has been identified as a key stumbling block.

Having now outlined the background and aims of this book, we provide an insight into corporate and local ownership definitions and patterns before providing a summary of the book's chapters.

AN OVERVIEW OF OWNERSHIP AND ASSESSMENT OF NATIONAL PATTERNS

Strachan et al. (2006) indentify four types of corporate wind ownership around the world: (i) large utility companies and developers with a portfolio of generating capacity; (ii) independent wind farm developers; (iii) wind turbine manufacturers and companies involved in the supply of component parts, such as blades, gearboxes, and generators; and, (iv) companies providing specialist services. In Spain, the United Kingdom, and the United States the vast majority of wind farms are financed and constructed by large electricity suppliers and independent companies specializing in renewable energy. We refer to some of these companies in the country summary later in this chapter, and also in the main chapters in the book. However, it is useful to flag some interesting points. One interesting feature is the trend toward multinational concentration of wind-power ownership. In Europe, multinational links are being forged in the electricity industry. E.On, for example, has been active in buying up wind-power capacity in the United States, and also developing wind farms in the United Kingdom, although paradoxically, it owns practically no wind power in its German homebase, and even criticizes the German wind-power programme. Iberdrola, the leading Spanish electricity company (and owner of Spanish wind power), has bought up Scottish Power, which is a major British wind-power developer. Meanwhile, among the wind-generator manufacturers, Vestas based in Denmark has so far retained its position as an independent concern. It also retains its position as having the largest share of the world's wind generator manufacturing market, and is followed in importance by GE Wind (United States), Enercon (Germany), and Gamesa (Spain).

However, the existence of significant trends toward local ownership in several countries is interesting given that the electricity industry is otherwise generally dominated by corporate and multinational ownership. Local ownership, or at least ownership that is independent of major traditional or investor-owned electricity companies, is common in Germany, Denmark, Ireland and The Netherlands.

Toke (2007) notes that 'local ownership of wind power can mean several things'. Often, definitions focus on local cooperatives as the purest and most desirable form of ownership. Local wind farm cooperatives have most famously been implemented in Denmark, whereby the wind turbines are owned fully by local residents. Along with Denmark, wind-power cooperatives are also very common in Germany, and have been named 'Burgerwindparks'. The method of financing and investing in such wind-power cooperatives does vary. In Denmark, for example, wind turbines have been financed primarily from equity capital, with no or little money borrowed from banks. The German 'Burgerwindparks' follow a more standard project financing method, with banks lending a large proportion of the required capital, but shareholders and other investors also playing an important role.

Toke (2007) notes, however, that ownership which falls outside the major electricity companies might also include nonlocal and noncommercial cooperatives and farmer ownership. First, examples of nonlocal ownership can be found occasionally in the United States, but particularly in Germany, where normally higher income earners invest in wind farms and earn a good return on their investment. Further, in The Netherlands, many wind-power cooperatives can perhaps be best described as ethical investor operations, where collections of private investors might or might not necessarily be local. It is interesting to note that commercial cooperatives in Germany might also be best described as 'corporate-ownership'. Second-farmer ownership dominates in Denmark, where farmers own a limited liability company, sometimes in collaboration with other farmers. Such farmers tend to borrow the bulk of the money needed to finance the project from a financial institution.

Having briefly examined different forms of ownership, this section now outlines other wind-power development patterns in the countries which are predominantly featured in this book.[1]

United States

Although wind power has been a predominantly European phenomenon since the 1990s until now, other parts of the world, including, particularly, the United States, are catching up fast. The United States is unlikely to surpass total European deployment for some time yet, but projections indicate that it is likely to have the largest deployment of any country in simple installed capacity terms by 2015. One study estimates that capacity will be around 49,000 MWe in 2015 (http://www.renewableenergyaccess.com/rea/partner/story?id=49091). However, this will still leave it lagging behind Europe as a whole, which had this capacity installed at the start of 2007.

Most of the wind power in the United States is being manufactured by a combination of US-owned GE Wind and the Danish-owned Vestas. As described by Dennis Tänzler (Chapter 8, this volume), most of the US wind-power capacity will be deployed by large corporate bodies. The largest single developer is the FPL Group, which is owned by the Florida-based electricity utility, Florida Power and Light. Development companies are helped by the US 'production tax credit' system. This allows companies to invest in wind power so that, up to a certain point, these investments are offset against tax. However, this policy is also buttressed by the system of 'renewable portfolio standards' whereby electricity suppliers are obliged to meet targets for the expansion of renewable energy.

California blazed the trail for wind-power development in the early 1980s in what was called the 'wind rush'. However, California has been overtaken by Texas as the state with the most installed wind power. An interesting facet of US development is that Texas has become the leader in terms of installed wind-power capacity. One day, perhaps, Texas may be better known as the 'windy' state, rather than the 'oil' state. Certainly, development in Texas is performed by corporate firms. In addition to this, the Texas state government has managed to orientate its support policies to marshall some of the excellent wind resources in the United States. This is more than can be said for California, which has so far managed to lock up much of the renewables programme in an over-complicated renewable financial support system. However, not all of the developers in the United States are major corporations. Tänzler covers efforts to develop community wind farms, such as those found in Minnesota, another leading wind-power state, which, along with Iowa, is second only to Texas and Califorina in terms of quantities of installed wind capacity.

However, because of the massive size of the US electricity-generation market, 50,000 MWe of wind power will still supply only a little over 3 per cent of US electricity by 2015, while several European countries will be well ahead of this figure.

The Netherlands

Wind power in The Netherlands was generating just over 3 per cent of the national electricity demand on an annual basis by the beginning of 2007. Given the high population density of The Netherlands, the continuing expansion of wind-power capacity there deserves a good explanation. One of the factors has been the rise of independent generators. Initially, the electricity distributors led the way in deploying wind power. However, since the mid-1990s, farmers and other private investors have added the majority of the new capacity. By the middle of 2004, farmers owned around 30 per cent of capacity and a further 20 per cent was owned by other local investors. In fact, the locally owned wind farms generated well over half the electricity generated by wind power in The Netherlands (interview with Mathieu Kortenoever, PAWEX, 12 August 2004). Development has been especially strong in areas such as Flevoland and Noord Holland, where farmers have had a developmental attitude toward land that, historically speaking, has only relatively recently been recovered from the sea. Susanne Agterbosch (Chapter 4, this volume) analyses the contributions of different types of wind-farm owners in The Netherlands. She focuses in particular on the role of wind-power cooperatives, which have accounted for around 5 per cent of the wind-power capacity in The Netherlands. Regrettably, as far as The Netherlands is concerned, expansion in the crucial early period was insufficient to allow for the development of a strong Dutch wind turbine manufacturing industry. The Danish industry has done much better to become the world leaders, with Vestas having the biggest single share of the world wind turbine market. This Dutch/Danish comparison is discussed by Linda Kamp (Chapter 9, this volume).

We do not discuss Danish wind power as a separate chapter in this volume. This is largely because onshore wind-power development was halted by the ending of subsidies that was put into effect when a right-wing government was elected in 2001. Some off-shore development continues, and there is still a good prospect that the share of Danish electricity consumption provided by wind power will rise significantly above the 20 per cent that is currently being achieved in Denmark. As Kamp (Chapter 9, this volume) discusses, the pioneering trail blazed by the Danes involved grassroots enthusiasm which led to the large bulk of onshore capacity being owned by local actors.

Germany

Germany boasts the greatest wind-power capacity in Europe. By 2007, this amounted to over 20,000 MWe. Despite some predictions to the contrary, the amount of capacity is still expanding, partly because new sites are being developed in the East. The largest quantity of German wind power is installed in Lower Saxony, followed by the Eastern Lander of Brandenburg and Sachsen Ahalt. As Sylvia Breukers (Chapter 3, this volume) discusses, however, a more restrictive policy has been most recently applied in NRW where a centre–right coalition replaced the Red/Green Lander Government. Much future German wind-power development depends on repowering existing wind farms, but local regulations impede this through restrictions on the height of wind turbines. Germany's contribution so far has been impressive, considering its relatively low wind speeds compared to other countries, and, in recent years, the relatively low feed-in tariffs available for wind power under the EEG law.

By 2007, wind power in Germany was generating around 6 per cent of total electricity consumption. Much of this development hinges on the ability of the leading German wind turbine manufacturer, Enercon, to develop a close relationship between farmers and banks, whereby high levels of reliability are guaranteed by Enercon, thus enabling the projects to be financed at very low internal rates of return. The ownership of German wind farms has much in common with Denmark, where the large bulk of onshore capacity is owned by nonutility players. Nearly half of German capacity is owned by 'burgerwindparks', or local citizens—often collections of farmers. Some wind power is owned by individual farmers. Just over half of German wind power is owned by independent companies which were started off by wind enthusiasts who then formed companies to develop wind farms whose equity was provided by public share offers. This topic is discussed further by David Toke (Chapter 2, this volume).

Germany is notable for the lack of involvement by the major electricity companies in wind-power development. Indeed, big companies such as E.On and RWE have been critics of the EEG law, which offers a 'feed-in tariff' to renewable energy. One problem in the case of Germany is that the electricity companies have enjoyed a position of effective monopoly retailers in a market with a practically stagnant electricity demand since 1990. The electricity majors believe that new renewable energy, which by 2007, generated over 12 per cent of German electricity, takes income away from the coal and nuclear power stations run by the electricity majors. Nevertheless, the German government has adopted increasingly aggressive targets for renewable energy. It now aims for 27 per cent of total energy to come from renewable sources by 2020.

United Kingdom

The attitude of the electricity majors in the United Kingdom to wind-power investment is rather different from the German utilities. The large bulk of the wind-power capacity in the United Kingdom is owned by the country's six electricity majors. There are a few sites that have been developed by farmers or community-oriented groups, but the total capacity was less than

2 per cent of the wind-power capacity that was deployed by the summer of 2007. The United Kingdom is a member of the second division of countries with wind-power development, behind Germany, Spain, the United States, and Denmark, and alongside countries like France, The Netherlands, Italy, and Portugal—with Portugal picking up its speed of development and threatening to become a world leader in terms of actual percentage of electricity supplied by wind power.

The United Kingdom is widely acknowledged to have the best wind resources in Europe, but these are unlikely to be as fully exploited as other countries with lesser wind resources. Hostility from landscape protection organizations right from the start of the United Kingdom's wind-power programme have contributed to a context of generally restrictive planning practices, which the UK government and the devolved Scottish and Welsh administrations have struggled to overcome. Much of the United Kingdom's wind resources are in Scotland, and this results in another problem in exploiting the wind resources because the transmission system in Scotland is weak. Planning arguments have delayed the strengthening of the grid. Many hope that, despite the relative disappointment with the volume of onshore capacity, the United Kingdom will become the leader in offshore wind-power installations. Offshore wind power is usually less controversial than onshore wind power. As was the case in The Netherlands, the United Kingdom's own market was not developed with sufficient timeliness, size, and consistency to allow a significant wind-turbine manufacturing base in the United Kingdom.

There have been incentives for wind power since 1990 under a competitive tendering system, but this produced little capacity. However, the Labour Government launched the Renewables Obligation in 2002, which gave the electricity suppliers a target of supplying 15 per cent of UK electricity from renewables by 2015. The system has been criticized for its cost-ineffectiveness compared to the 'feed-in tariff' system used in Germany, Spain, and Denmark. However, by the summer of 2007, there were—in addition to the 2,200 MW of installed wind power—some 5,500 MW of wind power under construction or given planning consent, and a further 10,500 MW were in the planning system. A total of 2,200 MW of wind power represents around 1.6 per cent of UK electricity consumption, and if all the consented and half the proposed wind-power capacity is implemented, then wind power would be generating around 10 per cent of the UK electricity supply, perhaps by 2015, so potentially meeting two-thirds of the renewables target with wind power alone.

Spain

Like the United Kingdom, Spain has a good wind regime, but its social context for at least onshore wind power is much brighter. As in the United Kingdom, leading electricity companies, such as Iberdrola, Endesa, and Union, are leading owners of wind-power capacity, as well as Acciona, the construction conglomerate (interview with Alfonso Cana, APPA[2], 9 December 2004). There is even less community- or farmer-owned wind power in Spain than in the United Kingdom. Regional governments, which are strong in Spain, are very involved in the positive promotion of wind power and much wind power is deployed by, or at least subcontracted to, local companies.

The regional governments are responsible for planning policies. In contrast to local governments in many states, these regional governments tend to be more optimistic about wind-power construction possibilities than even the central government. Economic motives are strong here. Indeed, even the large corporations are induced to put money into localities. The bulk of Spanish wind power uses machines manufactured by the Spanish Gamesa company. This company was originally involved in the aeronautical industry, but has successfully diversified into wind power.

Valentina Dinica (Chapter 5, this volume) describes the regional focus of the planning and the financial organization of wind power in Spain. As she says, there is little opposition on landscape impact to onshore wind power, and whilst a minority of wind-farm plans attract some opposition, very few are ultimately refused planning consent. In Spain, the money tends to be in the cities or on the coast, leaving the poor, depopulated municipalities of the interior (where wind power is usually deployed) to look for the sort of taxes and royalty revenues that wind power can provide. The northwestern region, Galicia, has the most installed wind power, followed by Castilla-Leon and Castilla-La Mancha (interview with Alfonso Cana, APPA, 9 December 2004).

Onshore wind power has gone from strength to strength aided by a 'feed-in tariff' system, as well as a quickly rising demand for electricity in a country where there are few indigenous energy resources. Spain will generate around 11 per cent of its electricity consumption in 2007, and at the beginning of 2007, around 11,600 MW of wind power was installed, a figure which is rising rapidly. The Spanish government's target for wind power has been successively raised, and now stands at 20,000 MW installed by 2010. There has been much debate about how much wind power the Spanish transmission system can accommodate. Spain has limited possibilities for exporting wind power, and so there is talk of how wind farms will act more like conventional power stations in coming offline when there is insufficient electricity demand.

So far, Spain's wind farms have been placed exclusively on land. However, there are big plans for offshore schemes. These are more controversial than onshore wind farms and are attracting criticism from fishing and tourist industries.

Ireland

Ireland, like the United Kingdom, Spain, and Denmark, has an excellent wind resource, especially given that it is a thinly populated island. However, the lack of a consistent and reliable financial support mechanism, as well as weaknesses in the grid infrastructure, has led to delays in deployment often locally developed. Nevertheless, by the autumn of 2007, around 800 MW of wind power was installed which will generate an average of around 7 per cent of electricity consumption in Ireland. The wind resource is strongest on the west and near the coast. So far, the largest amount of wind-power capacity has been developed in the county Donegal.

The Irish government has set a target of generating 15 per cent of electricity from renewable energy by the year 2010, and 30 per cent by 2020. However, the government has said that this is subject to 'technical' constraints, a reference to the fact that the transmission grid needs investments to upgrade it so that it can complement the connection of wind farms in many areas. Hence, a constraint on wind development in Ireland is the rate at which infrastructural investments will be brought forward.

As Ó Gallachóir et al. (Chapter 6, this volume) discuss, the Irish government has used a suboptimal policy of competitive tendering in the past (the Alternative Energy Requirement), which has resulted in a misalignment of planning and contract issue policies and a generally uneconomic price for many wind farms. The policy has been replaced with a feed-in tariff, although the wind industry remains dissatisfied with the level of this payment. Ireland follows California, France, and the United Kingdom in abandoning a competitive tendering policy for funding wind power and renewable energy schemes.

Although Ireland has not spawned its own major wind-turbine manufacturing company, it has been the home of Airtricity, which has become one of the world's major wind-power developers. Indeed, its portfolio of the projects it operates and which are under construction is considerably larger than Irish wind-power capacity. Airtricity sold off its US interests to E.On in October 2007. One of Airtricity's forward-looking projects is to encourage the development of a marine-based European 'supergrid' that will help develop offshore wind power.

AN OVERVIEW OF THE CHAPTERS

This book has arisen as a result of international collaboration arising from three large wind-power tracks at the following conferences: (i) The 12th International Sustainable Development Research Conference in Helsinki, Finland, 2005; (ii) The 3rd European Consortium for Political Research Conference in Budapest, Hungary, 2005; and (iii) The 13th International Greening of Industry Network Conference in Cardiff, Wales, 2006. These sessions brought together a number of leading and new researchers from a range of countries in order to discuss emerging issues, and the latest thinking and practice in wind-energy policy, planning, and management practice with the aim of sparking a more critical, cross-national investigation of the key issues or factors affecting the deployment of wind power. This volume includes what the editors felt were a selection of some of the best papers from these events, plus other chapters that have been commissioned with the aim of ensuring coverage of some main wind-power programmes in the world today. Hence, our detailed focus on a range of countries, including Denmark, Ireland, Germany, the United States, The Netherlands, Spain, and the United Kingdom.

In Chapter 2, David Toke reveals that it is important to dispel, or at least criticize, wind-power myths, since otherwise they lead to faulty prescriptions for policy and actions. Chapter 2 focuses on three myths. The first is concerned with whether or not 'large' or 'small' wind turbines and wind farms are the most appropriate forms for the technology. Small turbines and small wind farms are often appropriate to particular conditions because of restrictions on land available, but there is no intrinsic benefit to turbines or wind farms being large or small. Indeed, smaller turbines are much less cost-effective. Second, he considers myths surrounding the benefits of corporate or local ownership of wind power. He argues that the answers to this depend on context. For example, the fact that wind power is dominated by corporate players in Spain has little bearing on its rate of deployment since there is relatively little opposition to schemes (or at least compared to other European countries). However, in places like Germany and the United Kingdom, local ownership has an important potential role to play in gaining community acceptance. Third, he considers myths regarding market based and feed-in tariff systems as a means of giving incentives for wind power. He argues that it is certainly the case that feed-in tariffs are more cost-effective and transparent. However, so-called 'market based' schemes are generally less effective in building up renewable capacity. The issues dealt with in this chapter are important and feature throughout the book.

In Chapter 3, Sylvia Breukers outlines that wind-power development in NRW started with grassroots initiatives, and policies from the late 1980s onward were well tailored to these initiatives. Support for wind-power implementation was mobilized from the bottom upward, through locally based project development. This precluded early opposition. Increasing implementation laid the basis for a new expanding industry, which further strengthened political backing. Wind power has become embedded in society as an environmentally acceptable energy source, a new economic sector, and a socially acceptable alternative for conventional energy generation. On the other hand, the rapid maturing of the wind sector in the course of the 1990s rendered locally based project planning less self-evident. Moreover, giving priority to wind farms in the building law in 1997 eased siting, but at a cost of garnering support at the local level. Hence, local opposition increased, but only when installed capacity had already reached impressive levels.

Susanne Agterbosch analyses in Chapter 4 the main types of wind power entrepreneurs in The Netherlands, their capacity to implement wind energy, and the social and institutional conditions that affected their investments during the last fifteen years. Wind cooperatives are one of the main types of entrepreneurs that own the total capacity installed in The Netherlands. The other entrepreneurial groups are energy distributors, small private investors, and new independent wind-power producers. Comparing wind cooperatives with small private investors and energy distributors based on the total capacity installed, Agterbosch comes to the conclusion that wind cooperatives have been of minor importance. She shows, however, that their inferior position on the market coincides with some exceptional organizational characteristics. Some interesting comparisons are made with Denmark and Germany.

In Chapter 5, Valentina Dinica reveals that Spanish wind-power development is organized almost completely by the main utilities, and that there is no farmer or cooperative ownership. This chapter maps and reveals what influenced the entrance and domination of utility companies since the early 1980s, and shows how they have managed to deliver very impressive results in the deployment of wind—Spain is one of Europe's leading players in wind power. In explaining the success of wind power in Spain, a number of important observations can be gleaned: (i) there is less concern about landscape issues than in other European countries; (ii) there is a low population density; and (iii) the taxation system ensures that the wind farms provide local municipalities with an income stream. The latter is a significant community benefit of wind power.

Brian Ó Gallachóir et al. outline in Chapter 6 that, despite having an onshore wind resource that is among the best in Europe, wind-energy deployment in Ireland has been slow until recently. The first wind farm was commissioned in 1992 with an installed capacity of 6.45 MW. By December 2005, there were 64 wind farms operational in Ireland, with a combined installed capacity of 496 MW (onshore and offshore). Ireland will require an installed wind capacity of approximately 1,100 MW by 2010 to meet the EU Renewable Energy Directive indicative target, which presents a significant challenge to policy makers and to the wind-energy industry in Ireland. This chapter also assesses the development of wind energy in Ireland since the first wind farm was commissioned, and critiques the successes and failures of wind-energy policy in addressing the social and planning barriers to increased deployment. It discusses the role played to date by Independent Power Producers and highlights the obstacles to meeting the short-term 2010 targets, and to increasing deployment beyond 2010.

In Chapter 7, Afolabi Otitoju, Peter A. Strachan, and David Toke critically evaluate the performance of the Renewables Obligation (RO)—the main incentive scheme since 2002 to be used to promote the expansion of renewable energies in the United Kingdom. They conclude that the RO has underperformed and still has a long way to go to catch up with other EU support schemes, such as the German Feed In Tariff (FIT) system, and the level of installed capacity in countries such as Spain, Germany, and Denmark. However, they add that this state of affairs cannot solely be blamed on the RO, which is certainly a lot better than having no renewable support scheme at all, and is also better in promoting renewable volume than the previous UK support mechanisms adopted prior to 2002.

Dennis Tänzler examines the role of corporate and community wind-power players in the United States in Chapter 8. He notes that the current regulatory framework is mainly aimed at the expansion of renewable energies by large companies in order to achieve major steps toward a greater energy independency of the nation and the states, respectively. He argues that while this is a positive policy objective from both a national security as well as a climate change standpoint, it is not necessarily the best way to proceed to meet the social aspects of an overall sustainable energy system. He provides the example of Minnesota to show that there is an active cooperative movement at the local level to generate renewable energies. Tänzler argues that there is a distinct requirement for a greater degree of economic involvement of the local population, and furthermore, this need should be encouraged and supported by the national and regional government, as well as regional enterprise networks. A further feature of this chapter is that Tänzler evaluates the development of policy and support instruments in the United States which have been designed to support wind-power deployment.

In Chapter 9, Linda Kamp reveals that in both The Netherlands and Denmark, policies to develop a wind-turbine industry aiming for a large wind-turbine capacity began in the 1970s. However, the outcomes of these policies were very different. In Denmark, a flourishing wind-turbine industry developed, whereas in The Netherlands, a few companies started building wind turbines in the 1980s and 1990s and today, no wind-turbine producers now exist. How can this be explained? On the basis, again, of national comparisons, she outlines a number of factors: (i) different technological choices were made; (ii) different support policies and mechanisms were chosen; and (iii) the opinion and strategic approaches of the utilities regarding wind energy in both countries was very different. This chapter is vitally important for our analysis because Kamp reveals that the growth of renewable energy technologies is likely to be more effective where governments offer long-term support for research, development, and demonstration and take steps to ensure the quality and functionality of such technologies.

CONCLUSION

When drawing up renewable strategies, the chapters presented in this book highlight a number of lessons that future-deploying countries must consider, if their ambitions to generate more sustainable energy systems are to be met. First, countries are more likely to achieve success when they establish an important place for renewable energy sources in their national energy policies, and further set demanding national targets for wind and other renewables. Related to the achievement of such demanding targets, governments must also offer appropriate subsidies to foster expansion. While this must include stable, favourable, and long-term financial arrangements, it is also clear that supportive conditions for grid connection must also be considered. Ó Gallachóir et al. (Chapter 6, this volume) further notes that resource mapping and assessment is important. Breukers, Toke, and Tänzler state that the nature of corporate and local ownership—and control of the technology—can also affect levels of social acceptance. Finally, it is important to understand how the innovation system and learning processes that support the development of renewable energy technologies operate. Kamp states that, wherever governments offer long-term support for research, development, and demonstration—and take steps to ensure the quality and functionality of renewable technologies—then those countries are more likely to succeed. Finally, it is clear that when renewable technologies lead to domestic manufacturing capacity, further economic support can be anticipated.

While it is possible to identify such pragmatic policy and management lessons, it is clear, however, that many institutional, social, and cultural gaps remain, even in countries where wind power has now a strong footing. The chapters by Toke, Breukers, Tänzler, and Ó Gallachóir et al., in particular, have identified three important gaps. The first is related to ownership and control of wind resources, and it seems clear that corporate wind ownership and the lack of community benefits in countries such as Ireland, the United Kingdom, and the United States is a stumbling block. The second is related to ensuring appropriate and secure financing and policy support mechanisms, even in some countries that have successfully employed feed-in tariffs in the past. The third is related to the ongoing problems in the planning and regulatory environments which have been well documented in this book.

NOTES

1. Statistics used in the summary of country case studies are drawn from the following sources, except where otherwise stated: Wind Power Monthly, http://www.windpower-monthly.com/, and sites of national wind-power associations, including the Budesverband Wind Energie, http://www.wind-energie.de/de/statistiken/; the British Wind Energy Association, www.bwea.com; the American Wind Energy Association, http://www.awea.org/; and the Irish Wind Energy Association, http://www.iwea.com/index.cfm/page/home.
2. APPA: Asociación de Productores de Energías Renovables.

REFERENCES

Tole, D., Breukers, S., and Wolsink, M. (2008) 'Wind power deployment outcomes: how can we account for the differences?', *Renewable and Sustainable Energy Reviews*, 12 (4):1129–1147.

Blok, K. (2006) 'Renewable energy policies in the European Union', *Energy Policy*, 34(3): 251–55

Commission of the European Communities (CEC). (1996) 'Energy for the future: renewable sources of energy (Green paper)', CM (96) 576, 20 November.

———. (2001) 'Directive 2001/77/EC of the European Parliament and of the Council of 27th September 2001 on the promotion of the electricity produced from renewable energy sources in the internal energy market', *Official Journal of the European Communities,* 27 October: L 283/33–40.

Cowell, R. (2007) 'Wind power and the 'planning problem': the experience of Wales',. *European Environment,* 17(5): 291–306.

Cowell, R. and Strachan P. A. (2007) 'Managing wind power deployment in Europe', *European Environment,* 17(5): 285–90.

Department of Trade and Industry. (2005) *Community benefits from wind power. A study of UK practice and comparison with leading European countries,* report to the Renewables Advisory Board and the DTI, 05/1322.

Meyers, N. (2007) 'Learning from wind energy policy in the EU: lessons from Denmark, Sweden and Spain', *European Environment,* 17(5): 347–62.

Strachan, P. A. and Lal, D. (2004) 'Wind energy policy, planning and management practice in the UK: hot air or a gathering storm?', *Regional Studies,* 38(5): 551–71.

Strachan, P. A., Lal. D. and von Malmborg, F. (2006) 'The evolving UK wind energy industry: critical policy and management aspects of the emerging research agenda', *European Environment,* 16(1): 1–18.

Toke, D. (2005) 'Community wind power in Europe and in the UK', *Wind Engineering,* 29(3): 301–308.

Toke, D. (2007) 'Local ownership, wind power and sustainable finance', in D. Elliott (ed.) *Sustainable Energy.* London: Palgrave.

Warren, C. R., Lumsden, C., O'Dowd, S. & Birnie, R. V. (2005) ''Green on green': public perceptions of wind power in Scotland and Ireland', *Journal of Environmental Planning and Management,* 48(6), 851–73.

2 Wind-Power Outcomes
Myths and Reality

David Toke

INTRODUCTION

This chapter is focused on what the author sees as crucial gaps between perceived, conventional wisdom regarding the factors which influence wind-power policy outcomes and the empirical evidence. The outcome of wind-power policy is defined as the type and amount, relative to a particular country, of wind power that is deployed.

The terms 'myths' and 'reality' are used advisedly. Different types of 'myths' and 'realities' will apply to pro-wind-power discourses as opposed to anti-wind-power discourses. Onshore wind power, and occasionally offshore wind power (this chapter deals mainly with onshore issues), is a controversial policy topic in the United Kingdom and various other places. Hence, the notion of 'myths' and 'reality' discussed in this chapter are related to a general disposition in favour of maximizing wind-power deployment in onshore, as well as offshore, locations. A central theme running through this chapter is the examination of the usefulness of some commonplace but challengeable beliefs about how wind-power deployment can be maximized.

This chapter draws from careful empirical and theoretical analysis by various researchers, including the author's own research, in order to expedite this objective. When the text refers to conventional wisdom, it refers not only to what seems to pass for popular beliefs, but also to key entrenched views held by important opinion streams, as represented by different discourses on wind power.

A discourse, in this context, is a vocabulary and language that is usually associated with particular interest groups. The argument makes a careful distinction here, in that it does not assume that the discourses flow from economic positions. The point to make here is that people's material interests are themselves socially constructed and open to debate, interpretation, and reinterpretation.

Therefore, it is necessary to engage in a discussion of what people usually call facts (or at least statements that may be commonly agreed on between wind-power supporters) in order to correct misinformation. This is, in turn, an interpretive exercise, since the selection of which facts one emphasises makes a big difference, as does the context in which the same facts are placed. For example, apparent 'facts' about the planning advantages of local owner-ship which are discussed in this chapter are relatively meaningless in con-texts, such as those widespread in Spain, where there is little local resistance to wind-power schemes compared to other countries. This author has dis-cussed the theoretical issues of discourse analysis elsewhere, both in theory as related to other empirical topics (Toke 2000, 2004a), and also as a theory of methodology related specifically to research into wind power (Haggett and Toke 2006). There is a range of literature on discourse approaches, with Hajer (1995) being prominent in the field of environmental policy.

Of course, if discourses cannot be explained by being reflections of, or mainly dictated by, material interests, how can we explain them? How can we explain beliefs which may, plausibly, be mistaken? One analytical approach is that of historical institutionalism (Pierson and Skocpol 2002; Hall and Taylor 1996; Thelen 1999). This approach focuses on institutions (something which is interpreted widely to include includes rules, norms, and agreements) and on how previous decisions and outcomes have influenced later events. This is the notion of 'path dependence'. Hence, there is an effort to put forward plausible historical institutionalist explanations for prevailing institutions and domi-nant discourses in different fields. In adopting this mainly social construction-ist approach, this is not meant to invalidate the usefulness of rational choice theory. Indeed, this theory has been deployed to help explain wind-power outcomes (Toke 2002). However, rational choice theory is just one of various different methodological approaches. It is most useful where one can clearly model self-interest and the choice sets that confront actors. However, if we are to explain the construction of self-interest and how it is that actors in different contexts seem to face different choice sets, we need other modes of analysis to help us explain how these different contexts emerged.

It is important to dispel, or at least criticize, myths since they other-wise lead to faulty prescriptions for policy and actions. There is a focus on three main areas of mythology: first, the debate about whether 'large' or 'small' wind turbines and wind farms are the most appropriate forms for the technology. Second, debates about the benefits of local or corporate ownership of wind power; and third, the debate about market and feed-in tariff incentives for wind power. All are important areas of debate in wind-power policy, and there will be an elaboration of their importance in the discussions in the following sections. First, let us look at the debate about whether wind power should be 'large' or 'small'.

WIND POWER—'LARGE' OR 'SMALL'

The debate about the size of wind turbines is a key element of the public policy debate. For example, the Ramblers Association (a British organi-zation) says:

> We want to see support redirected from industrial scale, land based
> wind farms (often involving wind turbines over 100 metres tall) to-
> wards smaller, community based schemes, designed to meet local gen-
> eration needs (Ramblers Association 2005).

This may echo, or at least may be *thought* to echo, the experience of Danish
wind power. Indeed, there has often been a call from a number of quarters
for smaller schemes based on the Danish experience with windmills owned
by the local people who would be supplied with the electricity. In its evidence to the Dyfi Enquiry in 1991, the Council for the Protection of Rural
England (CPRE) commented:

> Of particular importance in influencing public attitudes is the relation-
> ship between local communities and windfarming. . . . In Denmark . . .
> windfarms that are owned and used by local wind energy co-operatives
> or other local users enjoy considerable support. By contrast windfarms
> put forward by public utilities often encounter fierce opposition from
> local people who appear to regard the machines as foreign elements
> imposed upon them (Caldwell 1991: 17)

This sentiment is accurate as far as it goes, and the issue of local ownership will be discussed later. However, the point which needs to be made
now is that when people talk about small, locally owned projects, they
are indeed conflating two things, i.e., small sized and locally owned, two
concepts that are not necessarily the same things at all. Indeed, cooperative, or farmer-owned wind-power schemes are not always small, and small
schemes are not necessarily locally owned. This shall also be discussed later
in this chapter.

For the moment, the issue is size; even here, it is important not to confuse
two different issues. First, is the issue of the advantages and disadvantages
of different sizes of wind turbines, and second is the issue of small or large
wind farms. Let us look at the issue of turbine size first.

Of course, this does not mean that small wind turbines are a bad
thing—quite the contrary. There will be many circumstances where it is
not possible to construct a commercially sized wind-power scheme. At the
time of writing, there is a campaign for 'microgeneration', including rooftop wind turbines, in the United Kingdom. These could be a useful, and
also populist, way of spreading wind-power technology. However, they are
a supplement to, rather than a replacement for, commercial wind power.
Rooftop-mounted windmills of 1 Kw capacity are being sold. They avoid
the transmission and distribution losses suffered by grid-connected wind
turbines. However, such losses amount to around 9 per cent (OFGEM
2003: 16), whereas these small turbines will produce less than half the
output per installed kilowatt of capacity compared to commercially sized
wind turbines in the United Kingdom. The small machines will also cost

more per kilowatt in capital costs, especially including installation costs. In short, the annualized power costs would be considerably more than twice as expensive as commercial wind turbines. If 10 per cent of British houses had 1-Kw machines, they would generate around 0.5 per cent of UK electricity (this figure is based on my own calculations given known capacity factors).

SIZE OF WIND FARMS

This section discusses commercially sized schemes; that is, more than the approximately 15-Kw size that can be fitted on to a tower of no more than 12 m or so in height. The issue of which size of wind farm may be most likely to gain planning acceptance is the source of much confusion. It is easy to read off Danish experience in the 1980s and 1990s and conclude that small schemes are less likely to be rejected on planning grounds. Electricity utilities often encountered stiff planning opposition when they proposed what were usually relatively large wind farms, whilst locally owned schemes tended to be more popular with the planning authorities. Danish experience seems to have gone down in wind turbine folklore as some sort of bible among environmental activists. Yet, people are interpreting the record selectively. It happens to be that the cooperative or farmer-owned schemes were small compared to utility schemes. Indeed, Danish farmers were limited by law to owning one machine each.

However, various opinion surveys, cited in particular by Devine-Wright (2000), AIM A/S (1993), Lee (1989), and Wolsink (1989), suggest that the public prefers small wind-power schemes to large wind farms. There is no need to doubt the accuracy of the opinion surveys, but it may be useful to question whether they are necessarily particularly relevant to individual planning cases. The point here is that the opinion surveys report general public attitudes toward the issue of size—they do not survey actual planning outcomes, and distinguish even less between schemes according to whether they are locally owned. It is necessary to point to both empirical evidence and theoretical arguments which suggest that the issue is at least rather more complex than the interpretations drawn from the opinion research. First, the empirical evidence from my own survey of fifty-one British planning cases reveals no correlation between the size of a proposed wind farm and its chances of obtaining planning consent (Toke 2005a). There is no reason to believe that the sample in this study was unrepresentative. It may be significant that, in the United Kingdom, there are practically no locally inspired and locally owned schemes which may tend, on the European continent, to give many smaller schemes a planning advantage.

The more one examines the attributes of particular schemes, the more the dangers become apparent of trying to generalize theories of the planning acceptability of different-sized schemes. There are various factors which may confound the 'small is more acceptable' rule drawn from the opinion surveys. The issue of whether the schemes are locally or remotely owned has already been discussed. There are various other factors. For example, smaller wind farms often may be sited, by their nature, in relatively densely populated areas where there is insufficient room for a larger wind farm. Hence, they may attract the wrath of a number of aggrieved local residents, although this will depend on whether the area is seen as industrial in nature. Even semi-urban areas may be valued for their landscape features. On the other hand, many larger wind farms may be situated in less densely populated areas, and hence incur the anger of a relatively smaller number of local residents. In addition, larger wind farms have more money to give to local people and local causes, which can be effective in defusing planning opposition. This will be discussed more later.

There is a more fundamental point, and one that forms a key theoretical criticism of behaviouralist studies, which is that opinion surveys do not represent the actual conditions under which decisions are made. In addition, people may say one thing in opinion surveys, yet do another in their actual behaviour (Wahlke 1979; Somit and Peterson 1998). A development of this point is that local authority planning decision procedures do not mirror the contours of general opinion research surveys. Indeed, there is no particular reason why they should, since the planning process is supposed to enable different interest groups to engage in a public debate on specific proposals. That is, it is the people who perceive themselves to be affected the most by a particular proposal who tend to have the most influence.

There is certainly a resonance among green activists of the slogan 'small is beautiful'. This is the title of a seminal work by Schumacher (1973). This may encourage many greens who are influenced by Schumacher and who are natural supporters of wind power to assume that, in the case of wind farms, small must be more acceptable to local people. However, Schumacher never said anything about the optimum size of commercial wind farms. He may well have liked the idea of rooftop mini-wind turbines given his strictures about becoming more self-sufficient in the use of resources. On the other hand, his main focus was to make work more of a satisfying end in itself, in addition to arguing for the decentralization of large organizations. He was certainly very opposed to nuclear power. However, while we can see how green activists might see smallness in wind farms as resonating with Schumacher's discourse, the resonance is not as strong as one might think on a superficial level.

If we are generally supportive of wind power because it reduces reliance on fossil fuels and nuclear power, and because it combats air pollution (including increases in carbon dioxide emissions), then we should decide whether small or large wind farms are appropriate according to practical criteria. Size should not be an independent consideration. Of course, there will be many circumstances where smaller schemes are desirable, and it is important to realize that when it comes to commercial wind farms, small is not necessarily stupid at all, as Beckerman (1995) insisted in his bluntly labelled riposte to Schumacher. In many cases, there will be only enough room for a small wind farm. It may frequently be the case that grid connection costs may be proportionately lower for a smaller wind farm. Indeed, in relatively built up areas, there are unlikely, in normal circumstances, to be excessive grid connection charges for projects of, say, 2 MW and above. This is because smaller wind farms will be able to tap into relatively lower voltage distribution lines, while the larger wind farms may require access to higher voltage lines, or lines that require reinforcement because of the extra power load from a larger wind farm. Given that the discount on ordering large numbers of wind turbines as opposed to one or two is not particularly great, the economics of smaller commercial projects are quite favourable compared to bigger projects.

Of course, bigger projects may be able to obtain access to higher wind speeds on remote hillsides (e.g., the Scottish Highlands), although the grid connection charges for such projects are often also quite high. Offshore wind-power schemes can be built to very large sizes, but their grid connection costs are often a much higher proportion of capital costs than the bulk of onshore schemes. This is a painful truth for the British government, which is currently involved in an effort to persuade the National Grid Company to shoulder the costs of connecting Round 2 offshore wind-power schemes to the grid. High grid connection costs are also a serious problem bedevilling efforts to move forward on the German offshore wind-power programme (interview with wind consultant Wolfgang Paulsen, 18 July 2005).

The point that is being made here is that abstract prejudices about the size of wind-power schemes should not be allowed to obstruct the practical implementation of renewable energy projects. We need to adopt the schemes that are best suited to different conditions. This will produce wind-power schemes of lots of different shapes and sizes.

LOCAL AND REMOTE OWNERSHIP

The countries studied below (in Figure 2.1) for patterns of wind-farm ownership gained the following percentages of national electricity supplied from wind power at the end of 2006: Spain (11 per cent), Germany (6 per cent), Denmark (20 per cent), The Netherlands (3 per cent), England and Wales (0.5 per cent), and Scotland (8 per cent). The ownership patterns in Figure 2.1 are given using 2004 data, but it is unlikely that there were significant changes between 2004 and 2006.

In Figure 2.1, the ownership categories are divided into corporate, farmers, and cooperatives. In fact, the term 'corporate' can mean various things. It can mean traditional utilities, independent power producers, and other hybrids. The term 'cooperative' is used to include schemes that are participative in nature and either local or run for nonprofit 'ethical

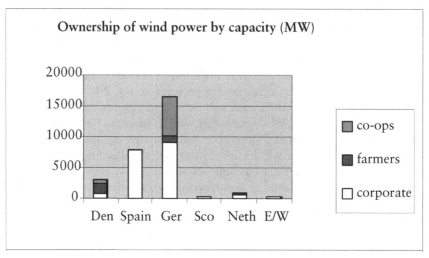

Figure 2.1   Ownership of wind power in selected European countries, 2004. Source: Toke, Wolsink, and Breukers 2008.

Note: the Danish statistics include offshore wind installations constituting around 14 per cent of installed capacity, most of which is owned by (corporate) utilities. Danish onshore wind power owned by the corporate sector constitutes 12 per cent of all wind power capacity.

investment' purposes. In Denmark and Germany, the cooperatives are, indeed, local, although in The Netherlands, living in the locality is not always a precondition for being able to invest in the company. Indeed, if a slightly different definition of cooperative was used to mean that the bulk of the equity was sold through public share offers, then it could be possible to call most wind-power capacity in Germany 'cooperative'. This is because companies known as *kommandistengedellschaften* have built around half of the wind-power capacity in Germany. These companies have been financed by public share offers to high income earners, although most recently, poor wind years, declining subsidy levels, and changes in tax systems have stilted their operations. In Germany, the tax rules allow people to offset their taxes against investments. Much of the rest of German wind power is owned either by local farmers, or *'Bürgerwindparks'* ('Citizens' wind farms') The 'citizens wind farms' are owned by local people on average incomes who, in fact, have no greater tax offset advantages compared to average British citizens.

Experience in Denmark certainly suggests that local ownership has planning advantages. A report from the Danish Ministry of Energy and Environment said:

> The local environmental disadvantages of wind power can lead to a lack of public acceptance of wind farms. Local ownership of wind

turbines (local farmers, co-operatives or companies) can ensure local acceptance of projects. In particular, co-operatives spreading owner-ship of a wind turbine between families in the vicinity of the wind turbine has been stimulated. . . . During the 1980s and early 1990s most new turbines were installed by co-operatives. Since the mid 1990s it is primarily farmers who have installed individually owned wind turbines' (Andersen 1998: 7)

In regard to the last sentence, it should be noted in that farmer ownership is much more prevalent than cooperative ownership in Denmark, as well as in other countries where there is an abundance of local ownership. The coop-eratives have played an important political role, but it is the farmers who have built up the capacity. Research also backs up the argument that local ownership has planning advantages, at least in the instance of schemes that are locally inspired. A thorough piece of research by Loring (2004) inves-tigated the detail of many cases in Denmark and the United Kingdom and concluded that active local networks promoting wind-power developments were associated with planning acceptance. Of course, the frequent position is that there are active local networks opposing wind-power developments. The point is that active, positive local networks can have an opposite effect and say, 'Yes in My Back Yard'. These active, positive local networks are associated in particular with farmers who are investing their own money in the schemes. It is plausible to assume that this self-interest drives local farmer–owners to put a great deal of effort into mobilizing their own con-tacts, or social capital, in support of the wind-power proposal. Farmers' roles are usually passive in the United Kindom. They will receive royalties if the schemes go ahead, but they will usually do little to promote the scheme at the planning stage. There are just a few notable exceptions to this trend, a couple of which have been discussed previously.

Of course, there are also cooperatives that are being organized by non-local actors, even though the intention is that preference will be given to local investors. This is the case in The Netherlands, where there is an active cooperative wind-power movement. Such efforts are to be lauded, although it is arguable whether they can mobilize local networks in the same ways as local farmers and, hence, achieve the same planning advantages. In The Netherlands, it is farmers in Nord Holland and Flavoland that have been largely responsible for the increase in capacity in recent years. In the United Kingdom, there are a small number of planned or actual cooperative projects. For example, there are plans to install a cooperative scheme at Awel Aman Tawe (Awel 2005). Another British cooperative—at Watchmill (Westmill Windfarm 2005)—has been inspired by a local farmer, Adam Twine, who is organizing a public share sale through Energy4All, an offshoot of the Baywind Energy Cooperative. Energy4All is cooperating with mainstream wind-power developers, Falck Renewables (Scotland) and Wind Prospect (Eastern England), to sell some of the equity to local people. Three farmers at Moel Maelogen in Wales have developed a 15-MW project which they own, although they are offering possibilities to the public to invest in the project in collaboration with the Triodos Bank. I mention these projects in the United Kingdom to demonstrate that there are possibilities for local ownership there. It also should be mentioned that locally owned (community-owned) wind-power schemes are *not* necessarily small. At the time of writing, two different schemes were reported to me for locally owned German schemes of each around 40–50 MW (interviews with wind power consultant Hans Detlef Feddersen, 2 September 2004; Henning Holst wind power consultant, personal communication, 27 May 205).

Henning Holst, a wind-power consultant who is active in Schleswig Holstein, commented:

> What happened after the EFL (Electricity Feed Law which subsidies wind power) is that many individuals have invested in local wind power schemes. These people have become 'energy experts', so people are much more aware about wind energy. Now everybody is aware that electricity doesn't just come out of a plug. Because there are thousands of investors in wind energy there is a strong lobby for good conditions for wind energy in the future. (Interview with Henning Holst 18/7/1999)

By contrast, there is no known, locally owned project in Spain. Wind-power development in Spain has been left totally up to the main electricity companies and energy agencies. However, it is doubtful whether this matters very much in planning terms. This is because there is, in comparison to other parts of Western Europe, much lower local opposition to wind-power proposals. Possible explanations for this include the low density of population in Spanish rural areas, and also the lower apparent value (relative to other countries) accorded to landscape factors. Certainly the socioeconomic profile of much of the Spanish countryside is one of depopulation and poverty among the farmers. There are fewer conflicts of land uses compared to, say, the United Kingdom. There are no landscape protection organizations active in Spain, in contrast to the United Kingdom. In Spain, the money tends to be in the cities and on the coast, not in the countryside. Interestingly, offshore wind farms seem to be more controversial in Spain compared to onshore wind farms, whilst the reverse is generally the case in the United Kingdom (Dinica 2003; interview with Alfonso Cano, APPA, 9 December 2004; interview with Gonzalo Saenz de Miera, Iberdrola Electricity Company, 9 December 2004; interview with Enrique Monasterio and Javier Marques, Basque Energy Agency, 10 December 2004).

Wind-power ownership in the United Kingdom and Spain has much in common, in that the large bulk of the wind-power capacity is owned by vertically integrated electricity majors, like Iberdrola and Endesa in Spain, and PowerGen (E.On) and Npower (R.W.E.) in the United Kingdom. In the United Kingdom, a significant share of wind-farm development is done by 'independent' companies, although these developers tend to be backed by major industrial corporations. The Spanish and the British electricity majors favour renewable development. The Spanish corporations are especially keen about wind power, partly because of the lack of indigenous Spanish fuel resources, and also because of the need to meet the rapid rate of expansion of Spanish electricity demand.

It is interesting to note that in Germany, RWE and E.On own very few wind farms and, indeed, are highly critical of the German renewable energy programme. Yet, these same companies have bought PowerGen and Npower (a large part of the British electricity industry), who are leading owners and developers of wind power in the United Kingdom. However, these companies have different interests in Germany and the United Kingdom. Not only has electricity demand in Germany been stagnant since 1990, but the German utilities are also keen to defend their 'sunk' investments in coal and nuclear power rather than lose income to renewable energy generators. In addition, the German electricity industry is still rather monopolistic compared to the United Kingdom, where there is a much greater emphasis on competing to seize new market opportunities.

However, we still have to explain how it is that local ownership is much stronger in some places than others. The notion of path dependence can help us here. In Denmark, Germany, and The Netherlands there was a strong, active, antinuclear movement in the 1970s and 1980s. This involved both mass antinuclear demonstrations and local energy activism, which focused on the development of alternative energy. Indeed, in the 1990s, many antinuclear activists in these countries became active at the grassroots level, promoting wind power and knowledge about the technology. In Germany, Denmark, and The Netherlands, a tradition of locally, populist-based energy activism connected to the antinuclear movement sprung up in the 1970s and 1980s (Jamison et al. 1990: 156–61). In Germany, the local activism was originally largely associated with the 'citizen's initiative' movement, a movement which became closely associated with the antinuclear movement (Markovits and Gorski 1993: 102–04). The Danish antinuclear movement was also very strong, and this spawned the highly populist, mass-based renewable energy movement called the Organisation for Renewable Energy (OVE) (Jamison et al. 1990: 95–109). The bulk of the Danish wind-power movement sprang from the OVE.

The British and Spanish antinuclear movements were much weaker, and there was little in the way of mass antinuclear protests. In Spain, environmental groups hardly existed as the country emerged from the Franco dictatorship, and there is even less of a tradition of energy activism there than in the United Kingdom. Even in the UK, the numbers of local wind-power activists have been small, and most wind-power activity in the United Kingdom is bound up in highly professionalized wind-power development companies and energy consultants (Toke 2004b).

It needs to be said, however, that local ownership is by no means the only way of involving local people. Giving local people or local government income generated by the project can also have important effects, and turn around indifference or hostility toward a project into support. In Spain, local people benefit in two ways. First, through payments to the landowners, which is usually the municipality itself; and secondly, through payments of taxes. Such payments can make a big difference to the balance sheets of what are small municipalities in the isolated Spanish countryside (interview with Alfonso Cano, APPA, 9 December 2004). In the United Kindom, royalties will go to landowners, who are usually farmers. As discussed earlier, British farmers invariably act merely as passive recipients in contrast to situations where they invest their own money in the projects. Tax receipts go to the government, not the local parish. However, in the case of the wind farm planned on the Isle of Lewis in western Scotland, the prospect of around £7 million a year in various streams of income to local people appears to have swung the local council around to support the project in the face of a very strong anti-wind farm campaign (Ross and Collins 2005).

WIND-POWER PROCUREMENT SCHEMES— FEED IN TARIFFS AND TRADEABLE GREEN ELECTRICITY CERTIFICATES

Another area where there may be a gap between myth and reality occurs in the debate between advocates of financial support systems for wind power who favour 'market-based' systems and those who favour paying 'fixed prices' for the electricity from wind-power schemes. Advocates of market-based schemes have, in recent years, usually talked about the benefits of systems involving so-called 'tradable green electricity certificates'. The idea behind this is that electricity suppliers are given requirements (portfolios or, under the British system, a renewable obligation) to supply a certain portion of electricity supplies from renewable energy sources by certain dates, and they are subjected to financial penalties if they fail to do so. They signify their fulfilment of their renewable obligation by purchase of green electricity certificates, which are awarded originally to renewable electricity generators in proportion with the amount of renewable electricity they produce. The idea of tradable green electricity certificates is generally also associated with support for the creation of a harmonized pan-European market for such certificates (Eurelectric Working Group Renewables and Distributed Generation 2004; Voogt et al. 2001). This type of thought has been described as being 'neoliberal' (Lauber 2004; Toke and Lauber, 2007). Its advocates claim that the system will lead to the cost-effective deployment of renewable electricity through market means. This neoliberal type of thinking has been welded onto notions of economic globalization, which give primacy to a perceived need to reduce barriers to multinational investment in order to increase economic efficiency.

On the other hand, the large bulk of European wind-power capacity has been developed using so-called 'renewable energy feed-in tariff' (REFIT) systems. These systems involve paying fixed prices for renewable electricity production. These prices are paid to generators of renewable electricity. The prices are set by the government or by law. The payments are guaranteed in excess of ten years, and twenty years in the case of Germany. Germany, Denmark, and Spain have used REFIT systems. Advocates of the REFIT model point out that the system has delivered considerable capacity in these countries. Indeed, the majority of the wind-power capacity existing in the world in 2005 was installed under REFIT regimes. It is claimed that this system will be more cost-effective than market-based systems, and also that the system delivers security to renewable generators that allows smaller renewable developers to be given sufficient financial confidence to develop projects (Hvelplund 2001).

We can make some comparisons between the 'market-based' and 'fixed-price' systems by comparing the biggest fully operational market based system, the British Renewables Obligation (RO) with the German REFIT. The British RO has only been running since April 2002, but at least in terms of renewable energy schemes being brought into the planning process, it seems to be having considerable success. By the spring of 2005, around 4 GW of (onshore and offshore) wind-power capacity had been given planning consent in the United Kingdom, and a further 6.6 GW was in the planning system (Hill 2005). Together, this would represent over 8 per cent of UK electricity consumption. Added to other new renewable energy sources (biomass and small hydro), this would provide the bulk of the United Kingdom's 2015 target of providing 15 per cent of UK electricity from wind power. The 2010 target for renewable electricity is 10.4 per cent of UK electricity supply.

Electricity suppliers must acquire 'renewable obligation certificates' (ROCs), from the renewable generators who earn the certificates. If the electricity suppliers fail to produce enough ROCs to meet their obligations, electricity suppliers have to pay a (inflation index-linked) penalty of 3p/KWh, or £30/MWh (2002 prices). This penalty is then recycled as a bonus in respect of each ROC. The addition of the recycled element means that the price of ROCs will be high if a low proportion of the target is being met, and relatively lower if more renewable electricity is being produced.

The system is supposed to produce competition, but in reality this has not happened. Indeed, there are theoretical reasons why this cannot happen due to the market structure. The electricity supply industry is dominated more or less completely by just six suppliers. They have a vested interest in ensuring that the price of ROCs does not crash, because that would jeopardize their own investments in renewable energy and undermine the contracts they have already issued for renewable electricity. Renewable generators normally want secure contracts. If this is the case, they will depend on the electricity suppliers to give them long-term contracts, in return for which the suppliers will take a big cut of the incentives. The incentives include the income for the ROCs, the baseload price, and exemption from the tax on electricity consumption. Fifteen-year supply contracts paying £50/MWh for renewable electricity are available (Toke 2005b). In fact, the RO has only been around 60 per cent fulfilled at the time of writing. (The target escalates upwards each year.) In addition, baseload electricity prices have been very high, meaning that developers are receiving such high returns (£70/MWh at the end of 2004) that they can afford to run on annual contracts for electricity suppliers. This means that the renewable operators can take most of the value of the incentives.

As a result, the RO is not very cost-effective compared with the German REFIT system. This system gives the equivalent of around £55/MWh for 20 years. However, if we compare the actual returns to wind-power developers, we can see that the returns to German wind-power operators are a lot lower than the British operators. This is because in Germany, the average wind energy captured by wind turbines is a lot lower because of lower ambient wind speeds. Indeed, whereas German wind-power plants operate with an average capacity factor of about 18 per cent, in the United Kingdom, the figure is more like 28 per cent (Toke 2005b; Lauber and Toke 2005). This means that even if you assume that British wind-power operators are only receiving £50/MWh, then the British operators are receiving returns that are around 30 per cent higher than their German counterparts. In fact, the gap, at time of writing, is rather bigger than 30 per cent because in practice (as is discussed earlier), British renewable generators are usually earning a lot more than £50/MWh.

Hence, we can say that as far as the experience of the British RO goes, it cannot be said that tradable green certificate schemes are more cost-effective compared to REFIT systems. Eurelectric (2004) may say that REFIT systems produce 'windfall' profits for the developers, but the comparison with the British RO does not bear this out. The tradable green electricity certificate scheme in Texas has been associated with low prices for wind power, but then the Texan target was a small one, the available wind speeds were high, and the system only worked as well as it did because of the federal subsidy in the shape of the production tax credit (Langiss and Wiser 2003). Hence, the alleged cost-effectiveness of 'market-based' schemes may be a myth.

The only sort of market-based scheme that has achieved low-cost results for renewable energy has been competitive bidding systems, such as those used in California, in the United Kingdom under the Renewable 'Non-Fossil Fuel Obligation' (Mitchell 2000), and then in Ireland (O'Gallachoir and McKeogh 2005). These systems involve prospective developers competing to submit the lowest bids, expressed in prices per kilowatt-hour, to be paid for supplying renewable electricity. Unfortunately, these systems have all, in varying degrees, been associated with dramatic underachievement of renewable energy targets. There is a tendency under such systems for prospective developers to make speculative bids which, in a high proportion of cases, prove to be uneconomic in practice. Interestingly, the UK electricity regulators, OFGEM, proposed such a system when the UK government considered reforms to the RO at the end of 2006. However, the priorities of OFGEM are concerned with reducing prices to the electricity consumer and not maximising volumes of renewable energy deployment. The Irish, of course, have most recently adopted a feed-in tariff system.

On the other hand, the notion that market-based schemes only co-exist with multinational capital rather than local owners may also be something of a myth. Spain, for example, which has a REFIT system, has a wind-power market which is dominated by the major electricity utilities. Local ownership is unheard of. In The Netherlands, there was, in the 1996–2002 period, a system of tradable green electricity certificates. However, this coincided with an upsurge in farmer ownership. The market liberalization that (coincidentally) took place actually seems to have benefited the farmer-owned sector. Farmers gained access to more than one supplier in their search for good contracts to supply electricity. The end of the supplier monopoly increased the farmers' bargaining position and allowed them to form an effective lobby for good terms from electricity suppliers (Breukers and Wolsink 2003).

There seems to be no financial or technical constraint preventing farmers or cooperatives from starting up wind-power schemes under the British RO. There was some problem with obtaining contracts to supply electricity at the start of the RO, but this situation changed after the British government confirmed, in December 2003, that 15.4 per cent of electricity should be gained from from renewable sources by 2015. There are a small number of cooperatives and farmers who are putting together project, and they seem to be enjoying good financial terms (Toke 2005c). The fact that there are not as many farmers in the United Kingdom compared to Germany, The Netherlands, and Denmark acting as developers seems to have little to do with financial or industrial structures, and a lot more to do with differences in culture (Toke 2004b). In particular, the lack of a cadre of local energy activists compared to some continental European countries, as dicussed earlier, has produced a path-dependent outcome, where the British wind-power industry is dominated by corporate developers.

In fact, the biggest financial problems in the United Kingdom have been faced by the companies who wished to develop offshore wind farms. These projects are more expensive than the onshore wind farms, which can be financed through the 15-year, £50/MWh contracts that were mentioned earlier. The major electricity suppliers have taken on the role of funding the schemes using their access to the full value of the ROC values. Progress has been slowed by financial issues. However, the United Kingdom's relatively greater experience with offshore energy developments may have meant faster progress compared to the German offshore wind-power programme. In Germany, and also in Denmark, multinational companies are not the only actors. In Germany, the Butendiek offshore wind-power scheme, for example, consists of a projected 240-MW scheme that would be owned by a cooperative investment venture.

Half of onshore investment in wind power is, in the case of Denmark, The Netherlands, and Germany combined, local in character. It is tied to local actors, mainly farmers. From this, it is possible to see that, if there was a harmonized European Union (EU) system of financing renewable energy (whether through a feed-in tariff or a tradable green certificate scheme), a lot of the investment might be lost because local actors in the less windy parts of Europe (especially Germany) would probably not put forward schemes if incentives were seriously reduced. Since their interest is usually in investing in a local project, it seems that many would not look for a scheme somewhere else.

Many projects on lower wind-power sites that are being exploited would not be replaced by alternative investment in higher wind-speed sites. There may be an abundance of potential, multinationally based investments for wind power. However, this would not help if there were less schemes being put forward. We would end up with significantly less capacity deployed compared to the present arrangement of nationally based financial support systems for renewable energy. Del Rio (2005) has suggested that a harmonized, tradable green electricity scheme in the EU might involve disadvantages to local communities.

Paradoxically, the neoliberal globalizers that favour harmonized EU-wide incentives schemes seem to be at odds with one of the original neo-classical icons, Ricardo. He was the early nineteenth-century author of the theory of comparative trade advantage. He noted the importance of local investment, commenting how 'feelings, which I would be sorry to see weakened, induce most men of property to be satisfied with a low rate of profits in their own country, rather than seek a more advantageous employment for their wealth in foreign nations' (Ricardo 1971).

CONCLUSION

The most central conclusion of this analysis is that, assuming that one is in favour of acheiving a rapid deployment of wind power, we should abandon ideological preconceptions about the size, type of ownership, and type of financial support system. Instead, we should focus on what seems to work in practice. The problems associated with deployment of wind power are too great to start making it conditional on a range of other criteria established because they conform to traditional green, left-wing, or right-wing discourses on economic and institutional issues. Analysis of wind-power planning and policy outcomes suggest that these different discourses often contain germs of truth, but also that these often contain myths.

Green activists are right to emphasize the planning advantages of local ownership, even though farmer ownership seems, ultimately, to deliver rather larger amounts of wind-power capacity compared to the more politically celebrated cooperatives. However, dominant green discourses about wind farms are misleading in other respects. First, large projects do not, because of their size at least, necessarily generate more planning opposition compared to smaller commercial schemes. The results of public opinion surveys concerning perceptions of small and large schemes do not mirror what happens in local authority planning processes, and the imagined vision of what a 'small' or 'large' wind-farm scheme may differ from what exists in practice. Second, the planning advantages that are associated with local ownership may be more complex than first thought. These advantages may rely heavily on the active support networks that are spawned by local wind-farm developers (usually farmers) who initiate the developments. This is as opposed to the fact of popular ownership itself, although popular equity ownership of wind-power schemes may have significant potential political advantages. Third, we can see from experience in Germany that locally owned projects are themselves not necessarily small. Banding farmers together and, sometimes (through cooperatives), the general public, can amass considerable amounts of equity capital.

Then again, it is also the case that in some countries, such as Spain, local ownership is not really necessary in order to encourage planning acceptance. In Spain, there is relatively little concern for the impact of wind power on landscapes. However, giving money to local people and causes seems to be good idea for wind power in most places, and this operates in Spain. The prospect of disbursement of significant financial incentives to local people and local institutions often gives a major boost to the prospects of the wind-farm proposal being accepted by local people and local governments. Indeed, large wind-power developments, whether in Spain or anywhere else, may have the resources to offer significant income streams to local people and insitutions. There is evidence that if wind-farm developers could offer more income to local people more often, then planning opposition might be reduced.

Green activists are by no means the only actors to hold misleading prejudices. If actors in the wind-power industry assert that local actors cannot develop cost-effective schemes, then they are proved wrong by empirical evidence. The wind industry may not recognize the advantages of local ownership, something in which it can engage by offering local people the opportunity to invest in wind-power projects. In addition, the belief of the electricity industry and conventional economists in so-called 'market-based' solutions is not always supported by the empirical evidence.

Tradable green certificate systems are not necessarily cost-effective compared to REFIT support systems. The success of tradable green cetificate systems depends very much on the right choice of design rules for incentives and penalties, and also on the need to have ambitious targets. It is not good for economists saying that they will set up a system based on incentives which will work in a free market situation. This is because electricity markets are a long way from being 'free' or perfectly competitive. On the other hand, it must be remembered that 'market-based' systems are not necessarily inimical to the interests of 'community' wind power.

The development of discourses that are associated with particular streams of thought can be understood by use of the notion of path dependence, whereby, for example, green antinuclear activists developed a preference for local energy activism as a response to nuclear power. Contemporary green energy-activist discourses reflect this historical tradition, and the strength of green energy activism seems path-dependent on the relative activism of antinuclear politics in different countries in the 1970s and 1980s. In contrast, discourses which stress reliance on multinational capital reflect a pastiche of current conventional interpretations of neoliberalism and globalization, which has been enrolled as a justification for the interests of the conventional electricity industry. Their prejudices against local ownership, small schemes, and against the cost-effectiveness of REFIT systems are misplaced. Set against this, however, we must remember that 'green' energy discourses themselves may be wrong if they exclude consideration of the benefits of large schemes and the enthusiastic involvement of the conventional electricity industry in wind-power development.

These findings go against the prejudices of different types of interests. An effective wind-power industry needs a diversity of sizes, types of ownership, and financial gearing, the optimum choices of which should be determined by context in which particular schemes are being developed.

REFERENCES

Andersen, P., (1998) *Wind Power in Denmark*, Copenhagen: Ministry of Energy and Environment.

AIM Research A/S. (1993) *Holdningsunderøgelse til vind energ*, report prepared for the Danish Wind Turbine Manufacturers Association.

Awel, A. (2005) 'Tawe proposed community windfarm', <http://www.awelamantawe.org.uk/> (31 May).

Beckerman, W. (1995) *Small is Stupid: Blowing the Whistle on the Greens*, London: Duckworth.

Breukers, S. and Wolsink, M. (2003) 'Institutional capacity in policy processes for wind energy in the Netherlands,' paper presented to ECPR Conference, Marburg, 20 September.

Caldwell, N. (1991) *Proposed WindFarm at Mynydd Cemais, Proof of Evidence on behalf of the Council for the Protection of Rural Wales (CPRW)*, Welshpool, Wales: Campaign for the Protection of Rural Wales, 16.

Del Rio, P. (2005) 'A European-wide harmonised tradable green certificate scheme for renewable electricity: is it really so beneficial?', *Energy Policy*, 33: 1239–50.

Devine-Wright, P. (2004) 'Beyond NIMBYism: towards an integrated framework for understanding public perceptions of wind energy, 8(2): 125–39.

Dinica, V. (2003) *Sustained Diffusion of Renewable Energy*, Enschede: Twente University Press.

Eurelectric Working Group Renewables and Distributed Generation. (2004) *A Quantitative Assessment of Direct Support Schemes for Renewables*, Brussels: Eurelectric, 16–18.

Hall, P. and Taylor, R. (1996) 'Political science and the three new institutionalisms', *Political Studies*, XLIV: 936–57.

Haggett, C. and Toke, D. (2006) 'Crossing the great divide—Using multi-method analysis to understand opposition to windfarms', *Public Administration*, 84(1): 103–20.

Hajer, M. (1995) *The Politics of Environmental Discourse*, Oxford: Clarendon Press.

Hill, A. (2005) 'UK breaks 1 GW barrier—and the next is already in the pipeline', *Real Power Magazine (BWEA)*, April–June: 8.

Hvelplund, F. (2001) *Renewable Energy Governance Systems: A Comparison of the "Political Price-/Amount Market" Model with the "Political Quota-/Certificate Price Market" System (The German and Danish Cases)*, Aalborg: Aalborg University.

Jamison, A., Eyerman, R., Cramer, C. and Læssoe, J. (1990) *The Making of the New Environmental Consciousness: A Comparative Study of the Environmental Movements in Sweden, Denmark and the Netherlands*, Edinburgh: Edinburgh University Press.

Langniss, O. and Wiser, R. (2003) 'The renewables portfolio standard in Texas: an early assessment', *Energy Policy*, 31(6): 527–35.

Lauber, V. (2004) 'REFIT and RPS: options for a harmonised community framework', *Energy Policy*, 32: 1405–14.

Lauber, V. and Toke, D. (2005) 'Einspeisetarife und Quoten-/Zertifikatssyteme: Erwartungen Der Europaischen Kommission und Erfahrungen aus dem Vergleich Zwischen Grossbritannien und Deutschland', *Zeitschrift für Neues Energierecht (Journal for New Energy Law)*, 2. 132–139.

Lee, T., Wren, B. and Hickman, M. (1989) 'Public responses to the siting and operation of wind turbines', *Wind Engineering*, 13: 188–95.

Loring, A. (2004) *Wind Development in England, Wales and Denmark—The role of community participation and network stability in project acceptance and planning success*. D. Phil. University of Sussex.

Markovits, A. and Gorski, P. (1993) *The German Left—Red Green and Beyond*, Cambridge: Polity Press.

Mitchell, C. (2000) 'The England and Wales non-fossil fuel obligation, Annual Review of Energy and Environment', Vol. 25, 285–312.

OFGEM (2003) Electricity distribution losses: A consultation document, January 2003 03/03, London: Office of Gas and Electricity Management.

O'Gallachoir, B. and McKeogh, E. (2005) 'Wind energy policy development in Ireland—a critical analysis', paper presented to 11th Annual International Sustainable Development Research Conference, June 6–8, Finlandia Hall, Helsinki, Finland.

Pierson, P. and Skocpol, T. (2002) 'Historical institutionalism in contemporary political science', in I. Katznelson and H. Milner (eds.) *Political Science: The State of the Discipline*, New York: WW Norton, 693–721.

Ramblers Association. (2005) <http://www.ramblers.org.uk/countryside/energy.html> (accessed 7 August 2005).

Ricardo, D. (1971) *On the Principles of Political Economy and Taxation*, Harmondsworth: Penguin, cited by John Gray (1998), *False Dawn—The Delusions of Global Capitalism*, London: Granta Books, 82.

Ross, D. and Collins, V. (2005) 'Councillors back world's largest windfarm on Lewis', *The Herald*, 29 June, <http://www.theherald.co.uk/news/42120-print. shtml> (accessed 30 June 2005).

Schumacher, E. (1973) Small is Beautiful, London: Blondand Briggs.

Somit, A. and Peterson, S. A. (1998) 'Review article: Biopolitics after three decades—A balance sheet', *British Journal of Political Science*, 28: 559–71.

Thelen, K. (1999) 'Historical institutionalism in comparative politics', *Annual Review of Political Science*, 2: 369–404.

Toke, D. (2000) *Green Politics and Neo-Liberalism*, Basingstoke: Macmillan.

———. (2002) 'Wind power in UK and Denmark: can rational choice help explain different outcomes?' *Environmental Politics*, 11(4): 83–100.

———. (2004a) *The Politics of GM Food*, London: Routledge.

———. (2004b) 'Wind power planning crisis—why its our fault', *Renew*, 153: 20.

———. (2005a) 'Explaining wind power planning outcomes, some findings from a study in England and Wales', *Energy Policy*, 33(12): 1527–39.

———. (2005b) 'Are green electricity certificates the way forward for renewable energy? An evaluation of the UK's Renewables Obligation in the context of international comparisons', *Environment and Planning C*, 23(3): 361–75.

———. (2005c) 'Community wind power in Europe and in the UK', *Wind Engineering*, 29(3): 301–308.

Toke, D. and Lauber, V. (2007) 'Anglo-Saxon and German Approaches to Neo-liberalism and Environmental Policy: the case of financing renewable energy, Geoforum 38, 677–687.

Toke, D., Wolsink, M. and Breukers, S. (2008) (forthcoming) 'Wind power deployment outcomes: How can we account for the differences?', *Renewable and Sustainable Energy Reviews*, 12 (4):1129–1147.

Toke, D. and Lauber, V. (2008) (forthcoming) 'Anglo Saxon and German approaches to neo-liberalism and environmental policy: the case of financing renewable energy', *Geoforum*.

Urquart, F. (1993) 'Protest over 'secret' wind farm plans', *The Scotsman*, 29 September.

Voogt, M. H., et al. (2001) 'Renewable energy burden sharing—REBUS—effects of burden sharing and certificate trade on the renewable electricity market in Europe', Energy Centre of the Netherlands ECN-C—01–030, Petten, The Netherlands, cited by Del Rio, P. (2005) 'A European-wide harmonised tradable green certificate scheme for renewable electricity: is it really so beneficial?', *Energy Policy*, 33: 1239–50.

Westmill Windfarm (2005) <http://www.energy4all.co.uk/Pages/Westmill10.htm> (accessed May 2005).

Wahlke, J. C. (1979) 'Pre-behaviouralism in political science', *American Political Science Review*, 73: 9–32, cited by Somit, A. and Peterson, S. A. (1998) 'Review article: biopolitics after three decades—a balance sheet', *British Journal of Political Science*, 28: 559–71.

Wolsink, M. (1989) 'Attitudes and expectancies about wind turbines and wind farms', *Wind Engineering*, 13: 196–206.

3 Local Social Acceptance Through Local Involvement

The Case of Wind-Power Implementation in North Rhine–Westphalia

Sylvia Breukers

INTRODUCTION

Implementation achievements cannot be explained with reference to technological, economic, or climatological conditions only. These conditions are no indication of the capacity that will be realized, for that depends on the motivation to invest in the technology, as well as on social acceptance of wind projects. It is this sociopolitical potential that we concentrate on when inquiring about the historical path of wind-power implementation in North Rhine–Westphalia (NRW) in order to understand its successful achievement—compared to other regions and countries in Europe (Breukers 2006).

We investigate how and to what extent wind power has become embedded within existing and changing practices, rules and routines of society—at the national and state level of policy-making, as well as the local level of land-use planning, decision making, and implementation. For successful implementation of wind power, numerous local decisions on siting and investments in wind farms are taken (Hull 1995; Pasqualetti 2001; Wolsink 1996, 2000). The outcomes of all such local decision-making processes eventually make up the aggregated installed capacity at the national or state level. Therefore, for our understanding of implementation achievements, it is important to address such local decision making as well.

CONCEPTUAL APPROACH AND METHOD

In line with historical new-institutionalist approaches, we define institutions as *rules, patterns, or procedures that structure behaviour and interaction.* These rules can be informal—norms, habits, and customs—or formal: written laws, regulations, and standards (Hall and Taylor 1996; Scharpf 1997). The institutional context structures actor orientations, interactions, actor configurations, and creates constraints on policy options and structures of incentives

(Scharpf 1997). Institutions empower some actors and enhance some perspectives at the expense of others. On the other hand, these institutions themselves can be challenged, altered, or reproduced by actors in processes of (strategic) interaction and in political conflict. This dynamic relationship between actors and the institutional context is a basic premise in our approach.

Case Study and Case Selection

The period under study runs from 1990 through 2005. This time frame is long enough to study stability and (institutional) change in a policy domain (Sabatier and Jenkins-Smith 1998). The organization of the case study follows Yin's case-study method (Yin 1994), using data from policy documents, stakeholder documents and meetings, and interviews with key stakeholders in the field of wind energy (see Appendix 3.1).

Because the policies and implementation achievements of Germany's several federal states differ so much, we decided to concentrate on a single state. Schleswig-Holstein, Lower Saxony, and NRW have been the three pioneering states in wind-power development. Until 2004, NRW ranked third among the German states with the highest installed capacity levels. NRW has performed well in terms of implementation, but also in terms of social acceptance of wind power. This land-locked German state is situated in the central–western part of Germany, bordering Belgium and The Netherlands. Though NRW is densely populated and boasts only moderate wind conditions, it has an impressive record of wind-power implementation (Table 3.1).

NRW produces around one-third of gross electricity production in Germany, and the major share of this is coal and lignite. In 1957, a first coal crisis set in that was caused by the supply of cheaper oil. An ongoing downward trend, together with a decline in the steel sector in the 1970s, has resulted in many job losses. The total collapse of the coal sector has, until today, been prevented through massive subsidies (Blotevogel 2003). NRW has attempted to transform itself from the former 'coal state' of Germany into the 'energy state', *NRW Energieland*.

Table 3.1   Cumulative Capacity Levels (MW) and Number of Turbines in NRW

Year	1992	1995	1998	1999	2000	2001	2002	2003	2004	2005
Installed Capacity (MW)	± 15	110	326	402	644	1,010	1,445	1,822	2,053	2,226
Number of Turbines	188	502	856	974	1,192	1,478	1,848	2,125	2,277	2,295

Source: Dewi 2006.

Elements of Inquiry

We first present an historical analysis of how institutional arrangements and changes in the *policy domains* of energy, spatial planning, and environmental policy have influenced policy processes for wind power and implementation (realization of wind projects) (Table 3.2). In a policy domain, both public and private actors directly or indirectly try to exert influence on the policy process (Sabatier and Jenkins-Smith 1999). Addressing relevant policy domains allows us to address processes and interactions outside of the formal policy-making arena. We address federal policy processes and politics as well in order to understand the developments and achievements in NRW.

Next, against the backdrop of this historical account, we inquire how actors have cooperated in their efforts to mobilize support for wind power. We discuss how stakeholders have 'assembled' over time around the issue of wind power (*policy community* formation). This wind-power policy community has evolved within the context of existing and changing routines and practices in the relevant policy domains, and has been more or less successful in mobilizing support for wind-power implementation—e.g., through influencing policy and at the level of implementation. In addition, we inquire into the position of 'conditional supporters', who support wind-power development if certain criteria are taken into account, and the rise of opponents against wind-power projects.

We assess historical patterns of support mobilization for wind-power implementation in and through policy making, project planning, and implementation practices in order to build social acceptance and commitment to wind-power developments. This allows us to draw some conclusions regarding the embedment of wind power in existing and changing institutional and social contexts and relate this to ownership structures and project development approaches.

Table 3.2   Elements of Inquiry

Elements of inquiry:	
• Institutional arrangements and changes in the energy-, spatial planning-, and environmental policy domains	Related to processes at the level of implementation: siting, investment decisions, and social acceptance.
• Rise and development of a policy community around wind power; interactions and cooperation, mobilization of support (locally, state level, nationally)	

Source: Author generated.

POLICY DOMAINS: ENERGY, PLANNING, AND THE ENVIRONMENT

Energy domain

NRW Sets an Example

Although the 1973 oil crisis primarily prompted the Federal Government of Germany to increase its support for hard coal and nuclear energy, it also triggered some attention for renewables. The federal government awarded a small part of the budget to the development of wind-power technology.

After the failure of a 3-MW turbine project in 1983, the government released its focus on large-scale applications and the remainder of research and development support was awarded to a diverse collection of both large and small projects. This prompted a variety of firms and academic departments into a process of experimentation and learning in wind technology (Jacobsson and Lauber 2006). The antinuclear and environmental movement inspired grassroots projects in turbine and project development. Also in NRW, such locally owned initiatives contributed to the mobilization of societal support and local social acceptance. The NRW government was responsive to grassroots developments, motivated by both environmental and economic reasons. In 1987, it adopted the comprehensive REN-programme,[1] which would serve as an example for other states later on. It was aimed at energy efficiency, cleaner conventional technologies, and new renewable energy technologies, and provided support that was well tailored to the needs of manufacturers and developers active at the grassroots level (MWMT 1994).

Environmental Concern Strengthens Support for Renewables

Wind-power developments accelerated after 1990. The Federal 100/250 MW programme provided investment subsidies for private developers, like farmers, and a subsidy per kilowatt-hour of electricity produced.

In 1991, the Federal Electricity Feed-In Act (StrEG)[2] was adopted (Table 3.3) after a joint lobby involving representatives of wind power, hydropower, biomass, and solar interests. The StrEG required the grid-owning utilities to connect renewable generators to the grid and to purchase their electricity. The tariff was coupled to the conventional electricity prices in Germany, and for wind, it was set at 90 per cent of the average sales price of electricity for end consumers. There was no limit to the amount of renewable electricity that could be fed into the grid. The StrEG did not apply to renewable electricity from applications that were 25 per cent or more owned by the federation, a state, or public utilities (Bundestag 1990). Hence, utilities would not receive extra benefits when producing renewable electricity themselves.

For private investors, the StrEG offered investment security, encouraging farmers, individuals, and businesses to invest in wind power. In the years that followed, private capital was mobilized on a large scale (Bergek and Jacobsson 2003). In addition, the government's banking institutions, *Deutsche Ausgleichsbank* and *Kreditanstalt für Wiederaufbau*, provided

Table 3.3 Main Legislation and Policy for Wind Power

Year	Law or measure	Focus
1987	NRW REN- Programme	Comprehensive support for renewables
1989	Federal 100 MW/ 250 MW Wind programme	Investment incentive Payment per kilowatt-hour for renewable electricity
1991	Federal Electricity Feed Law, amended 1998 (StrEG)	Feed-in tariff for renewable electricity Requirement for utilities to purchase renewable electricity Tariff wind power: 90% of consumer price electricity
1994	NRW changes Nature Protection Law	Facilitating projects of one or two turbines
1996	NRW Wind Ordinance (renewed in 2000, 2002)	Planning and permitting procedures and nature protection laws
1997	Federal Change Federal Construction Law	Privileging wind power in outlying areas Municipal designation of wind priority zones
1998	Federal Energy Reform Act, amending the StrEG	Geographical equalization of reimbursement obligation utilities
2000	NRW Wind Ordinance	Renewal of 1996 Ordinance
1999	Federal Ecological Tax Reform	Shift of tax burden from labour to pollution (Weidner 2005)
2000	Federal Erneuerbare- Energien-Gezetz (EEG) Renewable Energy Act	Feed-in tariff for twenty years Tariff decoupled from electricity price Differentiated for location and over time Requirement for electricity suppliers to purchase renewable electricity
2002	NRW Wind Ordinance	Renewal of 2000 Ordinance
2003	Härtefallregelung	Exemption for energy intensive companies to con- tribute to costs of renewables
2004	Federal Renewed EEG	Renewal of 2002 EEG Stronger degression in tariffs for wind power

Source: Author generated.

soft loans to project developers. The growth in installed wind-power capacity exceeded all expectations: it went from about 19 MW in 1989 to over 1,100 MW in 1995 in Germany; and from 10 MW in 1992 to 110 MW in 1995 in NRW (Hoppe-Kilpper et al. 1997; Keuper et al. 1992; Rehfeldt 1995). This rapid growth encouraged the demand for turbines, components, and services. Diversity was stimulated through national and state-level support, which triggered technological competition and improvement, resulting in marketable turbines (Borchers 1993; MWMEV 2001). Between 1990 and 1995, a firm basis was set for a booming home market for the upcoming domestic turbine industry.

Support for Wind Power at State and Federal Level

The NRW government aimed, simultaneously, to safeguard the coal and lignite industry (to prevent mass unemployment) and to encourage new renewable energy technologies (and investigate the potential for employment). At the federal level, the interests of the conventional and renewable energy sectors were more difficult to combine. Time and again there were fierce battles over the feed-in tariff system. Both the economic ministry as well as the energy sector have launched political and legal attacks to get rid of this support system several times without success. This shows the strength of the renewable energy lobby. However, the struggles did cause insecurity, especially in 1996–1997, when the StrEG was being amended. The economic ministry wanted to reduce the feed-in rates, but met with political opposition, which culminated in a joint protest demonstration in 1997 of the metalworkers union, farmer and church groups, and environmental and renewable energy associations (Hustedt 1998). In the end, the economic ministry lost out in the federal parliament (Lauber and Mez 2004).

In 2000, the Renewable Energy Act (EEG),[3] a feed-in tariff system but with more differentiations than its predecessor, was adopted (see Table 3.3). A new differentiation according to wind conditions turned out advantageous for locations with less favourable wind conditions, like in NRW. As a result, implementation in NRW accelerated, and the installed capacity level more than doubled from 644 MW in 2000 to 1,445 in 2002 (Table 3.1). However, with this acceleration, local resistance grew.

With the EEG renewal in 2004, heated discussions on its continuation again resulted in insecurity and a stagnation in the component-and-supply industry in NRW. The feed-in prices were lowered significantly, and the annual degression rate of the tariffs for wind was increased (Ragwitz and Huber 2005). In 2003, at the request of energy-intensive industries, a *Härtefallregelung* (legal amendment) was introduced, which exempts energy-intensive companies from paying a contribution for renewable electricity (interview with C. Wittek, Federal Economics

Ministry (BMWA, May 2004). Although it had to accept these changes, the renewables sector represented a significant political and economic interest, which made a drastic shift in the support system unlikely.

Industrial Impact for NRW

In a period of industrial decline of both the coal and steel industries, federal and state programmes created new opportunities for a cleaner technological sector in NRW. Specific state-level support provided backing in times of insecurity about national policies. Until the end of 2000, the NRW government supported 919 turbines (436 MW) with an equivalent of around 70 million. Although the turbine manufacturer that was based in NRW (Tacke) has gone bankrupt, technological developments, component supply, and services have increased and provided employment in NRW. After 2001, this market stopped growing, as domestic demand decreased and the potential of export turned out to be limited. The market is expected to consolidate rather than expand (any) further. In 2004, the component- and machine-building market for wind power in NRW provided 35,000 jobs and an annual return of 882 million Euros (Allnoch and Schlusemann 2004).

From Bürgerwindpark to Windfall Profit Funds?

With regard to project development, NRW shows a shift over the years: in the late 1980s and early 1990s many projects were initiated and realized by citizens, farmers, and local companies. These projects were characterised by financial participation from local community members. Over the years, more and more small and medium-sized companies specialized in the planning and development of wind projects, in doing so providing the option of financial participation. They developed turnkey projects or set up a wind project as an independent company, in which private individuals (e.g., farmers) and companies could buy shares. The initiative to develop wind projects increasingly moved away from members of the local community to 'outsider' companies. Some of these adopted a strategy of local participation—in the process design and/or financially—but this became less self-evident than it had been in the past. Local commitment and social acceptance accordingly decreased.

There are no data available on ownership for Germany, and company and ownership structures are heterogeneous and fluid. Estimates of locally owned projects for the whole of Germany range from 20 per cent to 50 per cent (interviews with H. Bartelt BWE, July 2003, 2004; and G. Benik Energieteam, April 2004). An estimate of farmer involvement states that over 50 per cent of the projects are realized with farmers—either as land renters, project owners, or as part of an operator group (interview with BWE, 2003).

As a general trend, NRW wind farms are increasingly planned without local financial involvement and with less local involvement in project planning. Various larger wind farms have been developed through investment funds, in which individuals could buy shares while benefiting from an investment tax rebate. This fiscal incentive was especially attractive for people with large incomes (Ruchser 2002). It is estimated that some 100,000 Germans hold a stake in a wind project (Greenpeace 2004). Buying shares in wind-power funds became very popular around 2000, but in the following years, some funds went bankrupt—e.g., Umweltkontor. This and the insecurity surrounding the EEG renewal dampened enthusiasm to invest in 2003 (interview with U. Steinhouser ABO Wind, November 2005). Project developers are increasingly looking abroad to develop projects. Within NRW, the best sites—with the least chances of conflict—have already been developed.

Spatial Planning Domain

In line with the federalist principle of the German constitution, the planning system involves a statutory division of competences and responsibilities between three distinct levels of government: the Federation, the sixteen states, and the local authorities. Germany has a decentralized zoning system, and the local development plan is the only planning instrument that is legally binding for public and private actors. A proposed wind project, in principle, has to be in accordance with the local development plan.

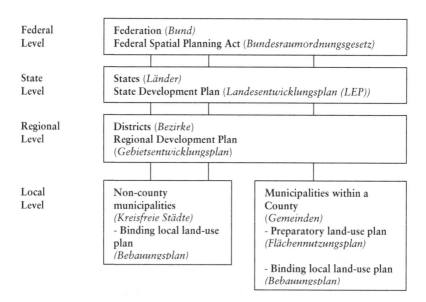

Figure 3.1 German planning at different levels of government. Source: EU (1999).

Generally, municipalities have increasingly been confronted with new decisions and regulations taken at higher levels, which has reduced their constitutionally granted right of local self-government. An example is the adoption of streamlining laws following the reunification of 1989, passed in order to facilitate development—e.g., housing—in the former German Democratic Republic. These speed-up measures invoked criticism for compromising environmental protection goals and restricting public participation (Jänicke and Weidner 1997; Turowski 2002).

Spatial planning in Germany has long been the prerogative of an 'inner circle' of experts, and is still generally regarded as highly complex, technocratic, and inaccessible. Efforts at participative local planning—beyond formal consultation—have not been widespread and, generally, public stakeholders show little interest in spatial planning (Kunzmann 2001). Although in NRW, the 1960s and 1970s were a period when planning was rather influential, in subsequent decades, planning had to tone down its ambitions because it was increasingly regarded as impeding economic development and growth (Kunzmann 2001).

Local Planning

Municipalities and cities make up the smallest administrative units (Figure 3.1). A distinction can be made between noncounty municipalities— cities or metropolitan authorities (*Kreisefreie Städte*)—and municipalities (*Gemeinden)* that are part of a county (*Kreis*). A municipality that is part of a county devises a *preparatory land-use plan*[4] that indicates the intended development. On the basis of this plan, a municipality can devise a land-use plan that is legally binding for both the government and the private sector. This *binding land-use plan*[5] covers only part of the area that the preparatory land-use plan addresses, and it is much more detailed. Noncounty municipalities or cities have no preparatory land-use plans.

Planning Support for Wind Power

In the early 1990s, it became clear that municipalities in NRW had difficulties in planning for wind power—e.g., in balancing different interests, dealing with nature and landscape impact issues, and in aligning their plans with regional plans (Allnoch and Schlusemann 1996; Borchers 1993). In order to facilitate planning for wind power, the NRW state government adopted the 1996 Wind Energy Ordinance,[6] which was renewed in 2000, and again in 2002. The Ordinance elaborates on planning and permitting procedures, the workings of the EU Birds Directive and the EU Habitats Directive, and the interests of nature and landscape protection, as formulated in federal and state legislation.

Wind-project developers in various states were complaining about local permitting procedures, which they regarded as lengthy, inconsistent, and complex. Their lobby resulted in a revision of the Federal Construction Law[7] (which lays down principles for land-use planning) in 1997. This amendment privileged the development of wind schemes in outlying areas where building or development is usually only allowed under strict conditions or when it accommodates specific agricultural functions (BMVBW 1997). An instrument to guide wind-power developments was introduced: municipalities could designate priority zones for wind-power development in their local land-use plans. Accordingly, they could identify low-conflict areas, where wind projects were unlikely to raise controversy, and exclude wind-power development in potentially conflict-rich areas. In principle, if municipalities have not indicated areas, a wind-project developer has the right to choose a site in the outlying area where wind power is 'privileged' (*Priviligierung*). This means that the project developer cannot be denied the right to realize the project, as long as it meets with the criteria needed to get building permission.

Initially, the idea was that all municipalities would have designated priority areas by the end of 1998. By the end of 2001, however, only half of the municipalities in NRW had done so, and around 2004, some two-thirds had designed priority areas (BMVBW 1997; WEAErl Entwurf 2005).

Wind-Power Project Planning

In principle, the criterion for approving a new development at the local level is compliance with the binding land-use plan, if there is one, and otherwise with the preparatory land-use plan.

Before a wind scheme application is submitted, the developer has to deliver studies on wind potential, technical issues, sound emissions, shadow, landscape impact, bird impact, economic impact, and, if required, an environmental impact study. Next, fine-tuning with permitting officials takes place—those with competences in Nature Protection, Building, and Aircraft Control, etc. An application for connection to the grid has to be filed with the regional energy supply company. When all these issues have been sorted out, the application for a building permission is submitted to the competent authority—either the local authority, the district, or the State Environmental Office, depending on the size of the project.

If a municipality has no binding land-use plan, there are three options. First, the application for a wind project can be expedited within the framework of the preparatory land-use plan, which means that many things will still need to be inquired into during the permitting process. In NRW, many municipalities only have a preparatory land-use plan with priority zones for wind-power development. A second option is that the municipality makes a binding land-use plan. A third option is that the developer or investor makes a project-based binding land-use plan[8] and bears the planning costs, while the municipality retains the right to indicate preferences and set criteria. This option was introduced in 1993 to accelerate planning.

Permitting Procedure in NRW

For one or two turbines, only a building permit is required. This process involves no consultation. Wind projects larger than two wind turbines go through the Immission Control Procedure.[9] Since the adoption of the Environmental Impact Assessment Act in 2001 (EU Directive 2001/42/EC), a preliminary environmental impact inquiry and/or an environmental impact assessment (EIA) is part of this procedure. Whether or not the EIA is performed depends on the amount of turbines and the outcome of the preliminary inquiry. Where previously formal stakeholder consultations only took place in the process of designating priority zones for wind power (changing the land-use plan), since 2001, consultation is also required during the Immission Control Procedure if it involves an EIA. Any appeals against the granting of permission should concern aspects that affect the complaining party personally (e.g., noise, shadow) and should be addressed to the permitting authorities. Generally, the permitting process is regarded as a clear process with unambiguous rules and procedures. This is because, next to the building permit, a single comprehensive permit is granted by the immission control authority (at district or state level). This authority coordinates the involvement of the various relevant authorities, which must give permission if the application complies with relevant legal provisions—i.e., land-use plans and sectoral laws and requirements (BMU 2003).

Privileged Turbines Become Controversial

In NRW, early wind-energy policies—and not planning institutions—supported a practice of locally based project planning. A project development approach in which (part of) the local community was involved helped to garner local social acceptance and prevented the early rise of local opposition against wind projects. Participative planning beyond formal consultation has generally not been a feature of NRW planning. Before the introduction of the EIA directive (2001), there was no formal obligation to involve citizens in the permitting process for wind projects. Consultation was only required in the process of designating priority zones for wind power, but municipalities usually did not extensively call upon their citizens to participate in this process (interview with M. Pletzinger, EnerSys, November 2005; Van Erp 1997).

Increasingly, larger and more impersonal investor groups have replaced the citizens' projects. The project development approach has tended toward less local involvement and local participation (financially or in project planning). After the *Priviligierung* in 1997, wind-power implementation accelerated, increasingly taking citizens by surprise (interview with M. Pletzinger, EnerSys, November 2005). Local opposition against wind projects also emerged from the side of municipalities. The refusal of half of the NRW municipalities to designate areas by 2001 may well be a sign of opposition against a perceived top-down prioritization of wind power and a curtailment of their powers of self-government. For instance, municipalities did not have the option to designate a location for a biomass installation and then be exempted from the requirement to designate locations for wind schemes. On the other hand, municipalities now also have an instrument that enables them to exclude wind-power developments by setting restrictive designations. In addition, it is the municipality that makes the decision, and not a higher tier of government. In taking a more proactive stance, the municipality can also create room for local (political) deliberation on the perceived costs and benefits of wind power for the local community.

After 2001, resistance against projects increased. Most new initiatives in NRW are confronted with opposing initiatives. To a certain extent, this appears to be due to the fact that the best sites have already been developed. New projects are increasingly planned in potentially conflict-rich localities (interviews with U. Steinhauser, ABO Wind, November 2005; M. Pletzinger EnerSys, 2005; and F. Musiol, Nabu NRW, April 2003).

NRW state planning follows broader political goals, and during the years of the SPD[10]—and after 1995, the SPD-Green governments—wind power could count on firm support. The Wind Ordinances attempted to encourage wind-power developments by clarifying the permitting and planning framework. Each new ordinance was preceded by consultation with various stakeholders. At one of these consultations in 2002, both planners and nature and landscape protection organizations called for the designation on a regional scale, in order to better protect nature and landscape interests (interviews with J. Tumbrick, Nabu NRW, Münster district, August 2003 and A. von Reth, Paderborn Municipality, April 2004). The new government coalition of CDU[11] and FPD[12] that came into office in 2005 has responded to such calls. The latest Wind Energy Ordinance aims at restricting wind-power developments, and this involves a rather drastic shift.

Environmental Policy Domain

In the 1970s, federal environmental policy was rather technocratic and characterized by a command-and-control approach (Jänicke and Weidner 1997). During the reign of the centre–right coalition in the 1980s, worries about *Waldsterben* and smog, as well as the entry of the Greens in the Bundestag in 1983, raised the profile of environmental policy. A separate environmental ministry was set up in 1986. The policy concept of ecological modernization gained support across political parties. It involved the idea that economic growth and pollution flows could be decoupled, and that environmental protection and economic growth could form a partnership (Weale et al. 2003). What made the concept attractive was that it aimed to improve ecological and economic efficiency within the framework of current economic and market dynamics (Weidner 2005). New green industries and technologies were supported and became the motor of ecological modernization, positioning Germany well in the international market for environmental technologies (Jänicke and Weidner 1997). The support for wind power fit well with this ecological modernization drive, as both economic and ecological aims were pursued.

After the waning of environmental concern resulting from reunification and economic recession in the early 1990s, the red–green coalition placed climate change firmly back on the agenda in 1998. Sustainable development and Local Agenda 21 (formulated at the Rio Conference in 1992) even became binding guidelines for spatial planning (Blotevogel 2000). However, the commitment to Local Agenda 21 activities, which emphasise broad, local, public participation, has not materialized (Weidner 2005). While the concept of sustainable development gained wide rhetorical support, concrete policies reflected a continued orientation toward the more practicable ecological modernization concept. The technocratic approach of the early years made way for market-based instruments, voluntary agreements, and (in)formal cooperation between the government, industry, and environmental organizations (Jänicke and Weidner 1997; Wurzel et al. 2003).

Institutionalization of Environmental Concern

By the 1980s, the German corporatist system had opened up to include environmental interests. Increasingly, environmental organizations have provided input into the policy process based on their expertise. The environmental policy domain has itself become institutionalized, helped by the early growth of the Green Party.[13] In 1979, the Greens were already represented in the state parliament of Bremen. After the 1983 federal elections, they entered the national parliament, and by 1994, they had become the third largest party in the national parliament. In NRW (as of 1995), as well as in several other states, they became coalition partners with SPD. Hence, because of the federal structure, the Greens could influence policy making by forming coalitions with the SPD (Jänicke and Weidner 1997; Weale et al. 2000). This has been of major importance for the uptake and acceptance of wind power in both society and politics. The specific focus of ecological modernization policies—combining environmental goals with economic aims—was apparent in the approach of the NRW government throughout the past decade and a half.

Policy Community Formation

The antinuclear and environmental movement from the 1970s inspired the search for alternatives to conventional energy generation, and engineers and technical universities took part in the development of alternative energy technologies. This movement formed the basis for the wind-policy community. Various organizations were set up in the 1970s and 1980s, such as the German Wind Energy Association (Bundesverband Wind Energy or BWE) in 1985. BWE had a decentralized structure from the beginning onward, and found supporters in politics at all levels of government. From early on, technological wind-energy research institutes brought together the manufacturers, developers, and the government. Until the mid-1990s, project developers were largely locally based—e.g., private individuals, self-employed people, farmers, and local utilities. Various citizens' wind farms (*Bürgerwindparks*) were set up in these years, encouraging local involvement, acceptance, and engagement (interview with W. Köhnlein, *Bürgerwindpark Baumberge*, November 2005).

In NRW, companies in component supply, as well as the metal industry, prospered due to the growth of the wind-power market. Industry-related actors, ranging from equipment producers to service providers, supported wind-power lobbies in times of political turmoil. The VDMA (German Engineering Federation), a large and influential industry branch, provided strong backing for a continuation of the feed-in tariff system.

Consolidation and Change

Wind projects in NRW have, over time, been developed by a variety of actors: farmers, local individuals, new developer companies, planning offices, turn-key developers, and a few energy companies. However, a project development approach that encourages local ownership has become increasingly exceptional. Although some developers still advocate an inclusive planning approach, newer entrants not necessarily prefer such a strategy, and the planning system does not encourage them to do so either. Moreover, as the opportunities for developing wind projects within NRW (and Germany as a whole) have become sparser, developers are increasingly looking abroad.

Unconditional and Conditional Support

The national environmental organizations, like Greenpeace and the World Nature Fund, unconditionally support wind power and have became more active in advocating wind power (interview with Sven Teske, Greenpeace, May 2004).

Nature, environmental, and landscape protection organizations, like Nabu[14] and BUND,[15] are historically strongly wedded to the cause of renewable energy by fighting nuclear power, coal, and lignite pollution. However, Nabu especially has become more reserved in NRW, and their local branches increasingly oppose wind projects. Nabu argued for the regional designation of wind-power zones so that sensitive areas can be better protected. Finding a balance between local nature protection and global climate protection has proven difficult, since local branches and members are often more critical of wind power than the national or state-level branches (interview with F. Musiol, Nabu, April 2004).

Citizens Against Wind Power

In NRW, citizens' initiatives against wind projects have mushroomed since the latter part of the 1990s, and especially after 2001(interview with BLS,

2003). Overall, these groups are not linked to nature protection organizations or their branches.

The Association for Health and Landscape Protection[16] claims to represent some 137 members, consisting of individuals, citizens' initiatives, and organizations in NRW. It provides information and advice for (potential) opponents or citizen groups. At the national level, the Darmstadt Manifesto (1998) has been signed by over a hundred academics who request an immediate withdrawal of financial support for wind power. In addition, some three hundred citizens' initiatives have signed a Resolution of Citizens Initiatives against Wind Turbines, addressed to all levels of government.

Utilities: Missed the Boat

The conventional energy sector, represented by Venband der Elektrizitätswirtzchaft (VDEW) (Association of German Utilities), realized too late how successful wind power was becoming. Traditionally, its political leverage on the various levels of government has been considerable. The economic ministry (Bunderministerium für Wirtschaftund Arbeit, BMWA) has historically represented the conventional and nuclear energy-sector interests. In the struggle to secure these interests for the future, this coalition has attempted several times to impede the continuation of the feed-in tariff system. Companies like E.On and RWE have become involved in offshore wind projects and in projects abroad, but within Germany, they are still at odds with the wind sector.

Government Performance

NRW ministries were better at collaborating than the federal ministries. The NRW government has supported wind power, and various departments have coordinated their efforts. In 1990, the NRW Energy Agency was set up to give advice to small- and medium-sized enterprises. In 1996, the State Initiative for Future Energies[17] was established as a strategic platform for industry, energy generators and users, manufacturers, research and science, and consultants. The aim was to facilitate market expansion and export. Different ministries took part in this initiative.

At the federal level, interdepartmental cooperation has been difficult; the environmental and economic ministries disagree on wind-power policy, and there has been constant conflict between the two. In 2002, the competence for renewables policy moved from the economic to the environmental ministry, which helped to safeguard support for wind, but did little to improve relations.

Mobilization of Support

In the 1980s, wind-power developments started at the grassroots level, where support was mobilized from the bottom upward. Policies that were well adapted to this level raised investments from many private actors and encouraged societal involvement in wind projects. The economic impact of wind-power developments garnered support from industrial and employment representatives. Wind-project developers and manufacturers also committed themselves to other renewables interests to exert leverage on the NRW and other state governments. They extended their lobby to improve the political, economic, and legal framework conditions at the federal level. The feed-in tariff system was introduced after a successful joint lobby with hydropower and other renewables interests. What began as a grassroots, environmentally motivated movement broadened into a coalition that represented environmental, economic, industrial, and employment interests, involving levels well above the grassroots and became powerful enough to withstand the established conventional and nuclear interests. The strength of the policy community around wind power lies in the diversity of interests and political affiliations, represented by actors at various levels. BWE has grown into a professional branch with representation from the regional to the EU level. Its decentralized organizational structure reflects the bottom-up roots. However, the constituency of the wind-power policy community has changed with the maturing of the wind-power sector and a decrease of locally based wind projects. Nevertheless, there are still professionalized companies that develop locally owned wind projects. The largest project in NRW (Sintfeld, 105 MW) is an example of a large commercial project that is developed in a participative manner and is owned locally. Still, overall, the ties to the local level of implementation have weakened, which is aggravated by the increase in mobilization of support against wind projects through citizens' initiatives at the grassroots level from the mid-1990s onward.

DISCUSSION

NRW: Decreasing Social Acceptance

The decentralized administrative structure provides room for states to adopt innovative policy (Wurzel et al. 2003). This is what happened in NRW, where policy from early on reflected efforts to combine environmental, economic, and employment concerns and, to a lesser degree, spatial planning objectives.

A major advantage of the feed-in system, in combination with other federal support programmes and NRW-level support, was that it enabled a diversity of actors to become involved in both the development of turbines and the development of projects. This diversity enabled technological learning and investment security-encouraged local ownership. Wind projects represented concrete political, economic, and environmental goals that were attractive at a local level, since local stakeholders were involved. This forestalled early local opposition against wind projects. The fact that the conventional energy sector was not involved in wind power helped the development of this diversity, but caused bitter confrontations as well.

Wind-power developments started locally and support was mobilized from the bottom upward. Local ownership and existing grassroots energy initiatives ensured this process of embedding. Through the creation of a new wind-power sector, local and supralocal economic benefits were generated. A closely knit but heterogeneous policy community evolved and both national and state-level governments responded to demands from this network. In the early 1990s, the basis was laid for a new industry, which further broadened a supportive basis. A path-dependent development took place, whereby wind power as an environmentally acceptable energy source, a new economic sector, and a socially acceptable alternative for conventional energy generation became embedded. The early institutionalization of environmental concern in society and politics was important to provide political legitimacy to a development that was rather costly to start up.

Throughout the course of the 1990s, both the maturing of the wind sector and the *Priviligierung* affected the conditions for wind-power project planning locally. Together with the absence of a participative planning tradition, this resulted in the decrease of local involvement in project planning and development. The prioritising of wind turbines in planning facilitated implementation, but also triggered resistance from municipalities, nature protection organizations, and citizens' groups. Resistance increased especially after 2001, albeit at a moment when an impressive level of installed capacity had already been reached (1,010 MW in 2001).

Areas of Contention

The tensions between proponents, opponents, and conditional proponents concern both conflicts at the level of national politics, and conflicts at the level of implementation. The conflicts of a national level existed from the beginning onward and concerns the continuing struggle between the renewables proponents on one side, and the coalition of the federal economic ministry, the conventional energy sector, and energy-intensive industry on the other side (Breukers 2006).

The conflicts at the local level, however, are of more recent origin. Wind projects have been confronted with a decreasing acceptance from those worried about landscape impact, nature, and environmental protection interests.

Wind power has outgrown its grassroots, but in the process, it has lost out in terms of local support. The wind-power sector has increasingly focused on political lobbying to safeguard economic feasibility and facilitate siting, while losing touch with actors at the level of implementation.

The general trend in planning is to prioritise the 'common good' (fighting climate change with wind power, in the case of wind power) over local concerns. Project developers and other proponents of wind energy easily brush aside concerns that motivate opposition against wind projects, hence denying the legitimacy of local concerns. This attitude passes over the fact that local social acceptance once formed the basis of successful developments. Moreover, in reaction to the increasing dissatisfaction at the local level, municipalities—but also regional and state governments—can adopt more restrictive rules. In other words, if sociopolitical support decreases at various subnational levels, there are several possibilities to effectively impede further implementation or repowering (replacing old turbines with new ones), regardless of a continuation of the feed-in tariff system.

This is what happened recently, when the coalition government of CDU and FDP replaced the SPD/Greens coalition in NRW. At this point, wind power had already become a controversial topic in NRW. The new coalition explicitly stated the aim to steer wind-power implementation more restrictively to protect the landscape and the people against the unbridled placement of wind turbines. The renewed Wind Energy Ordinance, among others, included restrictions in terms of a heightened minimum distance (of 1,500 m) between wind turbines and houses. In the ensuing discussion, both BWE and BUND strongly criticised the new policy. BWE states that the distance of 1,500 m will effectively hinder the replacement of older turbines with newer ones (repowering) because most will not get a building permission for the new turbine under the new Ordinance. In doing so, the Ordinance will also negatively affect the service and component-supply industry (and therefore, employment) in NRW. The nature protection organization Nabu, on the other hand, was satisfied with the new Ordinance, arguing that, finally, the (emotional) discussions have become part of the appraisal process and that the position of landscape protection, bird protection, and the protection of other animals has been strengthened in the light of the *Priviligierung*.

Legitimacy Through Local Ownership and Participative Planning

In NRW, inclusive approaches resulted from the type of projects and actors in the beginning period, rather than from local planning institutions. Areas of contention relate to local decision making about development and land-use, where economic, environmental, and political goals and aims are often not reconcilable. How to weigh the benefits of decreased global warming against the value of cherished landscapes or local quality of place? The former is hard to express in numbers (e.g., of carbon dioxide reduction) that are meaningful at a local level; the latter inherently includes value judgements (Owens 1994).

The conflict issues highlight the need for an approach with inherent, institutionalized priorities that take account of other (environmental, economic, and local) interests. Social acceptance relates to a commitment at various levels in society and to a variety of reasons to support or oppose a development. The diversity of motives for support, as well as motives for opposition, should be recognized. A strategy that enhances social acceptance entails the institutionalizing of participation in project planning and local decision making (democratic legitimacy), so that there is room to deliberate and negotiate on the costs and benefits of a wind project, together with an approach that encourages local ownership (legitimacy through cost–benefit sharing).

APPENDIX 3.1. OVERVIEW OF RESPONDENTS

Name	Organisation	Stakeholder type	Month & Year
Mr. G. Benik	Energieteam	Wind project developer: medium-sized company	April 2004
Mrs. U. Steinhauser	ABO Wind	Wind project developer: medium-sized turnkey developer	November 2005
Mr. W. Köhnlein	Bürgerwindpark Baumberge	Citizens' wind project	November 2005
Mr. J. Lackmann	BWE NRW; BEE[18]	NRW wind energy branch; national renewables branch	April 2004
Mr. H. Bartelt	BWE	National wind energy branch	July 2003
Mr. F. Musiol	Naturschutz Bund (Nabu) Germany	National nature protection organisation	April 2004
Mr. J. Tumbrinck	Naturschutz Bund (Nabu) NRW	NRW nature protection organisation	August 2003
Mr. S. Teske	Greenpeace Germany	National Environmental Organisation	May 2004
Mr. D. Krämer	Bundesverband Land-schafts Schutz (BLS)	Antiwind group (locally active)	July 2003
Mr. A. von Reth	Paderborn Municipality	Municipality	April 2004
Mr. K. Lauer	Bezirksregierung Mün-ster	District	August 2003
Mrs. C. Viertel	Bundesministerium für Umwelt, Naturschutz und Reaktorsicherheit (BMU)	Federal environmental ministry (responsible for renewables policy since 2002)	May 2004
Mrs. C. Wittek	Bundesministerium für Wirtschaft und Arbeit (BMWA)	Federal economic min-istry (responsible for energy policy; responsi-ble for renewables policy until 2002)	May 2004
Mrs. M. Pletziger	EnerSys	Company involved in project planning and development	November 2005

NOTES

1. REN stands for Rational Use of Energy and the Use of Renewable Energy Sources.
2. *Stromeinspeisungsgesetz* (StrEG).
3. *Erneuerbare Energien Gesetz* (EEG).
4. *Flächennutzungsplan.*
5. *Bebauungsplan.*
6. *Windenergie Erlass.*
7. *Baugezetzbuch.*
8. *Vorhabenbezogenes Bebauungsplan.*
9. *Immissionsschutzrechtliches Verfahren* (Since the end of 2005, all projects enter this procedure [interview with M. Pletzinger, EnerSys, November 2005]).
10. *Sozialdemokratische Partei Deutschland* (SPD): Social Democratic Party of Germany.
11. *Christlich Demokratischen Union* (CDU): Christian Democrats.
12. *Freie Demokratische Partei* (FDP): Free Democrat Party.
13. *Die Grünen*; after 1989, *Bündnis 90/Die Grünen* (amalgamation with civil rights activists)
14. *Naturschutzbund Deutschland* (Nabu).
15. *Bund für Umwelt und Naturschutz Deutschland* (BUND): the German Friends of the Earth.
16. *Verband für Gesundheits und Landschaftsschutz e.V.*
17. *Landesinitiative Zukunftsenergien.*
18. The respondent was from both these organisations, as well as a former wind developer.

REFERENCES

Allnoch, N. and Schlusemann, R. (1996) *NRW-Gemeindeumfrage zur Flächenausweisung von Windkraftanlagen, Studie im Auftrag der Landesinitiative Zukunftsenergien NRW*: Internationales Wirtschaftsforum Regenerative Energien (IWR) [Municipal survey in North Rhine-Westphalia on the designation of areas for wind energy. Study for the State initiative Future Energies (*Landesinitiative Zukunftsenergien*] International Economic Forum Renewable Energy.

Allnoch, N. and Schlusemann. R. (2004) *Zür Lage der Regenerativen Energiewirtschaft in Nordrhein-Westfalen 2003, Studie im Auftrag es Ministeriums für Verkehr, Energie und Landesplanung des Landes Nordrhein-Westfalen (MVEL)*: Internationales Wirtschaftsforum Regenerativen Energien (IWR) [About the situation of the renewable energy economy in North Rhine-Westphalia in 2003. Study commissioned by the North Rhine-Westphalian State Ministry for Transport, Energy and Spatial Planning. International Economic Forum Renewable Energy].

Bergek, A. and Jacobsson, S. (2003) 'The emergence of a growth industry: a comparative analysis of the German, Dutch and Swedish wind turbine industries', in S. Metcalfe and U. Canter (eds.) *Change, Transformation and Development: Schumpeterian Perspectives*, Heidelberg: Physica/Springer, 197–228.

Blotevogel, H. H. (2000) 'Rationality and discourse in (post)modern spatial planning', in W. Salet and A. Faludi (eds.) *The Revival of Strategic Spatial Planning.*

Proceedings of the Colloquium, Amsterdam, 25–26 February 1999, Amsterdam: Royal Netherlands Academy of Arts and Sciences, 121–34.

BMVBW. (1997) *Federal Building Code (Baugesetzbuch—BauGB)*. Berlin: Bundesministerium für Verkehr, Bau- und Wohnungswesen (BMVBW).

BMU (2003) *Report by the Federal Republic of Germany on achievement of the indicative target for the consumption of electricity produced from renewable energy sources in 2010*, Berlin: Bundesministerium für Umwelt, Naturschutz und Reaktorsicherheit.

Borchers, S. (1993) *REN-Programm 1988–1993, Ergebnisse der Breitenförderung, Sachstandbericht*, Düsseldorf: Ministerium für Wirtschaft, Mittelstand und Technologie.

Breukers, S. (2006) *Changing Institutional Landscapes for Implementing Wind Power, A Geographical Comparison of Institutional Capacity Building: The Netherlands, England and North Rhine-Westphalia*, Amsterdam: Amsterdam University Press.

Bundestag. (1990) *Gesetz über die Einspeisung von Strom aus erneuerbaren Energien in das öffentliche Netz (Stromeinspeisungsgesetz)*, Bonn: German Bundestag.

Dewi, A. (2006) *Statistics: Aufstellungszahlen der Windenergienutzung in Deutschland*, <http://www.dewi.de> (accessed 14 June 2006).

EU Directive 2001/42/EC of the European Parliament and of the Council of 27 June 2001 on the assessment of the effects of certain plans and programmes on the environment. Luxembourg, Official Journal of the European Communities http://www.environ.ie/en/Publications/Environment/Miscellaneous/FileDownLoad,1805,en.pdf.

EU. (1999) *The EU Compendium of Spatial Planning Systems and Policies: Germany*, Luxembourg: Office for Official Publications of the European Communities.

Greenpeace. (2004) *Windforce 12—A Blueprint to Achieve 12% of the World's Electricity from Wind Power by 2020*, Hamburg: Greenpeace and European Wind Energy Association.

Hall, P. A. and Taylor, R. (1996) 'Political science and the three new institutionalisms', *Political Studies*, 4(4): 936–57.

Hoppe-Kilpper, M., et al. (1997) *Strom aus Sonne und Wind. Stand und Perspektiven der Windenergienutzung in Deutschland—Ergebnisse aus dem Wissenschaftlichen Mess-und Evaluierungsprogramm*. Berlin: Forschungsverbund Sonnenenergie.

Hull, A. (1995) 'Local strategies for renewable energy: Policy approaches in England and Wales', *Land Use Policy*, 12(1): 7–16.

Hustedt, M. (1998) 'Windkraft—Made in Germany', in F. Alt, J. Claus, and H. Scheer (eds.) *Windiger Protest—Konflikte um das Zukunftspotential der Windkraft*. Bochum: Ponte Press, 163–68.

Jacobsson, S. and Lauber, V. (2006) 'The politics and policy of energy system transformation—explaining the German diffusion of renewable energy technology', *Energy Policy*, 34: 256–276.

Jänicke, M. and Weidner, H. (1997) *National Environmental Policies: A Comparative Study of Capacity-Building* (ed.) Berlin: SpringerVerlag.

Keuper, A., Molly, J. and Stuckermann, C. (1992) Wind Energy Use in Germany—Status 30.6. 1992. DEWI Magazin, 1.

Kunzmann, K. R. (2001) 'State planning: A German success story?' *International Planning Studies*, 6(2): 153–66.

Lauber, V. and Mez, L. (2004) 'Three decades of renewable electricity policies in Germany', *Energy and Environment*, 15(4): 599–623.

MWMT. (1994) *REN-Report—Landesprogramm "Rationelle Energieverwendung und Nutzung unerschöpflicher Energiequellen"* ["Rational Use of Energy and Application of Renewable Energy Sources"], Düsseldorf: Ministerium für Wirtschaft, Mittelstand und Technologie des Landes Nordrhein-Westfalen.

MWMEV. (2001) *Zukunftsenergien aus Nordrhein-Westfalen* [Future energies from NRW] Düsseldorf: Landesinitiative Zukunftsenergien; Ministeriums für Wirtschaft und Mittelstand, Energie und Verkehr (MWMEV) des Landes Nordrhein Westfalen.

Owens, S. (1994) 'Land, limits and sustainability: a conceptual framework and some dilemmas for the planning system', *Transactions of the Institute of British Geographers*, 19(4): 438–56.

Pasqualetti, M. J. (2001) 'Wind energy landscapes: Society and technology in the California desert', *Society and Natural Resources*, 14(8): 689–99.

Ragwitz, M. and Huber, C. (2005) 'Feed-in systems in Germany and Spain and a comparison', Karl Stuke Fraunhofer Institute for Systems and Innovation Research.

Rehfeldt, K. (1995) 'Wind energy use in Germany—Status 31.12.1995', *DEWI Magazin*, 18–20.

Ruchser, M. (2002) 'Analysis of the legislation regarding renewable energy sources in the EU member states: Financial report of Germany', Bonn: Altener, ENER-IURE Project Phase III, Forum für Zukunftenergien (Forum for Future Energy).

Sabatier, P. A. and Jenkins-Smith, H. (1999) 'The advocacy coalition framework: An assessment', in P. Sabatier (ed.) *Theories of the Policy Process*, Boulder: Westview Press, 117–66.

Scharpf, F. (1997) *Games Real Actors Play: Actor-Centered Institutionalism in Policy Research*, Boulder: Westview Press.

Turowski, G. (2002) *Spatial Planning in German: Structures and Concepts* (ed.) Hannover: Akademie für Raumforschung und Landesplanung (ARL).

Van Erp, F. (1997) *Siting Processes for Wind Energy Projects in Germany: Public Participation and the Response of the Local Population*, Eindhoven: Technische Universiteit Eindhoven.

Weale, A., et al. (2003) *Environmental Governance in Europe: An Ever Closer Ecological Union?*, 2nd edn, Oxford: Oxford University Press.

Weidner, H. (2005) 'Global equity versus public interest? The case of climate change policy in Germany', discussion paper no. SP IV 2005–102, Berlin: Wissenschaftszentrum Berlin für Sozialforschung.

WEAErl (2005) *Windenergie Erlass (Entwurf)—Grundsätze für Planung und Genehmigung von Windkraftanlagen* [Wind Energy Decree (Draft)—Fundamentals for the planning and permitting of wind energy applications.], Düsseldorf: Ministerium für Bauen und Verkehr, Ministerium für Wirtschaft, Mittelstand und Energien, Ministerium für Umwelt und Naturschutz, Landwirtschaft und Verbraucherschutz [the State Ministry for Building and Transport, the State Ministry for Economy, Economy, Small-and Medium sized business (or Self-employed) and Energy; and the State Ministry for Environment and Nature Protection, Agriculture and Consumer Protection.]

Wolsink, M. (1996) 'Dutch wind power policy—Stagnating implementation of renewables', *Energy Policy*, 24(12): 1079–88.

———. (2000) 'Wind power and the NIMBY-myth: institutional capacity and the limited significance of public support', *Renewable Energy*, 21(1): 49–64.

Wurzel, R., Jordan, A., Zito, A. and Brückner, L. (2003) From high regulatory state to social and ecological market economy? New environmental policy instruments in Germany', *Environmental Politics*, 12(1): 115–36.

Yin, R. K. (1994) *Case Study Research: Design and Methods*, 2nd edn, London: Sage Publications.

4 The Wind-Power Market in the Netherlands

Assessing the Performance of Wind Cooperatives

Susanne Agterbosch

INTRODUCTION

This chapter analyzes the performance of Dutch wind cooperatives. It is part of a comprehensive study focusing on wind energy for electricity generation, analyzing the evolution of the wind-power market in The Netherlands. This study analyzes the main types of wind-power entrepreneurs, their capacity to implement wind energy, and the social and institutional conditions that affected their investments in three successive market periods: *'Monopoly powers'* (1996–1997) *'Interbellum'* (1996–1997), and *'Free market'* (1998–2004) (Agterbosch 2004, 2006, 2007).

Wind cooperatives are one of the main types of entrepreneurs that own the total capacity installed in The Netherlands. The other entrepreneurial groups are energy distributors, small private investors, and new independent wind-power producers. Comparing wind cooperatives with small private investors and energy distributors, based on the total capacity installed over the last fifteen years, one comes to the conclusion that wind cooperatives have been of minor importance. It will be shown that their inferior position on the market coheres with some exceptional organizational characteristics. Wind power exploitation is not a way to make money for wind cooperatives, but rather a way to promote a sustainable society based on renewable energy sources. This idealistic background, just like the voluntary character of the organizations, influenced their behaviour in each of the three market periods and clearly distinguished this entrepreneurial group.

All twenty-five Dutch wind cooperatives were founded during a relatively short period, from 1986 to 1992. By now, eleven of these have been disbanded or have merged. The majority of the cooperatives that continued to exist are small organizations with only a limited number of turbines. It will be shown that the few cooperatives that performed better changed their character: they chose to professionalize to a more or less degree.

In addressing wind cooperatives and their market performance, special attention is paid to community ownership in some other countries. We will see that Dutch wind cooperatives deviate from cooperative arrangements in

Denmark and Germany, i.e., countries in which community ownership has played a major role in the successful development of wind power.

The chapter is organized as follows. First, the analytical concept of implementation capacity, which provides a description and explanation of differences over time in the performance of different types of entrepreneurs, is outlined. Second, important background information is provided on the development of the wind-power market in The Netherlands. Important entrepreneurial groups are defined and market shares are given. This market description is coupled with the division of the period 1989–2004 into three successive market periods. Third, there is a focus on wind cooperatives: their characteristics and market performance are also explained. Fourth, Dutch wind cooperatives are compared with community ownership in Denmark and Germany. Finally, key conclusions and reflections are outlined.

IMPLEMENTATION CAPACITY

Central to the analyses are the institutional context regulatory framework and the social context as explanatory variables for the emergence and performance of different entrepreneurial groups. The actual results of their investment behaviour, in terms of the amount of wind-power capacity actually implemented, has been analyzed using the concept of *implementation capacity* (IC). This concept is defined as the capacity of wind-power entrepreneurs to implement wind turbines. The IC is determined by the sum of the relevant economic, technical, institutional, and social conditions and mutual interdependencies. These conditions affect the decisions made by wind cooperatives on investments in wind power and determine the opportunities for this entrepreneurial group to actually implement wind-power projects. Every type of condition is necessary, but not in itself sufficient for implementation. To analyze (changes in) implementation capacity, the research specifically focused on two groups of conditions and their interdependencies.

The first group of conditions is the group of institutional conditions: explicit formalized policies and rules on different government levels, imposed on all stakeholders by top-down decision-making procedures, such as the Electricity Act (EA), the Spatial Planning Act, National Environmental Policy Plans, the Environmental Management Act, and spatial planning and permitting procedures. Enforcement is guaranteed by a formal sanction system that makes the imposed rules of the game operational.

The second group of conditions is the group of social conditions: the ways in which different stakeholders deal with prevailing institutional conditions. Social conditions are actions of, and cooperation or competition between, a variety of stakeholders involved (wind-power entrepreneurs, government authorities, landowners, environmental organizations, and local residents), in line with their interests, strategies, resources, and power positions.

Third, the research focuses on the interdependencies between these institutional and social conditions. In particular, the research focuses on changes in institutional conditions, the consequences of these changes for investment behaviour, and the possibility to implement wind turbines.

THE DEVELOPMENT OF THE DUTCH WIND-POWER MARKET

The Dutch wind-power market is not a homogeneous set of actors. In this section, market developments over the last fifteen years will be outlined, showing that, in fact, we need to distinguish at least four different types of entrepreneurs. They own the total capacity installed in The Netherlands (Figure 4.1):[1]

- *Small private investors* (mainly farmers): -ower exploitation is a form of supplementary income for this entrepreneurial group. Their core business lies outside the energy sector.
- *Electricity sector* (energy distributors): Wind-power exploitation is a small but growing business component for these companies. Their core business is in producing and selling a portfolio of (renewable) energy sources.
- *New independent wind-power producers*: Wind-power exploitation is a (new) part of their core business, which is most likely related to the renewable energy sector.
- *Wind cooperatives*: For this entrepreneurial group, wind-power exploitation is not a means of making money, but a means of working toward a sustainable society.

Each of these types of entrepreneurs has been active since the end of the 1980s, but they followed very different development paths and performed differently throughout the years. At the beginning of the 1990s, energy distributors dominated the wind-power market. Comparing energy distributors and small private investors on the basis of the total capacity that was installed, one comes to the conclusion that while the contribution of small private producers increased, the role of the electricity sector decreased in importance. Over the last few years, small private investors have caught up with—and in 2002, even surpassed—the electricity sector in terms of total capacity installed over the whole period. Also, the relative importance of new independent wind-power producers increased considerably over the last few years, and even surpassed energy distributors. Wind cooperatives, however, remained marginal on the wind-power market. Their market share fluctuated between 0 per cent and 4 per cent, with an exceptional peak in the year 2000, when they realized 9 per cent of total capacity installed. Though the number of cooperatives almost equalled the number of new independent wind-power producers, they seemed less well equipped to deal with the new setting of the liberalized market since the end of the 1990s.

Windmill Capacity Installed Per Year (MW)

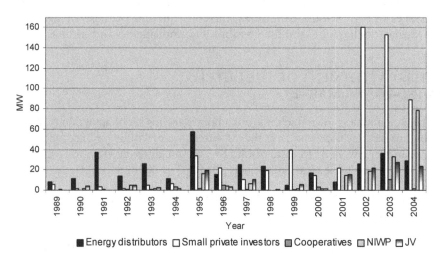

Figure 4.1 Wind-turbine capacity installed per year (MW). Sources: KEMA 2002/2003; Wind Service Holland 2003/2004.

Contribution to Windmill Capacity Installed Per Year %

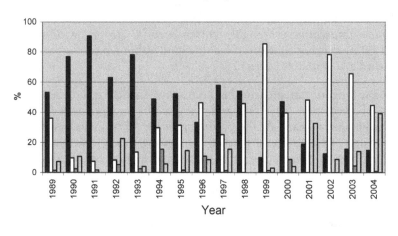

Figure 4.2 Contribution to wind-turbine capacity installed per year (%). Sources: KEMA 2002/2003; Wind Service Holland 2003/2004.

From this market description, we can deduce three successive market periods. This division is based on the performance of the four categories of entrepreneurs, changes in institutional conditions, and changes in relationships between the main categories of actors on the electricity market, such as generators, suppliers, consumers, and authorities at different levels of government.

Monopoly powers (1989–1995), the first period, started with the implementation of the EA in 1989, which separated electricity production from electricity supply and consumption. This was a major turnabout in the vertically integrated monopolistic electricity supply sector of those days. It was the very beginning of competition with energy distributors entering into decentralized generation. A lengthy tradition of interrelatedness between the Ministry of Economic Affairs and the traditionally state-owned electricity sector determined policy developments in this period. Policies on renewables consisted of voluntary agreements, in which a central role was assigned to the energy distributors, which were regarded as the main implementers of large-scale wind technology. The financial incentive system focused on the electricity supply side: It mainly consisted of investment subsidies. There was no green electricity market. Energy distributors dominated in terms of the number of turbines and total capacity installed annually in this period.

Interbellum (1996–1997), the second period, started with the publication of the third White Paper on Energy in 1996, which outlined the essential elements of future Dutch electricity policy: liberalization of the electricity sector and promotion of a sustainable energy supply. The years 1996 and 1997 were intermediate years devoted to laying the groundwork for the new liberalized market. The focus of the financial incentive system changed. Stimulation of supply was no longer considered feasible under free-market conditions. Accordingly, the financial incentive system switched from a subsidy to a fiscal system with demand-side measures, such as voluntary pricing schemes. During these intermediate years, small private investors overtook the electricity sector with regard to the number of turbines and total capacity installed annually.

Free market (1998–2004), the third period, started with the passing of the EA in 1998, which created the framework for the liberalization of the market. The liberalization of the market improved the bargaining position of private power producers, who were no longer obliged to sell their electricity to the regional energy distributor. In July 2001, the green electricity market was the first segment of the retail market that was fully opened to competition. Simultaneously, due to the greening of the tax system, suppliers were able to offer green electricity for the same price or even cheaper than electricity from fossil fuel sources. The economic conditions for wind power had never been as favourable in The Netherlands. New suppliers entered the market and started to treat consumers as customers with freedom of choice. A drastic increase in demand for green electricity occurred. Small private investors started to dominate the wind-power market in terms of the number of turbines, the number of projects, and total capacity installed annually. The relative importance of new independent wind-power producers also increased, and even surpassed that of energy distributors. Wind cooperatives were the only type of private investors which remained of minor importance in terms of projects and capacity installed.

In showing the correlation between changes in institutional conditions and social conditions and the performance of wind cooperatives, we will need to discuss the dynamics in these conditions in each of the three market periods. We will do this in the sections on the periods 1989–2002. First, we will go into the specific characteristics and market performance of this entrepreneurial group in the next two sections.

CHARACTERISTICS OF DUTCH WIND COOPERATIVES

The Dutch wind cooperatives are organizations in which citizens have a common interest in producing and selling wind power on the electricity market. The following characteristics describe these organizations:

1. They have a strong idealistic background; ideological incentives are the main driving force behind activities.
2. They are locally or regionally oriented organizations.
3. The members are citizens with no professional connection to the electricity sector.
4. The members serve to generate social support and they originally provided for the financing of the organization.
5. The organizations are managed by volunteers, although some work with a paid staff.
6. There exists a rather closed collaborative approach among the cooperatives.

The first feature of the Dutch wind cooperative is the idealistic background. The origin of the Dutch wind cooperatives is strongly linked to the Dutch Organisation for Renewable Energy (*Organisatie voor Duurzame Energie* [ODE]). ODE was itself established in the 1970s as a renewable energy pioneer's association. In the 1980s, workers from ODE visited all kinds of local groups, including environmental protest groups, to explain and promote the concept of wind cooperatives. ODE focused its attention on the coastal areas because the efficiency of wind turbines in the inland section of the country was insufficient in those days. As a result, twenty-five cooperatives were established during a relatively short period, from 1986 to 1992, especially in what are known as 'wind-abundant (coastal) areas'. In the meantime, eleven of the wind cooperatives have been disbanded or have merged. Most of these mergers have taken place between small cooperatives from the same region, which experienced problems due to a lack of human capacity.

The founders of the cooperatives objected to nuclear power and wanted to offer an alternative. This idealistic background clearly distinguishes this type of entrepreneur. Idealistic incentives, such as environmental considerations, are the decisive input to investment decisions.[2] The main interest is not to make money by wind-power exploitation, but to promote a sustainable society based on renewable sources. Cooperatives try to achieve this aim by developing wind projects based on strong local support and public participation. For some cooperatives, the main purpose was (and is) to demonstrate the feasibility of wind-power exploitation in their region.

In addition to developing wind-power projects, most cooperatives also develop other activities at the local or regional level. They inform the local population and politics through demonstrations and fairs, lectures at schools, newsletters, and websites. The majority of cooperatives lobby to influence local and regional policy making on wind energy, i.e., the adoption of wind energy in the municipal and regional land-use plan. Lobbying at the national level is left to the umbrella association ODE. This national wind lobby, however, never lived up to its promise, as will be shown later.

A second feature of the Dutch wind cooperative is the local or regional orientation in wind-power generation. At the end of the 1980s, wind cooperatives mutually agreed on the working area of each cooperative so no competition could occur: investments are restricted to the locality of the organizations. In addition, two wind cooperatives apply a strict residence requirement for membership. Although the other twelve cooperatives do not apply such a residence requirement, in practise, most of their members are citizens of the region where the cooperative is located.

Third, in 2002, the cooperatives together had 5,879 members (Figure 4.3) (Loenen van 2003: 24). This means that 0.05 per cent of the Dutch population owns a stake in a wind cooperative. Members are citizens with no professional connection to the electricity sector. In the beginning years, members were willing to accept a below-market return or no return at all in order to support the cooperative: 'We did not know whether wind power exploitation was financially feasible when we started and we did not expect to earn a profit (Loenen van 2003: 23)'. Although at present, members receive an annual dividend, which is way above market level, nearly all of them reinvest their dividends. In general, cooperatives actively recruit members only at the moment that new turbines are installed. Considering that the majority of cooperatives have not realized any projects since 1995, membership figures have stagnated or declined since that year. Three of the four largest wind cooperatives are exceptions: membership figures of Zeeuwind, Deltawind, and Kennemerwind kept on growing. These large cooperatives are also the cooperatives that were most successful in terms of the number of turbines installed (see also Figure 4.4).

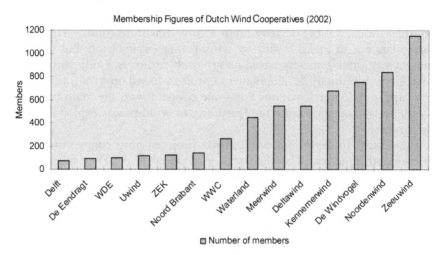

Figure 4.3 Membership figures of Dutch wind cooperatives in 2002. Source: Loenen van 2003: 24.

The fourth characteristic is that wind cooperatives originally raised all of their capital from the members. This financing strategy has changed over the years. Since the mid-1990s, they have also used mortgages and the proceeds of wind electricity sales to finance their activities. Members do not serve any longer to raise finances for new projects, but primarily to generate social support.

The fifth characteristic of the Dutch wind cooperative is the voluntary and amateurish character. The active members, who put much effort into the cooperative in the early years, are still the backbone of the organization today. Rejuvenation of active members, or membership in general, hardly occurred.

The dependence on volunteers impeded the operational process of wind-power implementation for half of the cooperatives. For three of them, a lack of human capacity even prevented them from project development at all. The governing boards of cooperatives consist of members who work full time, having little time left to devote to the cooperative. 'We have big plans, but not enough people to realize them (Loenen van 2003: 44)'. More-over, the scope and structure of knowledge at the side of these volunteers is usually limited, which is—in view of the complexity of procedures and the rather dynamic electricity market—a relative disadvantage.

The other half of the cooperatives experienced fewer problems with attracting sufficient human capacity. Four of them—Zeeuwind, Del-tawind, Kennemerwind, and Noordenwind—have decided to profession-alize, and now work with a paid staff. 'We have decided to engage people in an early stage to guarantee continuity in labour. Project development needs unbroken attention, which volunteers can insufficiently deliver'.[3] These four cooperatives own a share of 62 per cent of the turbines and a share of 80 per cent of the capacity ever installed by this entrepreneurial group (Figure 4.4).

The final characteristic is the collaborative approach among the Dutch cooperatives. Communication lines between the Dutch wind cooperatives are short. Wind cooperatives meet four times each year at the umbrella association, ODE. At these meetings, they discuss wind-power developments in The Netherlands and abroad, as well as problems they encounter in the operational process of wind-power implementation. The meetings contribute to knowledge and expertise building amongst of the cooperatives. Besides these meetings, some wind cooperatives maintain telephonic or written contact on a bilateral and very irregular basis. Personal features and actual developments in ongoing projects drive these contacts. By means of their websites and newsletters, they also inform their fellow cooperatives.

Being an exceptional type of investors—the only type of investor managed by volunteers and with ideological incentives serving as the main driving force behind investments—the question arises of how wind cooperatives have performed.

MARKET PERFORMANCE OF
DUTCH WIND COOPERATIVES

The performance in terms of realized capacity in the different Dutch provinces over the last fifteen years can be described based on the following features:

1. A continuous minor position on the market.
2. A strong decrease in the number of projects and a decrease in solitary installations.
3. Moderate but increasing lead times of the projects.
4. A strong concentration in ownership of wind-power capacity within this entrepreneurial group.
5. A limited employment of the joint ownership strategy with other entrepreneurial groups.

The first feature—the position on the wind-power market—has been described (see Figures 4.1 and 4.2). Wind cooperatives have been of minor importance as far as the statistics on the total capacity installed are concerned. The annual contribution fluctuated between 0 per cent and 5 per cent over the last 15 years, with some exceptional peaks in the years 1994, 1996, and 2000, when they realized 16 per cent, 11 per cent, and 9 per cent of total capacity installed, respectively.

Table 4.1   Characteristics of Projects Realized by Wind Cooperatives

Size of project	1989–1995		1996–1997		1998–2004	
	Number	%	Number	%	Number	%
Solitary	39	81.3	4	57.1	3	42.9
2 or 3 turbines	6	12.5	1	14.3	3	42.9
4 or 5 turbines	1	2.1	1	14.3	0	0
6 to10 turbines	0	0	1	14.3	1	14.3
11 and above	2	4.2	0	0	0	0
Average number of projects per year		6.9		3.5		1
Average number of turbines per project		1.3		2.3		2.1
Average capacity per project (MW)		0.2		0.8		2.3

Source: Author generated.

The second feature of the performance of this entrepreneurial group is the strong decrease in the number of projects in the second and third market periods (see Table 4.1). They deviate on this aspect from the other two private entrepreneurial groups. The average number of projects per year installed by small private investors and new independent wind-power producers increased in the third market period. As the number of projects strongly decreased, the average number of turbines per project increased during the course of the years. The dominant position of solitary installations disappeared. Also, the average capacity installed per project increased considerably, which is a combined consequence of the increase in the average number of turbines per project and technological progress.

The third feature of the performance of this entrepreneurial group is the moderate but increasing lead-times of the projects. We conducted a survey among the fourteen Dutch wind cooperatives with regard to projects realized in the period from 1989 to 2004.[4] The survey showed that the average lead-time required for the authorisation of the projects was forty-one months. This is the time required for authorisation, including the time required for informal deliberations and terms for appeal. None of the projects was completed within 1 year, 25 per cent of the projects were completed within 2 years, and only 50 per cent were completed within 3 years. Formally, planning and licensing takes eighteen to twenty-four months,[5] which implicates that, on average, seventeen to twenty-three months were required for informal deliberation, handling of formal protests, and construction. Cooperatives are in between energy distributors (lead-times of an average of more than six years) and small private investors (lead-times of an average of one to two years) with regard to the average lead-times.

The fourth feature is the concentration of ownership within this entrepreneurial group. Currently, 2 of the 14 wind cooperatives own 75 per cent of the wind-power capacity installed by this type of wind-power entrepreneur. These two wind cooperatives are Deltawind and Zeeuwind. The dominance of the cooperatives Deltawind and Zeeuwind is less pronounced in terms of the number of turbines installed. The number of turbines installed by Noordenwind and Kennemerwind are of the same magnitude (Figure 4.4).

The final feature is the limited employment of the joint ownership strategy with other types of entrepreneurs, at least in terms of the number of projects realized. Over the last fifteen years, only four out of ninety-three projects realized by cooperatives (4.3 per cent) have been realized in joint ownership with other types of entrepreneurs.

Looking at these features and comparing them with the market performance of small private investors and energy distributors,[6] some similarities and differences can be observed. All entrepreneurial groups show a geographical concentration in investments in the coastal provinces. Looking at the average project scale and the average lead-times, we observe that cooperatives are in between energy distributors and small private investors. Conversely, wind cooperatives do not occupy an intermediate position in terms of the number of projects and capacity installed. The limited number of projects and capacity installed, moderate lead-times notwithstanding, are in fact the most striking features of the performance of wind cooperatives as a group. However, the organizational characteristics and the market performances show that we may distinguish different subgroups: The first group encompasses the eleven wind cooperatives, which have disbanded or have merged. The second group encompasses the wind cooperatives, which continue to exist, but are moderate in size and own just a limited number of turbines. The third group encompasses the four larger cooperatives, who have more or less professionalized and who have established the majority of turbines installed by this group. These cooperatives are Kennemerwind, Noordenwind, Deltawind, and Zeeuwind (Figure 4.4).

In the next sections, we shift to a combined regional and national perspective to analyze the performance of these subgroups. Here, we analyze the relative importance of the organizational characteristics in view of changing social and institutional conditions, such as changing legislation and changing financial incentive schemes. The discussion will focus on how the three subgroups have reacted upon changes in social and institutional conditions in each of the three market periods.

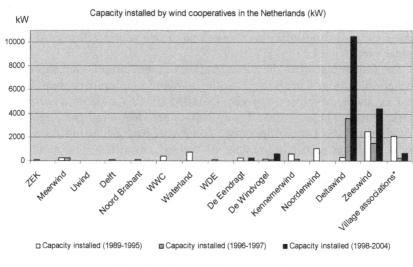

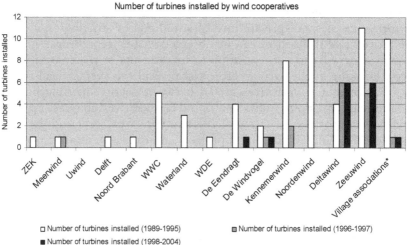

Figure 4.4   Capacity and number of turbines installed by wind cooperatives in the Netherlands. Several local communities or village associations in the province of Friesland implemented wind turbines in order to stimulate the use of renewable energy sources, simultaneously generating financial resources for social and cultural activities in their villages.

Source: Author generated.

MONOPOLY POWERS (1989–1995)

The major institutional change that determined implementation capacity developments in this period was the 1989 EA. This Act prescribed that energy distributors had to pay 'the most stimulating compensation' for renewable energy. However, 'the most stimulating compensation' turned out to be an ambiguous formulation: the law was not clear on this aspect. The methods for calculating this compensation were set out in the 'Standard Arrangements for Redeliveries' (SAR), part of the EA, and were revised annually. Payback tariffs consisted of the avoided costs component (SAR) and the Milieu Actie Plan (MAP) levy. Energy distributors imposed the MAP levy on consumer tariffs, which enabled them to support the generation of wind energy. Both the SAR and the MAP levy were institutional conditions with a strong element of self-regulation: energy distributors decided on the distribution of the MAP subsidies, and the actual conditions for the payback tariffs had to be agreed upon on a case-by-case basis. This peculiar configuration of institutional and social conditions was far from ideal for private investors. Private investors, who were obliged to sell their electricity to the regional energy distributor, were dependent on the energy distributor for both the SAR component and the MAP subsidy—a company that was also their competitor on the wind-power supply and green electricity market. Although the payback tariffs differed per energy distributor, they were low in general.

Looking at the total configuration of national institutional and social conditions, the same conclusion must be drawn for all private investors during this period: that of a rather weak implementation capacity (see Figure 4.5, arrow 1). This conclusion seems at odds with the fact that it was precisely during this period that cooperatives put into place most of the turbines they would ever implement.

How can we explain this? First, cooperatives did not follow the same rationality as the other types of entrepreneurs. They did not intend to make money out of their wind projects, and therefore, they were less concerned about hampering financial conditions. Their idealistic background made them rather insensible to low profits or even to no profits at all. Cooperatives were a new phenomenon in The Netherlands, and they were youthful associations with enthusiastic volunteers. The expansion in membership that took place between 1986 and 1995 applies to all cooperatives. Research into cooperative associations shows a correlation between increase in membership and dedication or level of activities undertaken by members (Meadowcroft 2002). This period of membership growth, combined with idealistic tendencies, constituted a social context that seemed to nullify other impeding conditions, in a certain sense (Figure 4.5, number 2).

In addition, impeding national social and institutional conditions were nullified by bilateral agreements between some wind cooperatives and their regional energy distributor. A few energy distributors were willing to pay a rather attractive compensation per kilowatt-hour produced by the regional wind cooperatives. These favourable agreements resulted, as a rule, from specific regional or local social conditions, such as short communication lines and the accidental enthusiasm of employees with sufficient high positions within the regional energy distributor. These positive local social

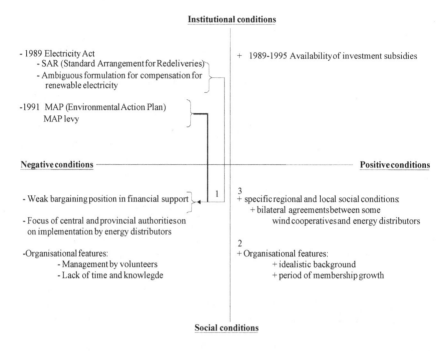

Figure 4.5   Constituent conditions of the implementation capacity for cooperatives in the Monopoly powers (1989–1995). Source: Author generated.

conditions turned out to be the basis for the success of the third subgroup of cooperatives who would establish the majority of the turbines (Figure 4.5, number 3).

A first important breakthrough was the increase of the payback tariff by the regional energy distributor in the province of Friesland in 1990 (Wind Service Holland 2004). The Noordenwind cooperative was able to take advantage of this favourable payback tariff, and of the circumstance that most municipalities in this province were helpful in planning at the beginning of the 1990s: 'We implemented all our turbines between 1989 and 1995. Implementation went rather easy. Municipalities cooperated in planning and there were no opponents. Lead times were 1 to 2 years'.[7]

A second example of positive local, social conditions concerned the cooperative Deltawind. The director of the regional energy distributor on the island Goeree Overflakkee, in the province of Zuid Holland, was president of this cooperative at the same time. A very favourable payback agreement emanated from the negotiations for the first wind turbines of Deltawind in 1990 and 1993. 'Successors of that director must have wondered about the terms of that agreement. However, these successors came from outside the island, at a time that the regional energy distributor was already taken over by Eneco'.[8]

A third example applied to the wind cooperative Zeeuwind, which received a very favourable compensation per kilowatt-hour. The energy distributor in the province of Zeeland paid 100 per cent of the consumer price for a maximum of 750 kWh per member of this cooperative. This rule additionally stimulated Zeeuwind to recruit new members, and it currently is the largest wind cooperative by far (see Figure 4.3).

A final example concerned the energy distributor Provincial Energiebedrijf Noord Holland (PEN) in the province of Noord Holland. PEN allowed the cooperative Kennemerwind to establish wind turbines in a wind-power plant originally built and exploited by PEN. It moreover adopted a very favourable payback tariff for cooperatively owned wind turbines (almost double the payback tariffs for private producers). Due to this favourable payback tariff and an investment subsidy of 35 per cent, returns were about 28 per cent during the first 5 or 6 years of the existence of Kennemerwind.[9]

These examples of positive regional and local social conditions correlate with the four cooperatives which performed best in terms of the number of turbines installed. The examples illustrate the importance of regional and local conditions for the implementation capacity of a particular cooperative. Differences in these regional and local conditions laid the foundation of the tripartition in different subgroups.

INTERBELLUM (1996–1997)

Nonprofit organizations, like cooperatives, were unable to make full use of the fiscal arrangements that were gradually introduced in this transitional period. The switch in governmental financial incentive system (from a subsidy to a fiscal system) deteriorated the competitiveness of cooperatives on the wind-power market. In addition, the unfavourable national institutional conditions (SAR and MAP) of the previous period still existed (see Figure 4.6, arrow 1). These conditions resulted in a weakening of implementation capacity. Only five cooperatives established turbines in this period, and the total number of projects installed by wind cooperatives decreased by half. The division in different subgroups, which had its origin in the former period, perpetuated. Three of the four successful wind cooperatives, which performed well in the first market period, established more than 80 per cent of the turbines installed by wind cooperatives in this second period. The exception was the cooperative Noordenwind. Noordenwind performed well in the first market period, but not in the second. Regional institutional regulatory and social developments in the province of Friesland, which is the working area of Noordenwind, explain this reversal in performance. Halfway through the 1990s, an increase in social resistance affected the operational process of policy making in this province. Municipalities became less inclined to cooperate in planning. Moreover, administrative discussions within the provincial authorities indicated a new policy direction, which would make the installation of new solitary turbines impossible.

The gradual introduction of fiscal instruments led to a change in funding strategy (Figure 4.6, arrow 2). Originally, cooperatives had raised all of the capital from their members, but now they started to consider bank loans. The introduction of the environmental impact assessment-scheme, the Vamil-scheme, and Green Funds[10] made it far more attractive to take out a mortgage. Dutch banks were looking for green projects to invest in with their Green Funds, and cooperatives were able to take advantage of the environmental impact assessment-scheme and the Vamil-scheme by means of a 'sale and lease back' plan. Continuing technological developments additionally stimulated this change in funding strategy. The increasing amount of capital needed to build larger turbines became very difficult to collect solely from individual members. The new funding strategy partly undermined a central point of departure of the wind cooperatives: developing wind projects based on strong local support and public participation. Members were no longer needed for financing the organizations and the projects. Membership figures stabilized or declined slightly. Registration of new members hardly occurred after 1995 (Figure 4.6, arrow 3).

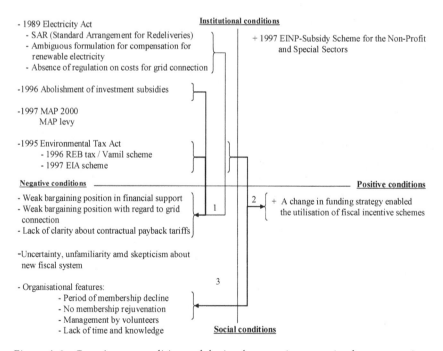

Figure 4.6 Constituent conditions of the implementation capacity for cooperatives in the Interbellum (1995–1996). Source: Author generated.

Like small private investors, wind cooperatives encountered problems due to a lack of clarity about contractual payback tariffs after the introduction of the Regulrende Energiebelasting (REB) tax or ecotax (Art. 36o of the new Environmental Tax Act) in 1996. However, while the Union of Private Wind Turbine Operators De Vereniging van Particuliere Windenergie Exploitatanten (PAWEX) and some small private investors in the provinces of Noord Holland and Flevoland went to court to obtain clarity about the interpretation of the Environmental Tax Act, ODE and the wind cooperatives awaited these judgments.[11]

FREE MARKET (1998–2002)

During this third period, national institutional conditions improved for cooperatives and for all private investors. The major improvements were: (1) liberalization of the wholesale market and the accompanying rules for grid connection; (2) the greening of the fiscal system; and (3) the liberalization of the green consumer market. However, unlike small private investors, wind cooperatives were largely unable to seize the opportunities provided by the liberalized market and to adapt to the requirements set by increased competition. It will be illustrated that this inability to seize these opportunities can also be explained by their voluntary character.

The 1998 EA created the framework for the liberalization of the wholesale electricity market. It was the first important institutional change in this period. Although in general it brought advantages for wind cooperatives, it also brought some difficulties. The major advantage was that it caused the disintegration of the monopoly powers of energy distributors. The bargaining power of wind cooperatives theoretically increased because they were no longer obliged to sell their electricity to the regional energy distributor (Figure 4.7, arrow 1). However, the sale of electricity in the new, somewhat more competitive, setting turned out to be problematic:

> Until recently, the sale of electricity was in a sense an automatic action. It was a matter of arranging a sufficient price with the regional electricity company. Nowadays, things are a bit more complicated. More professionalism is required to reap the rewards of liberalisation and to stipulate a good payback tariff[12] (Figure 4.7, arrow 2).

Moreover, it has already been shown that short communication lines and a good understanding between wind cooperatives and a few regional energy distributors had been an important condition for success. The amalgamations that took place among energy distributors at the end of the 1990s put pressure on these short communication lines. For energy distributors, feelings of solidarity with a certain region or wind cooperative lessened.

The second institutional change, the greening of the fiscal system, led to favourable economic conditions for wind-power implementation, which enlarged the implementation capacity of wind—power entrepreneurs in general. Moreover, the implementation of the Green Label system in January 1998, which was replaced by the green certificate system in 2001, additionally improved the bargaining position for private producers and, thus, for wind cooperatives. These economic policy instruments replaced the MAP levy and added to the bargaining position of private producers in financial support for installing new wind turbines. These institutional changes led to the emergence of many new market players, mainly small private investors and new independent wind-power producers (Figure 4.7, arrow 3). Different entrepreneurs were more frequently competing for the same location, a situation for which cooperatives were less well equipped than professional entrepreneurs. The more professional competitors on the market often possessed more human capacity and/or capital to hold on to a location. This competitive setting forced some wind cooperatives to collaborate with other types of entrepreneurs:

> We were working on a location but could not keep up with developments. Because things went too slowly according to the landowner, he summoned us to cooperate with an independent wind power producer.

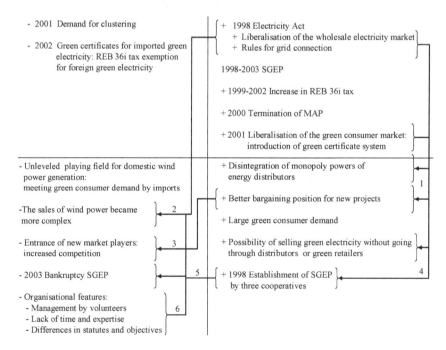

Figure 4.7 Constituent conditions of the implementation capacity for cooperatives in the Free Market (1998–2004). Source: Author generated.

Although this collaboration started as a marriage of convenience it in the end worked out alright.[13]

The liberalization of the wholesale market and the guaranteed access to the grid stimulated three cooperatives to establish the Association of Green Energy Producers (*Stichting Groene Energie Producenten* [SGEP]) in 1998. SGEP aimed to supply its members with green electricity without having to go through distribution companies or green retailers (Figure 4.7, arrow 4). The initiative anticipated the third institutional change in this period: the liberalization of the green consumer market in 2001, which would offer SGEP the opportunity to supply not only members with green electricity, but also other end users in The Netherlands.

SGEP is an example of a new social praxis that arose from changing institutional conditions. It can be compared with the cooperative Windunie, which was established by small private investors in 2002 with the aim of jointly selling green electricity on the electricity market. However, whilst Windunie became rather successful and added to the implementation capacity of small private investors, SGEP failed to survive on the liberalized market (Figure 4.7, arrow 5).

How can we explain this? First, the founding cooperatives encountered problems with acquiring production capacity due to their long-term contracts with distributors[14] (Marsman 2000; Radema 1999). However, the more important problems were organizational in character (Figure 4.7, arrow 6). Due to its voluntary nature, SGEP could not keep up with developments on the rather dynamic liberalizing market. In addition, differences in objectives and statutes of the founding cooperatives hampered collaboration in the area of electricity supply (De Windvogel 2003). These problems got worse due to some personal conflicts, which hampered efficient management.[15] Besides the three founding cooperatives, no other wind cooperatives supported SGEP. Other cooperatives joined broader market developments and started to sell their electricity to one of the emerging commercial green retailers on the market, like Echte Energie, Greenchoices, and Windunie.

Only four cooperatives established turbines in this period, and the total number of projects installed by cooperatives halved again (Table 4.1). Among the four wind cooperatives that established turbines were two of the four cooperatives that had chosen to work with a paid staff. These cooperatives, Deltawind and Zeeuwind, together established more than 80 per cent of the turbines installed by this entrepreneurial group in this period. The other two cooperatives that worked with a paid staff (Noordenwind and Kennemerwind) did not establish any projects. In the previous section, we saw that Noordenwind had to contend with difficulties in the area of local and regional policy making. The same applied for Kennemerwind. Kennemerwind started a new project in 1997 and met with a variety of problems, including slowness in policy making by the local authorities and problems due to provincial policy on ecological shores. This provincial policy was considered incompatible with the project, which still needs to be implemented.[16]

The vast majority of wind cooperatives did not establish any turbines in this period. They exploited the turbines that were installed in the first market period, and they had to contend with membership figures that stabilized or declined. This membership decline and the lack of recruitment of new active members became a problem for some cooperatives: 'The active members remained the same throughout the years. We previously were eager and devoted. However, our early enthusiasm has decreased somewhat' (Loenen van 2003: 44). The stagnation in the implementation of turbines and membership figures led to the disbanding of one cooperative in 2000, and to a number of mergers between small cooperatives in the province of Zuid Holland and Noord Holland in the period of 2000–2002.

COMMUNITY-OWNED WIND TURBINES IN DENMARK AND GERMANY

Before we step to the conclusions, this section compares Dutch wind cooperatives with community ownership in Denmark and Germany, i.e., countries in which joint ownership has played a major role in the successful deployment of wind power. These countries cover the majority of capacity growth in Europe over the last fifteen years.

Cooperative Arrangements in Denmark

The organization of wind-turbine development in Denmark is characterized by three types of ownership: wind turbines owned by wind cooperatives, wind turbines owned by single persons (such as farmers), and wind turbines owned by utilities.[17] From the 1980s until 1995, cooperatively owned turbines were dominant in Denmark. These turbines are owned and operated by about 2,100 wind cooperatives, which range in size from 100 to 200 people. Over 5 per cent of the Danish population owns a stake in a wind turbine, which increases public support for wind energy (Morthorst 1999; Toke 1999).

In 1978, about forty wind-turbine owners set up the 'Danish Windmill Owners Association'. This grassroots association negotiated collectively with electricity companies about the payback tariffs for private producers. In addition, this owners association and the 'Windturbine Manufacturing Association' coordinated lobbying efforts, and were able to influence national energy policy developments (Buen 2006; Kamp 2002: 152–53).

From the beginning of the 1980s, the national subsidy system in Denmark supported cooperative ownership, with a 30 per cent subsidy for individual and cooperative investments in wind energy. The subsidy was based on residence criteria: only people living in the district where the turbine was located were allowed to invest. Moreover, there was a limit on the amount any one investor was allowed to invest in a cooperatively owned wind turbine. These institutional conditions kept large commercial investors out (Nielsen 2002: 128).

A ten-year agreement in 1984 between the government, electricity companies, and the Danish Windmill Owners Association additionally boosted community ownership of wind turbines: electricity companies had to pay 35 per cent of grid connection costs and they had to buy wind electricity at 85 per cent of the consumer price.[18] In addition, an energy surcharge was introduced, which was paid directly to independent energy producers (Buen 2006: 4; Kamp 2002).

These policies and instruments to support community ownership matched the cooperative nature of the electricity supply system in Denmark. More than 100 power companies were responsible for the production and distribution of electricity at the time. Cooperative arrangements and municipalities owned these local power companies (Buen 2006; Vleuten van der & Raven 2006).

The dominance of cooperatively owned turbines remained until 1995. Since that year, single-owned turbines (mainly farmers) have dominated the market. This shift in ownership coincided with a relative decline in the internal rate of return for cooperatively owned turbines and a relative improvement of the internal rate of return of single-owned turbines. Although investments in wind power remained profitable for wind cooperatives, their market position declined due to competition by farmers (Morthorst 1999).

Although idealism was the principal motivator for wind cooperatives at the beginning of the 1980s, this quickly changed. The motive to invest in jointly owned wind turbines became a hybrid one, with both environmental and economic incentives being important for an investment decision (Morthorst 1999: 782). With revenues from cooperative investments being tax exempt, cooperative investments became extremely attractive for private individuals. The investments became tax driven (Buen 2006, 7–8).

Cooperative Arrangements in Germany

Wind power development in Germany started late compared to Denmark. Until the end of the 1980s, renewable energy faced a rather hostile electricity supply system, and only a few idealistic enthusiasts implemented wind turbines in those years. The situation changed with the 1991 Electricity Feed Act. This Act introduced guaranteed access to the grid and a proper remuneration price (90 per cent of the final consumer price) for private generators. Utilities were not entitled to receive any benefits under this Act.[19] The Act resulted in a market expansion of privately owned wind turbines, which, in turn, resulted in a growth of the political strength of the industry and owners association. This association was then able to add economic arguments to environmental arguments in favour of wind energy and had considerable influence on national energy policy developments (Breukers 2005; Jacobsson & Lauber 2006: 264–65).

The high and predictable income generation that resulted from the Electricity Feed Act motivated farmers, companies, and individuals to invest in wind power. Three types of private ownership of wind turbines emerged: small independent wind-power developers, farmer cooperatives, and 'burgerwindparks':

1. Farmer cooperatives organized themselves into informal cooperatives and developed their schemes incrementally. They owned about 50 per cent of Germany's wind-power capacity in 2004.
2. Small independent wind-power developers sold a high proportion of equity capital to local investors, mainly high-income earners. Individual investors could offset their marginal income taxes with wind-power investments. In 2004, about 40 per cent of wind-power capacity was developed this way.
3. Burgerwindparks consisted of wind-power projects owned and managed by a consortia of local citizens. Burgerwindparks owned about 10 per cent of Germany's wind-power capacity in 2004 (Toke 2005: 305). Only these burgerwindparks resemble the Dutch wind cooperatives, at least organizationally. However, they differ in objectives. Burgerwindparks principally aim at generating sources of income by way of supplying and selling wind electricity. They emerged at a moment that investing in wind energy became financially attractive for private individuals.

Comparing Dutch, Danish, and German Developments

When comparing Dutch wind cooperatives with cooperatives in Denmark and Germany, some remarkable differences can be noted.

First, in Denmark and in Germany, wind cooperatives capitalized on governmental incentives targeted specifically at cooperative or private ownership. In The Netherlands, conversely, there were no incentives for wind cooperatives in the period when they originated.

Second, the driving force behind the Dutch wind cooperatives was, and still is, idealism. Although idealism played a role in the emergence of cooperative ownership in Denmark and Germany, monetary returns became a more important driving force. Wind cooperatives in Denmark and Germany primarily aim at generating sources of income by supplying and selling wind electricity. They thus belong to the second type of cooperative arrangement distinguished previously in this discussion. Dutch wind cooperatives belong to the third variant.

Third, unlike in The Netherlands, joint ownership of wind turbines in Denmark and Germany is a widely spread social phenomenon, supported by strong associations. These associations have been able to influence national level policy making. Because community-owned wind turbines were strongly represented within these associations, they have been more powerful in negotiations at the national level than the wind cooperatives in The Netherlands.

REFLECTION ON THE MAIN FINDINGS

This chapter started with some background information on the main entrepreneurial groups in The Netherlands, their market shares, and the division of the period from 1989 to 2004 into three successive but distinct market periods. This was followed by a more detailed description of wind cooperatives and their market performance. The strong ideological inclination and the grassroots, voluntary character are the most notable characteristics of these locally oriented organizations. The most striking features of their market performance are the limited number of projects and capacity installed, notwithstanding the relatively moderate lead-times. Cooperatives continuously occupied a minor position on the market over the last fifteen years.

Ideological rather than economic arguments were decisive in the origin of the Dutch wind cooperatives. There were no national incentives in place when these organizations were set up. On the contrary, national social and institutional conditions during the first market period were very much to the disadvantage of the cooperatives. Despite these negative national conditions and limited organizational resources, such as finances and expertise, most cooperatives managed to implement one or a couple of wind turbines. This relative success depended on their own decisiveness and enthusiasm, combined with regional and local institutional regulatory and social conditions, such as willingness on the part of the regional energy distributor to pay a proper compensation per kilowatt-hour. Local social relations and short communication lines added to the implementation capacity of particular cooperatives. However, differences in these local conditions were huge and laid the foundation of a partition in three different subgroups, which followed different development paths and performed differently throughout the years.

The first subgroup consists of eleven wind cooperatives which have disbanded or have merged. The mergers took place in the first and the third market periods. Mergers took place between small cooperatives from the same region. A lack of human capacity and a lack of success in implementation prompted these mergers.

The second group encompasses the wind cooperatives who continued to exist, but which are moderate in size and own just a limited number of turbines. The vast majority of these cooperatives have not established any turbines since 1995. Compared to other professional entrepreneurial groups, they were less well equipped to deal with the depersonalization of the market, the increased competition, and the increase in the scale of wind-power projects. Their strong local roots and, in theory, large degree of public support turned out to be of less importance.

The third group encompasses the four larger cooperatives, who have more or less professionalized and who have established the majority of turbines installed by this entrepreneurial group. They worked with a paid staff and continued to realize wind-power projects in the second and third market periods. It seems reasonable to conclude that the degree of professionalism influenced the success in the operational process of implementation and determined the concentration in ownership within this entrepreneurial group. Only cooperatives that changed into more or less professional organizations working with a professional and paid staff have been able to hold their own as an investor on the market. However, the locality of these more successful cooperatives correlates to areas that had favourable payback agreements at the beginning of the 1990s. Moreover, two of the four cooperatives that work with a paid staff have not established any projects since 1996. They had to contend with difficulties in the area of local and regional policy making. Clearly, the degree of professionalism is not the only condition that determines the success of a cooperative. Regional and local social and institutional conditions are just as important.

Wind cooperatives as a group did not follow an economic rationality. The implementation capacity for wind cooperatives was always low in comparison to that of the other entrepreneurial groups. Nevertheless, they continued to strive for wind-power implementation. Looking at Figures 4.5 and 4.6, we notice the absence of positive national social and institutional conditions in the first and second market periods. In spite of this, it was during the first period that cooperatives put into place most of the turbines they would implement, which can be explained only by local and regional institutional regulatory and social developments. The third period is a different story. Looking at Figure 4.7, we notice national social and institutional improvements for wind cooperatives as for all private producers. However, while implementation by small private investors really expanded, it did not for wind cooperatives. Their amateurish and idealistic character kept them from seizing the opportunities provided by the broader process of liberalization.

The comparison with Denmark and Germany put the performance of the Dutch wind cooperatives in a broader perspective. Dutch wind cooperatives are cooperative arrangements for which ideological incentives are the decisive driving force behind activities. For cooperatives in Germany and Denmark, in contrast, monetary returns are more important. In these countries, cooperative arrangements capitalized on governmental incentives targeted specifically at cooperative or private ownership. The main reason for the expansion of cooperatively owned wind turbines in these countries is that cooperative investments became extremely attractive for private citizens. Especially in Denmark, wind cooperatives became a widely spread social phenomenon, supported by a strong wind-power association.

In The Netherlands, wind cooperatives remained a marginal phenomenon, and the umbrella association ODE never became influential, i.e., able to determine national energy development.

NOTES

1. One thing should be said about this distinction, which is based on ownership. During the period of 1996–2004, 13.1 per cent of the total capacity that was installed was realized in joint ownership. If a project is realized by a joint venture, the assignment of this project to particular entrepreneurial groups is based on proportion of ownership.
2. In addition, several wind cooperatives have used the proceeds of the sale of wind electricity to support financially unfeasible projects, such as the installation of solar panels or heat pumps at local schools. All these projects serve as demonstrations and education programmes and aim to generate public support for sustainable energy.
3. Springer, J. Personal communication, Zeeuwind, 20 March 2002.
4. The number of projects in the survey was limited. We received twenty questionnaires, twelve about projects realised before 1998, six about projects that had been recently completed, and two about projects that could not be implemented. Nevertheless, the survey covered 29 per cent of all projects, 45 per cent of all turbines, and 67 per cent of the capacity installed by wind cooperatives in The Netherlands. Moreover, all Dutch wind cooperatives participated, so no cooperative was overrepresented. In view of these figures, it is reasonable to assume that the results of the survey are a representative assessment of experiences of this entrepreneurial group.
5. The period required for authorization is 1.5 years (18 months) for the exemption of the municipal land-use plan, the assignment of the Construction Permit, and the assignment of the Environmental Permit, if each of these procedures is dealt with successively (apart from the terms required for appeal). This period is prolonged to 1.9 years (23 months) if the municipal land-use plan must be revised.
6. For a detailed description of the market performance of energy distributors and small private investors, see Agterbosch (2006).
7. Kruize, E. (Member of the board of Noordenwind), personal communication, 17 November 2004.
8. Tieleman, M. (Advisor of the board of Deltawind), personal communication, 6 January 2004; and Middelbos, A. (Employee Deltawind), personal communication, 12 January 2004.
9. Wind Service Holland, http://home.wxs.nl/~windsh/windsteun.html (accessed on 16 November 2005); and Gipe, P., http://www.wind-works.org/articles/Euro96TripReport.html (accessed on 13 January 2006).
10. Investors in green projects can obtain financing at lower interest rate from Green Funds. These funds are created from the savings of private individuals who are exempted from income taxes on interest received.
11. PAWEX took the view that the REB tax should be added to the contractual payback tariffs agreed upon in long-term contracts by distributors and private power producers. Energy distributors, on the contrary, were of the opinion that the tax should not be added in those cases in which the contractual payback tariff exceeded the sum of the avoided cost component (SAR) and the REB tax. The Ministry of Economic Affairs failed to provide for an unambiguous transitional arrangement.

12. Based on Springer, J. (Employee Zeeuwind), personal communication, 20 March 2002; Wiezer, F. (Representative ODE), Interview by Loes van Loenen, 8 July 2002; and Stoop, W.B. (Secretary Kennemerwind), Interview by Loes van Loenen, 11 June 2002.
13. Springer, J. (Employee Zeeuwind), personal communication, 20 March 2002.
14. To get started, SGEP needed production capacity and members to deliver the electricity. Both were acquired by means of a merger between SGEP and the cooperative Betuwind. The members of the cooperatives De Windvogel and Meerwind were also offered membership to SGEP, which additionally enlarged membership figures. However, the transfer of additional production capacity turned out to be a problem because of long-term contracts with energy distributors (Meerwind 1999, 2000).
15. Anonymous. (Member of the board of one of the founding cooperatives), personal communication, 4 June 2002.
16. Stoop, W.B. (Secretary Kennemerwind), written communication, 20 December 2004.
17. Wind turbines owned by utilities were mainly erected by the request of the government and played a minor role in the Danish wind power market (Morthorst 1999: 781–82).
18. Local ownership, imposed by the subsidy rules, stimulated the Danish wind-turbine manufacturing market. Danish wind-turbine buyers, being private persons or cooperatives, cooperated with the manufacturers to improve the turbines (Kamp 2002: 160).
19. In 2000, the Renewable Energy Sources Act replaced the Electricity Feed Act. Now, utilities qualify for a feed-in payment as well.

REFERENCES

Agterbosch, S. (2006) *Empowering Wind Power: On Social and Institutional Conditions Affecting the Performance of Entrepreneurs in the Wind Power Supply Market in the Netherlands*, Utrecht: Corpernicus Institute, Nederlands Geografische Studies 351.

Agterbosch, S., Glasbergen, P. and Vermeulen, W. (2007) 'Social barriers in wind power implementation in The Netherlands: Perceptions of wind power entrepreneurs and local civil servants of institutional and social conditions in realizing wind power projects', *Renewable & Sustainable Energy Reviews* 11: 1025–55.

Agterbosch, S., Vermeulen, W. and Glasbergen, P. (2004) 'Implementation of wind energy in the Netherlands: the importance of the social-institutional setting', *Energy Policy*, 32: 2049–66.

Breukers, S. (2005) 'Embedding wind power development: an international comparison on institutional capacity building for wind power implementation', paper presented at the European Consortium for Political Research (ECPR), Budapest. 9 September 2005.

Buen, J. (2006) Danish and Norwegian wind industry: the relationship between policy instruments, innovation and diffusion, *Energy Policy*, 34(18): 3887–3897.

De winduvogel. (2003) Wijzigingen m.b.t. zelf levering van 'groene energie', Windvaan7.

Jacobsson, S. and Lauber, V. (2006) 'The politics and policy of energy system transformation—explaining the German diffusion of renewable energy technology', *Energy Policy*, 34: 256–76.

Kamp, L. (2002) *Learning in Wind Turbine Technology. A Comparison between the Netherlands and Denmark*, Utrecht: Utrecht University.

KEMA. (2002/2003) *Dutch Windmonitor*, <http://www.windmonitor.nl>

Loenen van L. (2003) *Vechten voor Windmolens: Over windcooperaties in Nederland*, [*Fighting for Windmills: About Wind Cooperatives in the Netherlands*]— Final project: environmental studies and policy, Utrecht: Copernicus Institute, Utrecht University.

Marsman, A. (2000) 'Intentie tot samenwerking met SGEP', *Meerwind Nieuwsbrief*, 22: 4.

Morthorst, P. E. (1999) 'Capacity development and profitability of wind turbines', *Energy Policy*, 27: 779–87.

Meadowcroft, J. (2002) *Lecture as part of the course Sustainable Development at the Department of Environmental Studies and Policy*, Utrecht: Utrecht University, The Netherlands.

Nielsen, F. B. (2002) 'A formula for success in Denmark', in M. J. Pasqualetti, P. Gipe, and R. W. Righter (eds.) *Wind Power in View: Energy Landscapes in a Crowded World*, San Diego: Academic Press, pp. 115–132.

Radema, H. (1999) 'Voortgang samenwerking Meerwind', *Meerwind Nieuwsbrief*, 20: 12.

Toke, D. (2005) 'Community wind power in Europe and in the UK', *Wind Engineering*, 29(3): 301–08.

Vleuten van der, E. and Raven, R. (2006) 'Lock-in and change: Distributed generation in Denmark in a long-term perspective', *Energy Policy* 34(3): 1439–1451.

Wind Service Holland. (2003) <http://home.wxs.nl/~windsh/statistiek.html/> (2003)

———. (2004) <http://home.wxs.nl/~windsh/statistiek.html/> (2004)

———. (2004) *Windsteun*, <http://home.wxs.nl/~windsh/> (retrieved 16 November 2004).

5 Corporate Interests and Spanish Wind-Power Deployment

Valentina Dinica

INTRODUCTION

This chapter explores the deployment of wind power in Spain by investigating the factors that influenced the large increase in the installed capacity of wind power. The chapter highlights the role of corporate interests in the diffusion results achieved by 2007.

Spain has been one of the countries with the highest dependency on imported energy resources in the European Union. In 1973, domestic energy resources covered only 28.6 per cent of the total energy demand. Being severely hit by the oil crisis of mid-1970s, and given the absence of domestic gas resources and the limited availability of low-quality coal, two decades ago, the Spanish government developed a policy aimed at saving energy, energy efficiency, and the diversification of primary resources. In this framework, the use of all types of domestic energy resources and the promotion of fossil-free energy resources became top priorities.

A comprehensive national policy framework developed since the early 1980s covered the aspects of research and development, stimulation of a new industry for the manufacturing and operation of wind installations, and financial support for project developers. This was endorsed at the regional level, with governments of many Autonomous Communities[1] adopting ambitious regional plans for the long-term deployment of wind power.

After twenty-five years, the results are impressive, compared to other countries that attempted the introduction of wind-power technology worldwide. In 2006, wind power was generated in Spain at a rate of 22,199 GWh/year; that is, 8.8 per cent of gross electricity consumption. Spain reached 11,615-MW installed capacity in January 2007 (AEE 2007). By contrast, in The Netherlands, only 1,500 MW were installed during the same period of time, 1980–2006. In the United Kingdom, it is estimated that by 2010, around 3,000 MW will be operational, also taking into account the currently installed and already approved wind projects.

The, therefore, question emerges: How can the significant increase in the installed capacity of wind power in Spain be explained? What are the patterns of this increase throughout time, and what underlies them? To what extent are the factors affecting the patterns of diffusion and capacity increase unique to Spain, and affected by contextual factors, and to what extent are they replicable? The answer is significant, as the shift to a postcarbon society requires extensive and, above all, sustained diffusion of renewable energy technologies, while only a few countries have managed so far to sustain diffusion. The analysis of wind-technology diffusion in Spain reveals several groups of factors that affected diffusion outcomes in the last decades:

- National policy framework: energy research and development policies, renewable energy plans, and financing policy instruments; legal instruments for commercial support.
- The business culture and interests of financing agents.
- Business culture and interests of energy and industrial companies.
- Regional and local development policies and the business interests of public agencies and companies.
- Administrative, environmental, and social–local factors.

Each group of factors is discussed in separate sections below. But before that, it is necessary to examine the diffusion patterns of wind technology throughout time. This is important because the factors identified played different roles in different stages of diffusion. The chapter concludes with a summary of the main considerations and a short reflection on the prospects for the continued expansion of wind technology in Spain.

DIFFUSION PATTERNS OF WIND TECHNOLOGY IN SPAIN

In principle, the twenty-five-year period since the emergence of political interest for wind power can be divided into four parts:

- The decade of the 1980s can be described as the research and demonstration period.
- Market introduction phase, 1991–1994.
- Early market diffusion, 1995–1998.
- Accelerated market diffusion, since 1999.

The speed of the installed capacity increase was very different during the four stages. But there were also changes in the patterns of technology diffusion. It is useful to consider three indicators for diffusion patterns as departure points for understanding the factors that influenced wind-power deployment: the types of project developers, the types of financing schemes they used, and the sizes of projects. The results of investments at the end of each stage can be observed in Table 5.1.

Table 5.1   The Increase in Wind Power Installed Capacity in Spain

Year	1990	1994	1998	(January) 2007	Target 2010
MW	7	77	829	11,615	20,155

Source: AEE 2007.

There are two main forms of financial resources for any project, including wind projects: equity and capital borrowed in the form of loans, typically provided by banks. Project developers are the economic actors who initiate projects, take them through all necessary approval and construction steps, and provide equity financing for projects. Any economic actor may be a project developer: energy utilities/companies or an existing or newly established private or public company from any economic sector—including banks, public agencies, individuals, cooperatives, communities, etc. Different types of economic actors will have different financing potentials, and hence different abilities to provide equity to wind projects. But they will also have different prospects to access bank loans and will enjoy different financing terms for loans. Therefore, the types of economic actors interested in wind power are important, as this is relevant to the size of the 'financing reservoir' on which wind-power diffusion may draw.

A similar argument can be made regarding the types of financing schemes. Two categories of financing schemes are typically differentiated: 'internal financing schemes' and project finance. Internal financing schemes represent all types of financing where equity finance is either the only or the predominant (> 50 per cent) form of financing. In this category, the following schemes can be differentiated: private finance, participation finance, corporate finance, third-party finance, and multicontribution finance.[2] Under project finance, a bank loan is the dominant form of financing, and this is guaranteed by the assets and cash flow of the wind project. Since no claim is made on the assets or financial reserves of project developers, project finance may also be used by small developers, such as communities, cooperatives, or individuals. The accessibility of project finance dramatically increases the financing reservoir on which wind-power diffusion may rely. But many preconditions need to be met for project finance to be made available by banks. Some of these preconditions are also strongly influenced by the business culture of the financing agents active in a country. Since this did play an important role in wind-power diffusion in Spain, this will be discussed later in the chapter.

Finally, the size of projects also constitutes a useful indicator because when there are no legal constraints on this due to planning criteria or price support reasons, size may be related to the risk perception held by project developers and financiers at the time of the investment. The larger the projects, the lower the risk perception and the higher the speed of diffusion are likely to be. Broadly, investments in wind projects are assessed from the perspective of a wide range of risks: resource quality, environmental impacts, planning, social acceptability, technology risks, and commercial risks(in terms of the reliability of purchase contracts and price guarantees, etc). In the market introduction and early diffusion stages, most of these risks are typically (perceived as) high. This is reflected in the small dimensions of projects, an attempt to minimize financial losses when projects fail. A sustained increase in project sizes would, by contrast, indicate a lowering of the risk perception by project developers and/or banks, *ceteris paribus*. But project sizes may also be influenced by culturally biased business requirements. In some countries, or for some economic actors, larger projects may be more desirable, reducing the numerous components of project development costs. The following four subsections present briefly the diffusion patterns during these stages , which will underpin the discussion of the factors that most powerfully affected wind deployment in Spain.

Technology Development and Demonstration

The period from 1980 to 1990 was one of intensive research, development, and demonstration of national technical designs, and several imported turbine designs. By 1990, there were only 7 MW of wind power installed, but there were five original types of wind turbines on the Spanish market, offered by two Spanish manufacturers established during this time, Ecotecnia and MADE. By 1992, the offer jumped to 13 types of turbines in the range of 30 kW–330 kW, offered by 5 manufacturers, all with production factories located in Spain (Dinica 2003).

The only project developers in this period were the Spanish manufacturers—MADE and Ecotecnia, the energy utilities Endesa (the largest in Spain at that time) and Union Fenosa (third largest in Spain), the national energy agency IDAE (Instituto para la Diversificacion y Ahorro de la Energía), and a few regional and local authorities. IDAE was established in 1984, and the abbreviation stands for the Institute for Energy Saving and Diversification. Although the energy portfolio of IDAE is large, the stimulation of renewable electricity generation is one of its core areas of activities, nationally. MADE was, at that time, a department of the utility Endesa, and specialized in wind and solar power technologies (see the following web address for further details if the remit of IDAE—http://www.idae.es/index.php/mod.pags/ mem.detalle/id.222/relmenu.88/lang.uk). Ecotecnia was founded in 1980 by a small number of environmentally motivated engineers with extensive expertise and high expectations for the role wind technologies might play in the Spanish electricity supply.

All eleven projects developed up to 1990 were financed based on 'internal financing schemes'. Given the very early stage of technical development, technology risks were considered too high by banks to approve project finance. Six projects had equity contribution from IDAE, and all of them benefited from substantial investment subsidies based on the national renewable energy plans IDAE was managing. One project used third-party financing by IDAE and was meant to test one turbine designed by Ecotecnia. Four other demonstration projects were financed based on equity from energy utilities Endesa and Union Fenosa, also relying heavily on investment subsidies. The projects had very small sizes, aiming to demonstrate a few turbines of Spanish or imported design.

Market Introduction

Between 1991 and 1994, 70 MW of installed capacity was added, lifting the total power to 77 MW by 1994. Six groups of developers can be differentiated in this period:

- Manufacturers of wind technology: projects totaling 4 MW.
- Energy utilities: commissioning 6 MW total.
- Companies established for the construction and operation of a single wind project. These will be hereafter referred to as 'project-dedicated companies'. These companies collectively built projects totaling 53 MW; energy utilities were part of all seven project-dedicated companies. Other equity providers were: regional governmental agencies, water utilities, and manufacturers;
- One company dedicated exclusively to investments in renewable electricity generation: Energia Hidraulica Navarra (EHN) was the first company of this type—to be hereafterreferred to as a 'renewables-dedicated company'—and entered the market in 1994 with a 3-MW project.
- IDAE and local energy agencies were the only project developers in the case of some very small projects that totaled 1.5 MW.
- Research institutes: Technological Institute for Renewable Energy ITER of the Canary Islands and the national energy research center, CIEMAT, built three wind installations that together counted 1.5 MW.

Consequently, the first four groups of project developers mentioned in this list, who can certainly be categorized as 'large developers', were responsible for the commissioning of 66 MW of the total 70 MW of new capacity.

What is also important to note here is the market entry of the first 'renewables-dedicated company'. Beginning in 1995, such companies became the dominant investment formula. Some of these companies even created separate subsidiaries to focus exclusively on wind projects. EHN later became a leading investor in wind power, being 37 per cent owned by the energy utility, Iberdrola (second largest at that time), and 38 per cent owned by the development company, Sodena, of the regional government of Navarra. The rest of EHN was owned by the Spanish industrial corporation Cementos Portland. Interestingly, Iberdrola and Sodena were, at that time, also co-owners of the manufacturer, Gamesa Eolica, next to the Danish manufacturer Vestas[3] (40 per cent) with whom a technology transfer agreement was signed in 1994 (Dinica 2003). Hence, at the end of this short period of market introduction, an increase in corporations' interest for investments can be observed. Although only a few corporations showed interest by 1994, they were highly influential, tone-setting corporations.

All projects were initially based on internal financing schemes.[4] More than half of the projects developed were very small installations. Not only were turbine' sizes smaller at that time, but the number of turbines per project was also still low. The economics of the interaction between wind resource/regime and technology were still under exploration by the experimenting investors, while the planning, environmental, and social acceptability criteria for project approval were still not settled or not clear to investors. Therefore, although large developers were already dominating the picture of investments, the financing reservoirs on which diffusion drew at that time were smaller due to limitations on the use of internal financing schemes imposed by corporate managers. The management boards of corporations and public agencies were still unwilling to take greater risks associated with larger projects at that stage. During that period there were no restrictions on project sizes, which emerged later.

Early Market Diffusion from 1995 to 1998

In 1994, a new law was adopted to guarantee the purchase of renewable electricity by companies managing the networks for electricity transmission—the 2366/1994 Royal Decree. The price support per kilowatt-hour of wind electricity was made dependent on project sizes. When projects were below 25 MW, developers qualified for higher tariffs. But when projects were above 25 MW, special approval had to be obtained from the Ministry of Industry and Energy. When approval was not given, the alternative price was four times lower. Large projects started to emerge between 1995 and 1998 but small- and medium-size projects were still the dominant choice of investors.[5]

With the 1994 decree, commercial risks lowered slightly and more economic and financing agents became interested in wind power. Between 1995 and 1998, 752 MW of new wind capacity was added to the 77 MW already operating. The largest part of this capacity was installed by:

- Renewables-dedicated companies, including some dedicated exclusively to investments in wind power, which installed around 60 per cent of capacity, and
- Project-dedicated companies, which together commissioned 36 per cent of capacity (Dinica 2003).

The main actors forming these two categories of companies were: energy utilities, manufacturers of wind technology, regional and local public authorities, or public companies established by them for economic or energy development, local energy agencies, and large industrial corporations that were increasingly entering the wind-power business in this period. Initially, these were Spanish industrial companies coming from sectors facing economic difficulties. But later, the types of corporations entering the wind business diversified, and foreign companies also joined the growing sector. Some capacity was also commissioned by manufacturers and utilities as single investors per project, mostly for the purpose of testing new turbine models. Few private developers and three research institutes also accounted for a few megawatts.

Project finance was first used in 1995, but was only approved by banks when certain actors were involved with equity in projects: energy companies, large industrial corporations, wind technology manufacturers, and public authorities or agencies. However, the years 1995–1996 should be seen rather as a period of transition from internal financing schemes toward project finance. During these years, financing parameters were stricter than for the conventional business areas. The share between equity and loans in projects' capital structure was still not settled around levels that are typical for other longer-established economic sectors. Debt maturity was shorter and interest rates were slightly higher than for conventional industries.

At the same time, private corporations and public actors interested investing gained more trust in the technology and its operational preconditions, and were willing to approve more and larger projects based on internal financing schemes compared to the earlier period. This expansion of the accessible financing reservoir was reflected in the more significant increase in installed capacity in this short period.

Accelerated Market Diffusion Since 1999

Since 1999, the market capacity for wind energy expanded by 10,786 MW. On a global scale, this is an unprecedented rapid increase in such a short period. In January 2007, Spain had 11,615 MW of operating wind projects, and thousands megawatts more in various phases of approval procedures and development phases.

One of the factors that coincided with this was a change in the commercial support regulations in 1998, and the adoption of a special national policy plan for renewable energy in 1999. The 2818/1998 Royal Decree raised the ceiling for eligibility of commercial wind plants to 50 MW. Projects exceeding this limit have no guarantee on contracts and have to submit their output for trade using the power pooling mechanism. However, this did not stop investors from developing larger projects for which the higher payment per kWh was still secured. The explanation is that these large plants have more interconnectors to the grid, being split for permits and price eligibility into two or more separate wind parks. Since 1999, more than two-thirds of the new projects have capacities above 25 MW, and the number of projects installed annually that are larger than 50 MW has increased steadily. Hence, a dramatic increase in project sizes can be observed.

Project finance became the main financing scheme from the end of 1998, and financing terms started to take normal values. Without project finance, such a large number of such large projects are unlikely to have been possible. Except perhaps for manufacturers, corporations are typically unwilling to want to put all their financial reserves and assets only in wind energy. Most projects developed since 1999 are owned by:

- renewables-dedicated companies—which remain the dominating investment formula that was used for around two-thirds of the new installed capacity; and by
- project-dedicated companies.

The *number* of developers and financiers has increased enormously since 1999. Importantly, financing agents, such as banks and insurance companies, started to go beyond providing loans. Many also became equity providers in project-dedicated companies, or co-owners of wind/renewables-dedicated companies, adopting investment plans of hundreds of megawatt capacity. Some even became co-owners of the increasing number of manufacturing companies. For example, the Bank Bilbao Vizcaya Argentaria acquired shares in the manufacturer Gamesa Eolica, and was keen on financing projects using Gamesa technology.

These were the 'ultimate signals' that wind power has become a reliable business sector with low investment risks. As a consequence, increasingly more Spanish and foreign corporations entered the wind-power market as both manufacturers and developers of commercial projects. Hence, the financing reservoirs expanded enormously, which was a precondition for the thousands of megawatts installed since 1999. Although few projects were also developed by small companies, small municipalities, and individual investors with the help of special policy instruments, the main actors behind the two categories of investment formulas remain the same as prior to 1999: energy utilities, manufacturers, industrial corporations, regional authorities/agencies, and, to a smaller extent than before, IDAE; financing agents must be added to this list as key newcomers to the wind business.

This section has focused on *how* diffusion took place by presenting the diffusion patterns during the four stages of wind-capacity expansion. The gradual but steady increase in the available financing reservoir enabled more and larger projects, leading to impressive diffusion results by 2007. The opening up of the financing reservoir is a key precondition for diffusion. But which were the factors that stimulated and enabled this? And which other factors facilitated the implementation of developers' investment plans? The literature on renewable energy technology diffusion is rich with examples of failed attempts of market introduction and diffusion obstacles of all types—administrative, economic, social, environmental, political, and so on. Did such obstacles emerge in Spain as well? And if they did, how have they been overcome? If they did not, is there a reason for this? Can the lessons learned about wind diffusion in Spain be replicated elsewhere to facilitate the greening of the electricity supply? The following sections will address these questions to unveil *why* diffusion results could have such an impact for wind energy in Spain.

FACTORS AFFECTING DIFFUSION PATTERNS AND THE CORPORATE DOMINANCE OF WIND POWER INVESTMENTS IN SPAIN

Policy Support for the Manufacturing Industry through Financing Instruments

In Spain, the oil crisis of the 1970s generated a powerful political commitment for all forms of renewable energy. But political actors went beyond the goal of increasing the role of renewable resources in energy supply. Anticipating that, in the long term, a major shift away from fossil fuels would be needed worldwide, and expecting an increasing demand for renewable energy technologies and maintenance services, Spain aimed to be an early mover and develop a strong national manufacturing industry and service sector for such technologies. Spain's energy policies and renewable energy plans directly supported research and development (R&D) for the development of competitive Spanish designs of wind technology, as wind energy was seen as having higher chances of market success within short-medium term.

The first R&D program for wind power was launched in 1979, and resulted in a demonstration project of 100 kW at Tariffa, in 1982. The 1983 Plan for Energy Conservation and Saving launched some policy instruments for wind power in the context of a special R&D Program for Renewable Energy. From 1980 to 2006, four Renewable Energy Plans were adopted. The policy instruments used for their implementation displayed a remarkable continuous political commitment to renewable energy support, irrespective of the politics of the political parties in power. To implement its energy objectives for the reduction of fossil fuels, the government established in 1984 the energy agency, IDAE. The commitment of IDAE to develop implementation programs for renewable energy in general, and for wind energy in particular, as a form of saving fossil fuels was significant throughout time. IDAE became closely involved in the support of the innovation processes of Spanish manufacturers during the 1980s. Three instruments were used for this:

- R&D subsidies.
- Investment subsidies for demonstration projects, and later, market introduction projects.

- Direct financing, either in the form of equity contribution to project-dedicated companies or third-party financing for demonstration projects.

It is important to note the originality of IDAE in using direct-equity investments and third-party financing for projects with Spanish turbine design. Such instruments were seldom used in other European countries. According to IDAE experts (Concha and Cayetano 1996), in order to ensure renewables' market diffusion, 'IDAE tried to find out a replicability effect to speed up private investments, and to obtain an economically sustainable renewable energy market'. The involvement of IDAE in the direct financing of wind projects was based on criteria such as:

- Support of technological improvements. This was a high priority in the 1980s. IDAE aimed to speed up national technology development that typically encountered financing obstacles for the demonstration of technical performances. IDAE considered this a strategically good step, expecting international competition for wind-technology manufacturing in the coming decades.
- The need to overcome the commercialization obstacle through the 'mobilization of as many (financial) resources as possible, stimulating the entry of new investors in the sector, such as private companies, financing institutions, etc' (Ayuste et al. 1996); this criterion was important for IDAE, especially in early 1990s, during the market introduction phase.
- 'Promotion of wind installations at locations with difficult access, electrical infrastructure or with lower wind potential' (Ayuste et al. 1996) to demonstrate that these are not real obstacles, but rather solvable technical challenges. This became important around the mid-1990s, as the most economically attractive locations for projects started to be filled in; the aim in this stage was therefore to give a further impulse to market diffusion.

Next to financial resources, IDAE also contributed to projects during the 1980s and early 1990s by means of human resources—through the technical energy experts it made available for project development. IDAE's direct involvement managed to offer, therefore, both the technical and financial support necessary with excellent timing for the manufacturers and early developers' needs, also sharing in the risks of the investment.

Hence, the continuous political commitment to the objectives formulated in the energy R&D policies and the renewables energy plans, as well as the fine-tuning and reliability proven by the financing instruments deployed to reach them, spread the seeds of interest in wind- technology manufacturing and commercial projects among large corporations.[6] At the end of 1994, a potential investor could choose among nineteen types of turbines, of which seventeen were manufactured in Spain, and based on Spanish design or technology transfer agreements (Dinica 2003). By 2006, Spain had one of the strongest wind-technology manufacturing industries in the world. Almost all manufacturers active worldwide now have production factories in Spain, offering countless turbine types, sizes, and designs at competitive prices. The Spanish company Gamesa Eolica has become the uncontested market leader, having manufactured 5,195 MW of the capacity installed in Spain by early 2005. But more factors have contributed to this, as the following sections explain.

Legal Instruments for Commercial Support

For any investor in electricity generation, the commercial terms under which the investment is made are of crucial importance, namely the clarity and reliability of the legal framework regarding the purchase contracts and the price per kilowatt-hour likely to be received during the project's economic lifetime. This factor influenced not only how diffusion took place, in terms of diffusion patterns, but also why the developers observations since 1994, had showed that the market was dominated by such investments.

Since 1980, the Spanish political actors intended to give renewable electricity project developers three major legal guarantees—network connection, purchase contracts with grid companies, and a certain price per kilowatt-hour. However, the final wording of the legal instruments was flawed in some respects. It took a long time until the law offered the initially intended guarantees. The first instrument for the commercial support of wind-based electricity was the 82/1980 Energy Conservation Law. The price per kilowatt-hour was not specified in the legal text, and was supposed to be annually set by the Ministry of Energy and Industry. This was associated with high risk for many potential investors, because ministerial orders could be modified easily and unilaterally by the minister. The length of purchase contracts with grid companies was also not specified in the law, which was again associated with high risks. The law was completely silent regarding minimum contract length and renewal prospects or terms. The only clear guarantee was that of network connection, but this was obviously not convincing enough for many potential investors.

Therefore, the legal framework for commercial support applicable between 1980 and 1994 was exposed to high commercial risks. This played an important role in fact that the types of economic actors investing up to 1994 were limited to two energy utilities (Endesa and Union Fenosa), manufacturers operating as subsidiaries of utilities, influential corporations, or public authorities/agencies. When one of these types of actors was involved in project ownership, the likelihood of grid companies refusing a contract of reasonable length (in terms of investment recovery) or the renewal of an expired purchasing contract was considerably lower or absent (Lopez 2000).

In the early 1990s, the IDAE organized numerous roundtables and seminars where financing institutions were invited and asked to specify under what circumstances they would be interested in financing renewables-based projects. Special workshops for wind-energy investments were also organized. During these meetings, public authorities became aware of the policy and legislative shortfalls of the commercial support mechanism.

In 1994, a new electricity law was adopted, as part of a more general legislative change in the energy industry related to liberalization. This was followed by the special Royal Decree 2366/1994 for renewables commercial support, which brought changes that somewhat lowered the commercial risks for investors. The guarantee on purchase contracts was given for a minimum of five years. Moreover, prices for wind electricity were to be set by means of Royal Decree, and passed by the national government. This was associated with improved price reliability. The government acknowledged in the introduction of the Royal Decree 2366/1994 the "inadequacy of the current economic regime to the actual reality".

These legal changes created an atmosphere of higher investment interest among a larger number of economic actors. Developing confidence among energy utilities as investors was also crucial. After 1994, two of the four largest energy utilities at that time, Iberdrola and Hidrocantabrico, also opened special subsidiaries for renewables, with ambitious investment plans in wind energy. Some of the roundtables taking place since 1995 to expand the pool of potential developers and financiers were actually organized by utilities themselves, especially Iberdrola.

Later, the introduction of the 12 per cent target for the renewable-energy contribution to the electricity supply by 2010 in the 54/1997 Electricity Law, and the preservation of the special commercial regime terms through the Royal Decree 2818/1998, led to an atmosphere of real enthusiasm to invest in renewables in general, and in wind electricity in particular. The profitability enabled by the price-support level for wind energy was the highest among renewables. Through the 1998 Royal Decree, the price reliability improved even further, as the requirement that any price change needed the approval of the national parliament was introduced. In 1999, a special Policy Plan for the Promotion of Renewable Energy was approved by the parliament. The plan traces the main actions and support principles in order to reach a legal target of 8,974 MW of wind power by 2010. The investment frenzy generated since 1999 led to the bypassing of this target by 2005. Later, the government updated the target to 20,155 MW by 2010.

But as the number of developers expanded after 1994, and basically exploded after 1998, one cannot observe too much change in terms of the *types* of economic actors present in this booming business sector. Although large industrial corporations were the main newcomers since 1994, and financing agents were the surprise newcomers (with equity investments) from 1998, both these categories can only be referred to as large, financially strong companies. What influenced the persistence of large corporations as dominant wind project developers? Some answers emerge as extremely significant:

- The business culture and interests of Spanish financing agents.
- The business culture and interests of energy and industrial corporations.
- The regional and local policies aiming to maximize the regional and local economic and social benefits of wind-power investments, as well as the direct business interests of the regional and local public authorities and corporations. And
- A series of administrative, environmental, and social–local factors.

These factors help explain not only the dominance of corporate investments, but also the speed of diffusion through the basically unlimited availability of project finance since 1999, and the significant increase in project sizes.

The Business Culture and Interests of Financing Agents

In Spain, the business culture of the financing community is strongly biased toward large-scale projects. As a market analyst observed:

> Large banks often have a lending threshold well above the size of a small renewable energy project. For lenders, the ideal project suitable for project finance is 30–40 MW. (. . .) Small developers have often to form joint ventures with strong partners (utility, manufacturer, local authority) in order to secure financing (Ilex Associates 1996: 113).

Besides, financing agents are most likely to approve project finance when at least one—but preferably more—equity contributor(s) is an energy utility, industrial corporation, or public authority/agency. It is argued that, next to their valuable assets and financing reserves, in case of project failure, such actors are also more likely to possess qualified technical expertise. An energy utility/company or industrial company is more likely to be able to dispose of or hire qualified personnel for all stages of a project: design, permitting, construction, proper operation, and maintenance.[7]

The overwhelming majority of companies established for wind-power investments since 1994 were characterized by some striking features in terms of the actors, and the role each actor played. The joint ventures included almost the same types of actors, each fulfilling a clear role:

- There was a bank or another type of financing agent securing the necessary loan;

- A regional/local authority securing the necessary administrative or environmental permits and focusing on social–local approval.
- IDAE with a direct-equity investment.[8]
- A manufacturer supplying the technology and offering a reliable guarantee for technical quality (importance for the insurance), which was typically offered at lower costs than were available on the market.
- An energy utility offering the guarantee of grid connection and other network-related issues (the energy utility was often also the legal buyer of wind electricity, hence eliminating the contract risks in the legal support framework).
- Sometimes the land owner also has an ownership share in the wind plant, which is preferred by financing agents.
- And eventually, another local/regional agent that could bring extra benefits to the project.

Almost all project-dedicated companies in Spain have this actor formula. This emphasizes the crucial role of resource complementarity in the formation of companies for market introduction and early diffusion. When wind-dedicated companies and renewables-dedicated companies emerged, they displayed largely the same actor formula, with the main differences being that:

- IDAE was not involved in such companies anymore, as wind-power investments were not supposed to become its core activity.
- And industrial corporations from a wide variety of sectors entered the wind-generation business.

In this context, small developers have nothing to offer large investors, except for land use rights, for which a very small project ownership may be allowed. Financing agents prefer to lend to, and do business with, large companies and public authorities/agencies, as this is more likely to maximize project success throughout all stages.

Beside these business culture aspects, there is a direct business interest that many banks have in companies dedicated either to wind or renewable electricity investments. For example, Caja Madrid Bank and Mapfre Insurance Company have shares in the renewables-dedicated company Sinae, together with the fourth largest energy utility, Hidrocantabrico. Together they have had, since 1998, very ambitious investment plants amounting to almost 1,000 MW of wind power, which will require large financial resources. The fourth largest bank in Spain, the Sabadell Bank, already has equity shares in some wind-project-dedicated companies, and wants to invest equity in much more. The third largest bank in Catalonia, the Catalonia Savings Bank, is also involved, through direct ownership, in several wind projects. In some of these, it is also a partner of the regional energy agency of Catalonia—ICAEN. Consequently, there is direct competition between financing agents and companies of all types for financial resources to invest in windparks.

The Business Culture and Interests of Energy and Industrial Corporations

The business culture of energy and industrial corporations in Spain is also biased toward large-scale investments, and against the involvement of small developers. According to a environmentally motivated Spanish investor:

> Unlike foreign firms, Spanish organizations, both public and private, tend to harbor conservative business policies. This means that when a large company is joining a project, the size of the project is likely to increase well above the small/medium scale level that a small developer would attempt to join. (Ilex Associates 1996).

Energy companies gradually became very interested in wind power, as they understood that the political support from government for renewables put them in a 'sink or swim' situation. Since 1995, all four of the largest energy companies have had renewables-dedicated companies, and two of them also owned successful wind-technology manufacturers, with Endesa owning Made, and Iberdrola having ownership shares in Gamesa Eolica. Having management rights to electricity networks (directly or through subsidiaries or related companies), energy companies typically demand ownership shares when competing developers require grid connection to attach high profitability wind plants to 'their grid' (Lopez, C. Iberdola Cogeneracion Y Renovables, interview, April 2001).

However, energy companies also posed problems when competitors wanted to attach plants to 'their grid' in locations where these competitors also wanted to build plants through their own renewables-dedicated companies solely or in joint ventures with other preferred investors. As the law guarantees grid connection except for well-defended technical obstacles, energy companies may invoke technical reasons to refuse grid connection. As Spain is a country with low population density in the rural areas where wind resources are rich, the grid has typically low voltage there, and grid connection can be refused. Grid companies argue that wind power destabilizes the grid due to intermittent generation.

This technical obstacle could, however, be overcome through additional infrastructural investments and more interconnectors, in which energy companies have expertise. Besides, they, and other large developers, also have higher financial resources for these extra costs. Such costs can be compensated by the benefits of receiving project finance loans under good terms from banks. This constitutes another obstacle for small developers that benefits the energy utilities and their preferred business partners.

The investment preference of energy and industrial corporations with ownership shares in manufacturers is clearly aimed toward the economic actors able to maximize the megawatt order for their own wind technology. Small developers can be no competitors for the corporations, banks, as well as regional and local development companies of public authorities, who are willing to order hundreds of megawatts of a specific wind-turbine design.

Manufacturers remained key project developers because there was extra money to be made, based on the legal instruments for the commercial support of wind power. They used two strategies for this. Some, such as Desa, Made, and Gamesa, chose to establish separate companies with the exclusive economic activity of investing in wind projects using their own technology. Such projects were, in turn, most often developed under the investment approach of a project-dedicated company. The strategy used by others, such as Ecotecnia, Neg-Micon, and Bonus-Bazan, was to have small ownership shares in some of the projects using their technology. Since the competition for investment is so high among economic and financing actors, manufacturers have a clear preference for large corporations able to invest in large-size projects.

Regional and Local Development Policies and Business Interests of Development Companies

The market dominance of corporations is also a direct consequence of the approval criteria for wind projects used by regional and local authorities. The first 'filters for large corporations' were in the form of the *royalties and social welfare investments* which were received from developers since the early 1990s. Many sites where wind-rich resources were found, were located in rural economically depressed areas. Local municipalities saw a development opportunity in the increasing profits wind projects could generate based on the generous governmental price support. Local investments, such as village libraries, roads, or school endowments for computer equipment, became frequent preconditions for permitting wind projects. A third option emerged later in the form of land rents. Increasing fees were required for both public and private land renting. As more corporations were entering the market and competition among developers for sites sharpened, the required local royalties, land rents, and social investments also skyrocketed. These requirements added to the market-entry obstacle for small developers, such as small private firms, associations, cooperatives, or even individuals who were interested to invest locally. They are unlikely to develop projects with such high profitability that would accommodate these requirements.

But a much higher obstacle for small developers emerged when regional governments started to adopt, in 1995, *wind-power deployment plans*. Such plans emerged after the first change in the commercial support law in

1994, which generated a clear, increased interest from energy companies, industrial corporations, and financing agents in wind power. Regional authorities expected to see a significant contribution from wind projects to regional industrial development, and more investments for structural, economic, and social development. As many large areas had no other interesting resources, and in the context of advancing desertification in some parts of Spain, and the steady migration of rural population to urban areas, wind power was seen as the sudden miracle that could bring people and money back to rural areas. In many Autonomous Communities, developers have been asked to come up not with project proposals, but rather with large investment plants, that are able to develop manufacturing and other industrial companies within their territory. Once the regional governments approved the strategic investment plans of a group of company(ies), those developers could enjoy preferential rights to access sites within the region. Competing developers had to wait until the winning corporations explicitly discarded sites (WPM July 2000: 37).

For example, the plan formulated in 1995 by Galicia required that at least 70 per cent of the manufacturing process for any single wind farm installed in Galicia be carried out in the region. The regional energy agency stated that the 1995 plan created 12 industrial plants, with more than 1,000 jobs (WPM August 2000: 10). In addition, the personnel employed for all necessary preliminary studies, construction work, and maintenance operations, were also regionally recruited. The new, updated regional wind plan of Galicia estimates the addition of 2,000 direct jobs and 3,000 more indirect jobs to increase its installed capacity to 2,800 MW by 2010 (Aranda and Cruz 2000). In January 2007, Galicia already had 2,603 MW of wind capacity.

Other regions that have already attracted extensive manufacturing activities by early 2007 are: Castilla la Mancha, with 2,312 MW installed; and Aragon, with 1,549 MW (AEE 2007). They were both among the first to generate a consensus among the various regional public authorities and formulate attractive regional deployment plans. The new development plan of Castilla y Leon was adopted in 2000, envisaging the installation of 2,980 MW by 2010, which is expected to create over 10,000 jobs in total. Of these, 485 jobs will be permanent maintenance and operation jobs. In January 2007, Castilla y Leon was already accounting for 2,120 MW of wind capacity. The number of wind-related jobs was also high in Navarra. Most of the 916 MW of wind capacity installed there by January 2007 were produced in the region, where the largest manufacturer, Gamesa, has its headquarters.

In some regions, however, regional environmental departments were clashing with the energy and economic departments. Social opposition based on environmental grounds was stronger, and a longer social–political dialogue needed to be carried out first. This delayed the adoption of regional wind deployment plans substantially. For example, this was the case in Valencia, which only adopted its first plan for wind development in 2000, aiming to install 1,700 MW by the year 2010. Although the net technically exploitable potential is estimated at only 700 MW (IDAE 1999), this does not seem to inhibit neither domestic nor foreign market players to commission large investments in manufacturing plants regionally. The regional government expects that the plan will create 20,000 jobs, the key objective of the plan being to reduce by half the energy import dependency while bringing wealth and employment "to more socially and economically-depressed areas in the mountainous interior" (WPM November 2000: 32). By 2006, almost all of the Autonomous Communities had already adopted, or were in process of adopting, approval guidelines based on similar conditions.

But while regional and local authorities have had the merit of enhancing employment and regional economic development and welfare generally, they brought about two different types of obstacles for the market entry of small developers. Next to the requirements in the strategic wind-deployment plans, another obstacle can be seen in the direct involvement of regional governments, their energy agencies, and their companies for regional economic development, in the ownership of companies developing wind projects.

In Navarra, for example, most of the wind capacity was installed by Energia Hidraulica Navarra, in which the regional government holds 38 per cent of ownership shares through its regional development company, Sodena. In the Basque Country, the regional energy agency, Ente Vasco de la Energia, also has ownership shares in one of the few projects to be approved there. In Aragon, the regional government's company for the industrial development of Aragon (SODIAR) also participates in wind projects. Similarly, in Galicia, two public companies of the regional government are involved in wind projects: the Company for the Development of Galicia and Energy Management of Galicia.

While the participation of regional governments and their agencies and companies has played a crucial role in introducing wind technology to the market and accelerating its diffusion, by reducing the risk perception of other potential private investors, their continued participation in large-scale projects with powerful industrial groups and strong financing agents and can be seen as a market obstacle for small local developers. The obstacle is not so much direct, by refusing project permitting, but indirect, by reaping the information advantage public authorities may have directly or indirectly regarding the location of wind-rich sites, and their timely 'occupation' through early applications with the preferred investment partners. Land still remains available, but the quality of wind resources makes a project either less or not at all profitable under the applicable price support instruments. It is important to also note that in all the previously mentioned Autonomous Communities with the largest installed capacities by January 2007, the public companies associated with the regional and local authorities played a large role in investments.

Local Factors: Administrative, Social, and Environmental

Geographical factors have been in favour of wind-power expansion in Spain, as one of the European Union countries with lowest population density. In rural areas, localities are typically wide apart from each other and land availability has not been a problem. Sites with rich wind resources are, in many cases, remote from social and industrial sites and in difficult-access areas, which made landowners typically happy to accommodate wind projects for various forms of economic benefits.

The high speed of diffusion might leave the impression that there was no significant obstacle for wind technology in Spain, except for the market entry of small developers. But this image is not entirely true. The national government offered continuous and reliable policy support for overcoming technical, financial, and commercial obstacles. However, environmental, social, and administrative obstacles did emerge in many regions, while the national government has more restricted rules at subnational levels in these fields.

In the first place, it is important to note that, in contrast to other European countries, local opposition was sometimes grounded explicitly in economic considerations. The local population was often embittered by the fact that corporations and public companies may install large wind farms on municipal land or others' private land, making fast and substantial profits, while they have no access to project financing loans. As a consequence, private landowners adopted a double strategy. Some increased the rent required when approached by corporations, which can go as high as 1.5 per cent of the price received per kilowatt-hour. Others combined this price strategy with that of first asking local firms and individuals if they are interested in constructing wind plants on their lands with rich wind resources. Only when no local economic actor showed interest did landowners agree to rent to corporations outside their area. This approach was first used in Andalucia, where there are some sites with very good wind resources, such as Tariffa and Cadiz (Dinica 2003). This approach to overcoming the market-entry obstacle of small local developers is, so far, unique in Europe.

Administrative refusals of project proposals, or community opposition based on environmental grounds, were more than just isolated cases in Spain. This obstacle was sustained by the absence of a coherent national approach and set of criteria for analyzing environmental impacts, and the maximum impacts acceptable for the approval of wind projects, specifically. As the government acknowledged in its 1999 policy plan for renewable energy, although:

> the public image of wind energy is generally favorable, sometimes this is not sufficient for finalizing large wind-park projects. (. . .) While the most important environmental groups in the country are in favor of

wind energy development and act positively towards its implementation, local groups are frequently raising disproportionate objection against the visual impact, or the impact on birds and land of wind installations (IDAE 1999).

Besides these more classical types of environmental arguments, the complaint that environmental benefits do not accrue locally was also raised. In the Autonomous Communities, where the added wind capacity is exported to other regions in Spain—either because the wind farms are large and need to be directly connected to the high-voltage transmission grid or because the region already has a surplus of generation capacity—this argument also confronted developers. Another frequent reason for opposition has been the location of wind projects near or over sites with archeological remains. In some cases, developers were refused permission, while in others, additional investments had to be made to conserve the archeological site or even develop it for tourism.

In some regions, communities also protested out of fear that wind turbines will flood the landscape in the absence of a regional plan setting wind-deployment ceilings and a commonly agreed territorial distribution. When such plans were adopted, communities in some regions criticized them as lacking a foundation in social dialogue. Developers mentioned that local opposition based on environmental grounds can produce construction delays of three to five years. The overall percentage of projects ultimately refused due to administrative and/or community opposition based on environmental grounds or landscape-related reasons is low in Spain compared to other countries.

Mechanisms to overcome opposition on these grounds were developed and proved to work throughout time. Developers argue that when local economic benefits are increased, such as higher royalties or social welfare investments, this frequently also speeds up acceptance (Arrieta, J. Public Relations Energia Hidraulica Navarra, interview, April 2001; Lopez, C. Iberdola Cogeneracion Y Renovables, interview, April 2001). But these mechanisms worked in Spain because people have, on average, relatively low income compared to other European countries, while in rural areas, poverty among farmers is still common. Such mechanisms are unknown to Northern European countries, such as the United Kingdom, The Netherlands, and Germany, where the average income is quite high, especially in certain rural areas where real estate is pricy.

A study done in two cities in Catalunia regarding the visual impact of wind turbines showed that almost 60 per cent of interviewees considered visual impact acceptable, as long as wind parks can generate economic advantages for the municipality.[9] But this does not always remove the environmental opposition. When this became clear to developers and regional/local governments toward the end of the 1990s, initiatives emerged for communication and image-building campaigns. They came from three directions:

- Regional associations of project developers, which designed and carried out public information campaigns.
- Developers themselves, who also undertook such actions in the regions were they commissioned many or large projects.
- Regional/local governments in some regions, where it was decided to actively involve local communities in the design of strategic regional wind-deployment plans to avoid future opposition for individual projects.

Consequently, although environmental, social, and administrative obstacles did exist in Spain, they have been of lower magnitude than those obstacles in other countries, mainly due to the benefit of sufficient land availability with no alternative economic use and an environmental movement that supported, in principle, wind power as a clean resource, and opposed it only, at times, locally, based on some contextual reasons. The obstacles that emerged could be addressed to a large extent through (additional) local economic benefits offered by developers on the grounds of high employment in low-income rural areas. The instruments of communication with communities and image-building campaigns also have been introduced in the last decade and have been successful in most areas where they have been tried.

CONCLUSIONS

This chapter revealed the diffusion patterns of wind deployment in Spain, as well as the factors affecting them and the significant diffusion results until early 2007. A significant and continuous political commitment at the national level for the use of indigenous energy resources was the first and the most crucial factor for diffusion success. Irrespective of the political biases, all national governments and parliaments agreed it was better to subsidize domestic renewable energy resources than foreign fossil fuels.

An important role in diffusion was played by the renewable energy agency, IDAE. The direct-financing instruments it implemented helped overcome the financing obstacle and risk perception of potential investors between 1980 and the mid-1990s, and successfully addressed the commercialization obstacle still experienced in early 1990s. Hence, a contribution was also brought by the communication policy of IDAE through the organization of workshops and roundtables with potential developers and financing agents in the mid-1990s. Up to the mid-1990s, only few large companies were attracted by wind investments. However, importantly, these were well-known and highly influential economic actors.

The potential financing reservoirs on which wind projects could draw increased enormously during the 1990s. Since 1995–1996, project finance became the dominant investment tool, which helped increase the size of wind projects. The number of corporations investing in commercial projects and wind installation manufacturing companies skyrocketed after the 1998 change in the law for the commercial support of wind power, which lowered the investment risks significantly. An important role in risk perception reduction was also played by the market entry of financing agents as equity and manufacturing investors. This also influenced the rate of capacity increase, since financing agents in Spain are biased in favor of large investments, preferably projects above 30–40 MW.

These factors, which helped diffusion speed up, emerged, however, as obstacles for the market entry of smaller developers. While the number of developers increased since the mid-1990s, the types of developers remained, to a large extent, the same: energy utilities, manufacturers, public authorities, public companies, and a few industrial corporations, joined since 1994–1995 by industrial corporations and financing agents. Neither corporations nor financing agents are interested in projects with smaller developers in Spain. Their business culture draws them toward investments with other large companies that can bring obvious benefits to the success of projects.

Regional and local authorities also played a crucial role in the diffusion speed. While in other European Union countries they contribute often to the commercialization obstacle, in Spain, subnational authorities gave an exceptional impulse to diffusion speed. The contextual factors of large availability of land, restricted alternative resources of economic development in rural areas, the tendency of population migration toward urban areas, and the low income in employment in rural areas all contributed to the political commitment of subnational authorities to the support of wind-deployment plans. The ambitious regional wind-investment plans designed since the mid-1990s, in combination with their direct business interest as equity investors, opened the doors widely for project developers.

Environmental, administrative, and local–social obstacles also emerged in Spain. But they were lower in frequency and magnitude compared to other European countries. In Spain, landscape-protection organizations are uncommon and not really influential. They miss a national-level organization, coordination, and the financial resources necessary to support their lobbying activities. Also, in Spain, there is no history of landscape protection, which is typical in certain European countries, such as the United Kingdom. Landscape-protection legislation is also less demanding in Spain. Local opposition has been more often generated by the desire to protect archeological sites than by considerations on landscape quality. When local opposition emerged, some mechanisms deployed for overcoming these obstacles proved workable. The contextual factor of low income in rural areas played an important role in making such mechanisms work, as some involved highly appreciated financial compensations for the negative (perceived) impacts of wind power: (additional) royalties to local municipalities, higher land rent fees, or social welfare investments. Toward the end of the 1990s, communication and information campaigns for all sorts of stakeholders were implemented by developers and subnational authorities.

Comparing the factors that play crucial roles in wind-technology diffusion in Spain to those that affected diffusion in other European countries, some appear to have been unique to Spain:

- The direct financial involvement of the energy agency IDEA to spin-off investments.
- The need for employment and higher income, especially in rural areas, which were at the basis of the regional plans for wind deployment designed by regional public authorities.
- The business culture and interests of large corporations.
- The inability of local farmers to organize institutional finance for their investments plans, which is both culturally grounded, as there is no tradition of such initiatives, and business-imposed, as financing agents do not regard farmers and local communities as serious business partners.
- The poverty among farmers, willing to accept visual impacts and harness any extra income or even indirect benefits possible.
- The low social concerns for the landscape impacts of windparks, on the grounds of the absence of a strong, nationally coordinated landscape conservation organization.

The question that emerges after this analysis is how sustainable are these diffusion patterns likely to be in Spain? The national government increased the target to 20,155 MW by 2010. But at the same time, at the end of 2006 it lowered the price support for wind electricity guaranteed in the special regime (AEE 2007). Developers were protesting this change in early 2007, as many of the proposed projects were not feasible anymore under the proposed payment. An aspect less understood by public authorities with relevant competences is that market diffusion helps lower costs for some aspects or components of investments, such as technology costs and maintenance costs through economies of scale and competition. At the same time, however, the production costs for wind electricity are strongly affected by the location of wind projects relative to the grid connection and the quality of wind resources (Dinica 2003). As the close-to-grid locations are filled up and the wind resource-rich sites are occupied with projects, these two factors are likely to increase the costs of wind-electricity production, unless all the other cost components can be lowered at a faster pace. Hence, as diffusion expands, wind electricity might become more expensive than it used to be. Lowering the legal price support has two negative consequences: increasing commercial risks, as the political commitment for renewables' support becomes questionable in investors view, and lowering the economically feasible potential of exploitable wind resources. These threaten the sustained diffusion of wind electricity in Spain, and may reawake the commercialization obstacle of the early 1990s.

It remains to be seen whether wind deployment in Spain will remain a textbook example of accelerated diffusion until the complete exploitation of the technically available wind resources, or weather Spain will offer grounds for case studies on the unsustainable diffusion of wind technology in the future. The answer lies in the stability of the combination that characterized wind deployment so far in Spain, namely continuous and high political commitment for renewable electricity as an indigenous energy resource, and a series of economic and social contextual factors for Spain. Land availability, regional/local permitting, and social acceptability are necessary but not sufficient preconditions for a technology, which, under the failure to incorporate the environmental costs of fossil fuels in electricity prices, remains expensive for 'competition on the free market'. In this context, the key to the sustained diffusion of wind technology in Spain remains the combination of stable and economically feasible political price support on the one hand, and investment interests from financing agents and a wide diversity of companies on the other.

NOTES

1. The 1978 Spanish Constitution started a process of decentralization that led to the creation of seventeen Autonomous Communities. They represent an 'intermediate level of government between the State and the Local Authorities'. The current state organization resembles federal models, but 'national sovereignty resides over the whole Spanish population'. The responsibilities of the Autonomous Communities are more limited than in federal states (IDAE and SODEAN 1999).
2. The typology is taken from Langniss 1996, 1998. The 'multiple-contribution finance' scheme was added to this typology, and is defined as the case when equity comes from more than one economic actor.
3. At the end of 2001, Vestas sold its 40 per cent share to Gamesa Energia.
4. After 1995, when project finance became possible, some projects changed their financing schemes, as they managed to acquire bank loans.
5. Twenty-three projects had capacities between 15 and 25 MW, and six projects had capacities higher than 25 MW. Next to this, there were 15 projects with capacities between 5 and 15 MW, while the remaining 22 projects had less than 5 MW.
6. Manufacturer Ecotecnia is one of the few examples of companies that were small at the start. Developing high-quality models, the company managed to compete with large corporations and become a key supplier of wind technology nationally and internationally.
7. Interviews with Marta Fernandez, Sinae, April 2001, Madrid; Antonio Lara, Made, May 2001, Madrid; Marcel Bustos, Associations of Small Self-Generators, April 2001, Barcelona; Mariano Olmeda, Banco Central Hispano, Project Finance Division, Presentation "Analysis of risks of a wind project

from the perspective of the financing agent", Banco Central Hispano, Project Finance Division, Zaragoza Seminar, summer 1996.

8. Although, in the second half of the 1990s, its presence was not really necessary because the spin-off had been already created, IDAE continued to invest as part of its self-financing strategy.

9. "Attitude of population with regard to wind park installations. *International Journal of Organic Evolution* November 2000–April 2001". Interviews with 600 citizens of Tarragona and Tierras Altas del Ebre, Catalunia, 21 November 2001, www.gabinetceres.com/eolics.html.

REFERENCES

AEE. (2007) 'Espana alcanza 11,615 MW de potencia eolica instalada', news release at <www.aeeolica.org> (16 January 2007).

Aranda, F. A. (2000) 'The state of technological development of wind energy exploitation (in Spanish)', in *Energia Special Edition* May 2000: 28–34, Madrid.

Aranda, F. A. and Cruz, I. C. (2000) 'CIEMAT, Breathing ahead: Spain', *Renewable Energy World*, May–June: 22–29.

Ayuste, R., Hernández, C., Olmos, V. and Escudero, M. J. (1996) Experiencia del IDAE en el sector de la energieeolica, Madrid, Spain.

Concha, C. C. and Cayetano, H. G. (1996) (IDAE) 'Innovative financing instruments and renewable energy', conference paper for World Energy Council, available at <http://www.worldenergy.org/wec-geis/members_only.html>.

Dinica, V. (2003) *Sustained Diffusion of Renewable Energy—Politically Defined Investment Contexts for the Diffusion of Renewable Electricity Technologies in Spain, the Netherlands and United Kingdom*. Ph.D. Twente University.

IDAE. (1995) 'Third party financing for energy saving projects', October, Madrid: Spanish Government publications.

———. (1997) 'Energías renovables, Cogeneración', in *Documentos*, vol. 9. Madrid: Spanish Government publications.

———. (1998) 'Las energias renovables en España, balance y perspectivas 2000', November, Madrid: Spanish Government publications.

———. (1998b) 'Parques eólicos de pequeña y mediana potencia', in *Producto energético*: IDAE, November. Madrid: Spanish Government publications.

———. (1999) Policy Plan for the Promotion of Renewable Energy, Madrid: Spanish Government publications.

———. (2000) Energías renovables, Eólico, in *Documentos*, vol. 54. Madrid: Spanish Government publications.

IDAE and SODEAN (1999) *Report concerning fiscal measures in Spain*, report for the Ener-Jure EU Projects , 29 January 1999, Madrid.

Ilex Associates. (1996) 'A review of overseas financing mechanisms and incentives for commercial renewable energy projects', London: See document number ETSU K/FR/00026/REP/3: 113.

Langniss, O. (1996) 'Instruments to foster renewable energy investments in Europe a survey under the financial point of view', *Renewable Energy*, 9(1): 1112–5.

Langniss, O. (1998), 'Financing renewable energy systems (ed.)', European research project funded in part by the European Commission in the framework of the JOULE III Program, Stuggart, Germany: Hansadruk, Kiel.

Lopez, E. D. (2000) *The Legal Regime for Renewable Energy and Cogeneration*, National Institute of Public Administration, Madrid.

WPM. (2000) 'Strategy unveiled in face of protest—Basque country fight', *Windpower Monthly*, September: 25.

———. (2000) 'Regional plan gives boost to Galicia—first phase of Somozas line', *Windpower Monthly*, April: 39.

———. (2000) 'Renewed but tempered growth in Spain', *Windpower Monthly*, July: 37.

———. (2000) 'Valencia finally get wind strategy—favouritism feared', *Windpower Monthly*, November: 32.

———. (2000) 'Galicia revises wind strategy', *Windpower Monthly*, August: 10.

6 Wind-Energy Policy Development in Ireland
A Critical Analysis

Brian P. Ó Gallachóir, Morgan Bazilian, and Eamon J. McKeogh

INTRODUCTION

The renewable energy market support in Ireland prior to 1992 (Ó Gallachóir 2000) was essentially a form of feed-in tariff. This was utilized by small-scale hydropower producers who built electricity-generating plants, and consequently negotiated a tariff in order to trade in electricity with the then-monopoly electricity supplier, ESB. Deployment was rather slow but continuous, and these projects can be classed as being relatively small (typically < 1 MW). This limited scale resulted in a total of approximately 11 MW of installed hydro capacity, some of which was also supported with European Union (EU) funding for innovative energy technologies (the Energy Demonstration and THERMIE programmes). In addition to this, there funding was also available for renewable energy research and development projects in the period prior to 1992 (1976–1988 [International Energy Agency 2004]), which was the first form of support provided for wind energy. A competition was launched in 1990 for grant support from the EU VALOREN programme (Council Regulation [EEC] No. 3301/86, of 27 October 1986) to construct the first wind farm in Ireland. The successful 6.5-MW Bellacorrick wind farm was commissioned in 1992 and comprises 20 Nordtank 300-kW turbines and one 450-kW turbine. This growing interest in renewable energy led to an announcement in 1993 (Ó Gallachóir 2001) on the *Alternative Energy Requirement*, which was officially launched a year later. This marked the first renewable energy targets for Ireland, setting a goal 55 MW to be achieved by the end of 1997 (30 MW of which was to be wind power). This period also saw the establishment of a competitive tendering market support mechanism toward supporting initiatives in meeting renewables targets. Early attempts to build wind farms, in particular, raised a number of issues facing this new industry in Ireland, pointing to the need for a clearer policy framework. As a result, the period of 1993–2000 also saw the publication of the first renewable energy policy document, *Renewable Energy—Strategy for the Future* (Department of Transport, Energy and Communications 1996). Here, the new targets for renewable energy were more ambitious (100 MW to be achieved by 2000) and, in addition to this target, the strategy also put in place a series of measures to address the barriers that might impede the delivery of these innovative and proactive targets.

Thereafter, the period of 2000–2005 can be characterized as a period of increased ambition, with the introduction of the *Green Paper on Sustainable Energy* (Department of Public Enterprise 1999), which was published in 1999—and set a target of an additional 500 MW to be achieved in the period of 2000–2005. This policy document once again pointed to the challenges facing renewable energy in Ireland and committed to addressing these separately, through the establishment of a Renewable Energy Strategy Group (RESG). This group was mandated (Department of Public Enterprise, 1999) to, "examine all aspects of, and obstacles to, the further deployment of renewable energy technologies and to identify measures to redress constraints in the deployment of renewable energy, particularly in relation to economic costs, the planning process and grid connection" and to produce a report by mid-2000.

The setting of national wind targets for the period of 2005–2010 began with the 1996 strategy, which included a target of 30 MW per annum up to 2010. In terms of revising this target, a review of wind-energy policy was initiated in December 2003 with the publication of a consultation paper outlining future options (Department of Communications, Marine and Natural Resources 2003). Consequently, the Minister established a *Renewable Energy Development Group* (REDG) in May 2004 (Department of Communications, Marine and Natural Resources, 2004) in order to address issues relating to, *inter alia*, the next market support mechanism; research and development; the grid upgrade programme; and the applications backlog in windfarm grid connections. The REDG reported in November 2004 (Renewable Energy Development Group Short Term Analysis Group 2004), focussing on preliminary actions required and additional challenges to increased renewable energy deployment, with a particular focus on wind energy. A key development that had occurred between the two national policy developments (Green Paper in 1999 and REDG in 2004) was the finalization of EU Directive 2001/77/EC (European Union 2001) on the promotion of electricity from renewable energy sources. This effectively established a new target for renewable energy in Ireland, toward the achievement of 13.2 per cent of gross electricity consumption from renewable energy sources by 2010.

The renewable energy policy review process covering the period of 2005–2010 was completed in May 2005. The Minister for Communications, Marine and Natural Resources announced that the support mechanism would be changed from a competitive tendering scheme to a renewable energy feed-in tariff (REFIT) scheme. The initial target was to deliver a further 400 MW of new electricity generating plant to be built by 2010 in order to meet the 2010 target (Department of Communications, Marine and Natural Resources 2006a). When the results were announced in September 2006, REFIT contracts were offered for 609 MW of renewable plant (599 MW of which were wind power) (Department of Communications, Marine and Natural Resources 2006b). In addition, the national target for electricity from renewable energy was raised from 13.2 per cent to 15 per cent of gross electricity consumption by 2010 (Department of Communications, Marine and Natural Resources 2006c).

Against this backdrop, this chapter critiques the key policy developments in Ireland in terms of their capacity to deliver the targets set within the specific periods identified previously. This critique is structured around the three time periods, which were marked by significant policy timelines, i.e., 1993–2000 (first targets and first policy); the period of 2000–2005 (increased ambition); and finally, the period of 2005–2010 (preparing for the future). Within each time period, the chapter assesses individual measures and explores key interactions. In the period of 1993–2000 the key interaction of focus is between market support measures and spatial planning measures. In the period of 2000–2005, this shifts to the interaction between market support measures and measures relating to access to the electricity network. It is interesting to relate these periods (which are significant in terms of policy development) to the periods that were significant in wind-energy deployment terms. With this in mind, Figure 6.1 illustrates the annual deployment of wind power from 1992 to 2006. What is notable are:

• The concentration of activity at the end of each period.
• The delays in meeting the targets.

The period of 1993–2000 targeted the end of 1999 as the date to deliver projects; however, a significant proportion of these targets were delivered during 2000. Additionally, the policies for the period of 2000–2005 sought a steady increase in deployment but there was very little activity during 2001–2003, and considerable growth was realized during 2004–2006.

This chapter does not seek to detail the reasons for supporting wind-energy deployment, as these reasons have been detailed elsewhere (see reference list [O'Leary et al. 2004]) and, in essence, this reasoning relates to wind energy's contribution to national efforts in meeting greenhouse gas emission targets (Department of the Environment and Local Government 2000) and improving the security of energy supply by decreasing Ireland's 89 per cent import dependency (Howley and Ó Gallachóir 2005). Furthermore, supplementary evidence associated with a comparison of the various market support options for renewable energy options can be found elsewhere (Ó Gallachóir 2000; Renewable Energy Strategy

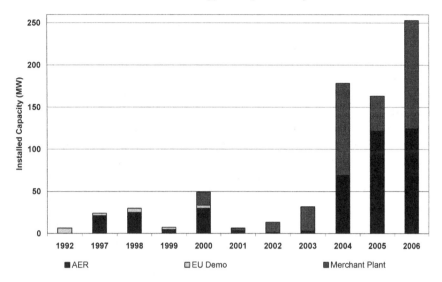

Figure 6.1 Annual deployment of wind power in Ireland from 1992 to 2006. Source: Author generated.

Group 2000). Consequently, this chapter discusses the remaining challenges that are required to meet the short-term 2010 target and toward increasing deployment beyond 2010. In addition, this chapter also identifies the areas where effective wind-energy policy will be able to deliver solid solutions to the renewables issue, and points toward the lessons that can be learned from the Irish experience.

WIND-ENERGY POLICY DEVELOPMENT 1993–2000

Ireland's market support mechanism for wind energy, the Alternative Energy Requirement (AER) was first announced in 1993 and officially launched in 1994. It was seen as a competitive tendering system, similar to the United Kingdom's Non-Fossil Fuel Obligation or France's EOLE 2005 programme. The AER was relatively distinct compared with both the UK and French mechanisms, and indeed with subsequent AER rounds, applicants were asked to bid on the basis of the capital grant being sought, rather than the average price per kilowatt-hour required. This was therefore related to the IR£15 million (€19 million) European Regional Development Fund (ERDF) support which was available for renewable energy projects through Ireland's Economic Infrastructure Operational Programme 1994–1999. As a consequence, the target which was set for wind energy was 30 MW (of a total 75 MW) by 1997, and based on the response, contracts were offered for 73 MW (of a total of approximately 111 MW). This response was, in part, related to the significant wind-energy resource in Ireland, which was quantified in terms of a 179GW feasible resource or a 2.2GW accessible resource (ESBI and ETSU 1997). Successful projects received fifteen-year power purchase agreements (PPAs) from the then-monopoly supplier, ESB Customer Supply, with the price per kilowatt-hour fixed at IR£0.04 (€0.051). The competition was based on the level of capital grant required, and the target was well exceeded, based on those who bid for a capital grant of zero (and in some cases, a negative capital grant was bid). The PPAs were offered for a fifteen-year period, with the price linked to the Irish consumer price index. Wind farms with a combined installed capacity of 46 MW (of a total 69.4 MW) were brought to the stage of construction and operation under this scheme. Notably, the target for wind energy was surpassed, illustrating the market appetite for wind-energy deployment. AER I as a whole did not reach the 75 MW target set—which somewhat pointed toward difficulties in the implementation of this particular initiative. The experience with AER I pointed to a number of challenges that would face wind farm development, namely:

- In securing planning permission.
- In access to the electricity network (grid connection).
- In finance.

Regarding the latter issue, Irish lending institutions viewed wind-energy projects as a new and unfamiliar technology and, hence, attributed an associated "higher" risk profile to such investments. This view was seen to diminish with experience and the certainties associated with a secure PPA—validated wind-resource assessment (and, hence, this particular revenue stream). Subsequently, Ireland saw the emergence of a positive approach toward PPA investment decision making by the financial sector.

The policy document issued in 1996, Renewable Energy Strategy for the Future contained a number of measures that were specifically designed to address the barriers identified during AER I, in addition to setting targets for 2010. These measures included:-

- An annual target of an additional 30 MW per year installed capacity from wind-power plants until 2010.
- Fifteen-year fixed price, index-linked PPAs for projects successful under the AER process.
- Guaranteed market access (in the form of a PPA) for projects successful under the EU THERMIE energy demonstration programme.
- Tax relief for corporate investment in wind-energy projects.

- Provision of third-party access to the electricity network for the direct sale of wind-generated electricity to customers.
- A national point of contact for information on wind energy (Renewable Energy Information Office).
- A Working Group on Grid Connection Issues Related to Renewable Energies.

In assessing this strategy, it is important to reflect on a key gap in the final document, which focuses on the discussion of spatial planning with regard to wind energy. Planning policy was the remit of a separate department in Ireland (Environment and Local Government). The development of market support policy for wind energy was therefore carried out in parallel with wind energy planning policy, but the two were not integrated successfully and this had significant consequences for target delivery. The AER I process led to a number of local authority planners processing planning permission applications for wind farms in the absence of a clear, coherent policy framework for assessment. On 7 May 1993, the first planning application for a wind farm in county Kerry was lodged with Kerry County Council (Daly 1999). The Department of the Environment Guidelines were not issued until September 1996 (Department of the Environment 1996), three years later. Of significant note, this misalignment between wind energy market support and planning policy has seen little change since 1993 and has, therefore, continued in the same ineffective vein.

AER III[1] was launched in 1997 in order to deliver 90 MW of wind capacity by 1999,[2] essentially rolling 3 yearly 30-MW targets into a single programme. In contrast to AER I, this process involved the inclusion of a fixed capital grant of IR£65 thousand (€82.5 thousand) being made available per megawatt installed—from ERDF funding. Here, proposers bid on the basis of the price per kilowatt-hour of electricity sought. Contracts were therefore offered for 138 MW of wind capacity, comprising 101 MW from large-scale (>5 MW) and 37 MW from small-scale (of a total 160 MW renewable energy plant). Progress was seen as being relatively slow, and this was primarily due to delays and difficulties in securing planning permission and, as a consequence, projects were offered a one-year time extension. Despite the additional time, AER III delivered 38 MW (Department of Communications, Marine and Natural Resources 2005) of the original 90-MW target. It is important to note that this failure to meet the target was not due to a failure in spatial planning policy, but a misalignment between planning and market support policies. This is evidenced by the fact that, in 1999, there were wind farms representing 155 MW that had planning permission but did not have AER III contracts (Renewable Energy Strategy Group 2000). The market support mechanism was therefore providing contracts—and the planning system was providing planning permissions—but wind farm deployment was clearly being stunted.

There were a number of positive elements arising from the Strategy for the Future. The Working Group on Grid Connection Issues relating to Renewable Energies was established to develop an agreed set of criteria governing the factors that influence the method of connecting renewable energy electricity-generating units to the electricity grid. This brought together—for the first time—the Distribution System Operator (DSO) and Transmission System Operator (TSO) with representatives from the wind, hydro, and biomass industries, in order to tease out the issues associated with grid connection. The Department of Communications, Marine and Natural Resources (DCMNR; at that time, the Department of Public Enterprise [DPE]) was also represented, and the national energy agency, Sustainable Energy Ireland (SEI—then known as Irish Energy Centre) facilitated the process. The main outcome of the work from this group was an improved understanding by the electricity system operators—and the renewable energy developers—of their respective positions and requirements. This understanding, in turn, allowed a trust to be developed (through the intensive dialogue that had taken place) and a consensus to be built—which was an important primer for the RESG that followed in 1999. In addition to wind-energy demonstration projects, and in particular, those who were successful in securing support from the EU THERMIE programme, they were offered a fifteen-year contract similar to that offered under the AER scheme. This mechanism delivered an additional 14.2 MW of wind-generating capacity in the period of 1993–2000.

The Electricity Regulation Act 1999 (Government of Ireland 1999) had provided third-party access to the electricity network to wind (and other renewable) electricity suppliers, which allowed them to sell directly to all final customers, irrespective of the customer's consumption. Under the Act, brown electricity suppliers could sell only to large customers (> 4 GWh per annum). Green electricity suppliers thus had total market access, and, in particular, to the sections of the market which paid most for electricity (commercial and domestic customers). This provided wind farm developers with an alternative to the AER route to the electricity market and resulted in 16 MW of wind capacity by the end of 2000, growing to a staggering 338 MW by the end of 2006. In terms of benefits for firms involved in this emerging industry, tax relief for wind-energy projects was introduced under Section 62 of the 1998 Irish Finance Act. Here, a company who invested equity from its profits into a renewable energy project, was allowed to invest those profits, without any subjection to Irish corporation tax. The tax relief was to be capped for a single project at 50% of all capital expenditure net of grants (excluding lands)—up to a limit of £7.5 million. Investment by a company or group of companies in more that one qualifying project was also capped, but the level was set at £10 million per annum. This support sent an important signal of support from the Department of Finance at the time of introduction, but the benefits associated with this scheme have diminished with the reduction in corporation tax over a number of years (International Energy Agency 2004), although this relief was extended to 2006 under Section 39 of the Finance Act 2004. Here, we see some of the distinct benefits for firms becoming involved in energy renewables, but a capping of these benefits is questionable as an effective means of sustainable development of a greening energy policy by the government. Consequently, a clearer understanding of the rationale of government thinking is required, otherwise, the diminishing benefits for the investor may be detrimental to this rapidly emerging renewables industry. By the end of 1999, there were 19 wind farms with a combined installed capacity in Ireland of 117 MW. There was significant market interest in wind-power development (279 expressions of interest in AER III representing 1,680 MW), and there were 155 MW with planning permission, a further 167 MW within the planning process and 217 MW at an advanced stage of preparation for a planning application. With the framing of a National Climate Change Strategy under way, Ireland was seen to be at a crossroads with a decision to take in terms of whether to take wind energy seriously, increase the targets and address the various barriers confronting stakeholders.

WIND-ENERGY POLICY DEVELOPMENT 2000–2005

The publication of the Green Paper on Sustainable Energy saw a significant increase in the government targets for wind energy (Department of Public Enterprise 1999). The target for renewable energy was an additional 500 MW by 2005, with wind energy delivering the bulk of this, i.e., 450 MW (Renewable Energy Strategy Group, 2000). This effectively trebled the previous target of 30 MW for the same period. Based on projected electricity-demand growth, this target implied that wind energy would account for 7 per cent (from 1 per cent in 2000) of gross electricity consumption and 1 per cent of total primary energy supply by 2005. The Department of Public Enterprise established an RESG in 1999 to examine the constraints in meeting the 2000–2005 targets and thereafter to recommend strategies in order to overcome the constraints by focussing on onshore wind energy in the first instance, and reporting to the Minister within six months. The mandate of the RESG is clearly specified in the Green Paper on Sustainable Energy as being to examine and report on:

- The economic costs of promoting a green electricity market.
- The economic and technical barriers to green electricity production.
- International benchmarks for trade costs, delivery times, and quality of service obligations in other green electricity markets.
- Grid connection issues, including capacity, price, and delivery times.
- Technical limits of the electricity grid including priority solutions to particular weaknesses and bottlenecks.
- Electricity market factors likely to impede or obstruct the development of a green electricity market including top up and spill, transmission, and metering.

- Planning support issues, including any emerging trends or weaknesses in planning consent applications.
- Factors impeding local and community-based green electricity-generating schemes.

Given the complexity and distinctiveness of the constraints, coupled with the need to address them in an integrated manner, the approach adopted in developing the strategy was seen as critical toward achieving success (Ó Gallachóir and McKeogh 2000). A number of factors in the approach adopted in this exercise were unique in an Irish, and probably EU-wide, context. The rationale for some of these factors was drawn from previous experiences in dealing with constraints associated with renewable energy deployment. With this in mind, the RESG further developed the consensus-building experience gained from the Working Group on Grid Connection Issues to develop the strategy. Firstly, the membership was broadened, in particular to include planning issues. The Department of the Environment, Heritage and Local Government (DEHLG; then Department of the Environment and Local Government [DELG]) was included, given their dual role in preparing the National Climate Change Strategy (published while the RESG deliberated), and having responsibility for planning guidelines issued to local authorities. The Irish Planning Institute (IPI), a professional association of local authority and private consultant planners in Ireland, was also represented. IPI had previously been interested in the spatial planning aspects of wind energy and took part in an EU THERMIE B-funded project entitled *Municipal Action and Wind Power* (Energie Cités et al. 1999). The City and County Managers' Association, which represents the interests of local authority management, who in turn make key decisions in relation to wind farms, was also represented in the RESG. As with the Working Group, the TSO and DSO were represented, as was DCMNR, SEI, and the Irish Wind Energy Association (IWEA). The work programme for RESG was structured on the basis of thematic meetings, dealing with specific constraints. The significance of the programme was in the examination of different areas (on an individual basis) where constraints existed, and this was followed by an integrated resource planning exercise to develop a comprehensive strategy. RESG identified and discussed the constraints under the three headings: electricity market, electricity network, and spatial planning, and we now look at these separately.

Electricity Market

RESG assessed the AER scheme and identified the following shortcomings, with conclusions in italics.

Market Access

In AER, market access opportunities have been restricted by the timing, categories, and quantities announced sporadically. It was difficult to reasonably predict when such competitions would be announced or success would be achieved in such competitions. This caused some project developers to with-hold planning applications and development work re: connections to the grid, until the results of competitions were announced. This introduced significant uncertainty, whereby it was unclear when the projects with PPAs would be actually commissioned. Of the 138 MW of wind capacity offered to PPAs in AER III, only 38 MW were commissioned. *Any clear signal to the market of future proposals would reduce this uncertainty.*

Administrative delays

The administration of competitions involved a preliminary assessment of projects and the financial ability of project proposers by DCMNR (or an agent on its behalf). Under the AER III competition, for example, the number of applicants at the technical stage exceeded the number of successful developers by a factor of ten to one.

Access to Finance for Wind Farms in the Liberalized Market

Wind farms were able to avail of the opportunities offered by the liberaliza-tion of the electricity market since early 2000. Indications were that projects may suffer from an initial lack of confidence among support players—banks and financiers, in particular—particularly in the early trading stages of the green electricity market. *Appropriate assistance for an interim period and for a limited amount of capacity would help these projects aimed at that market in securing loans to finance their respective developments.*

Electricity Network

The Renewable Energy Strategy Group examined the electricity network from two perspectives: (1) individual connections to the network (grid con-nections); and (2) the ability of the network as a whole to accommodate increasing amounts of intermittent wind-generated electricity *(capacity acceptance)*.

Grid Connection

The Strategy Group discussed a manifestation, which was becoming increas-ingly prevalent as the number of wind farms connecting to the network grew. In a number of areas around the country, there were only certain amounts of available capacity on the distribution network for accommodating wind energy locally. The normal business case for infrastructural investment for connections was bundled in its entirety—on the first or next entrant—and remitted if others connected to the additional capacity. Additionally, there were cases where, say, 2 MW of capacity was required, but due to a lack of available capacity on the network, the minimum upgrade required would have accommodated, say, 10 MW. This may have constituted a deal-breaker for new entrants, as the 2-MW wind farm would be required to pay the full costs of the 10-MW infrastructure. *This is an issue worth noting.*

Capacity Acceptance

Assuming that the targets that were set were actually met, and the wind turbines operated at their rated capacity—which was on average for 37 per cent of the year (taking into account wind availability, turbine efficiency, operation and maintenance, etc.)—the annual production of wind-generated electricity was estimated to reach 1,948 GWh by 2005, or 7 per cent of the total forecast electricity demand (27,035 GWh) for that year, and compared with just over 1 per cent in 2000. *A key question which arose was: How would these levels impact the electricity network, and arising from this, how much can the network as a whole accommodate these figures? Resulting from separate studies, IWEA maintained that a 20 per cent penetration of wind energy was not problematic, whereas for ESB the 7 per cent target posed a significant challenge.*

Spatial Planning

The planning system had approved the construction of a significant number of wind farm projects, but there was a misalignment between these projects and those who had secured a PPA through the AER process. Other constraints also existed within the planning system, and the RESG saw legislation as an important tool in dealing with these.

Lack of Cohesion Between Planning and Energy Policy

Within the planning system, decisions on strategic policies are frequently made in the context of planning applications in the absence of a clear policy framework for those decisions (Van der Kamp 1999). The reason for this is that development plans rarely contain sufficient detail to enable an applicant to make a reasonable assumption on the likelihood of a planning application for any particular site or in any particular region. This resulted in possible conflicts between the development of wind farms and other land use priorities for these areas, in particular, the industry of tourism and the important issue of amenity. The Irish planning system is seen as a discretionary rather than a 'plan-led system'. It is not surprising, therefore, that the initial consideration of applications for planning consent to construct wind-energy infrastructure took place in the absence of a local expression of spatial planning policy for wind energy.

Tools Required to Assess the Impact of Wind Turbines on the Landscape

Wind turbines represented a new feature on the Irish landscape. Planners did not have access to the appropriate training and necessary tools for assessing landscape character in those emerging and developing areas, which would be a first step to determining whether the landscape could visually accommodate these developments.

Strategy for Intensifying Wind-Energy Deployment

The principal conclusion of the Renewable Energy Strategy Group was that three principal elements required integration in a plan-led approach, namely appropriate location, adequate availability of the wind resource, and accommodating electricity network infrastructure. The strategy centred on a cohesive plan-led approach to market mechanisms, grid upgrading, and spatial planning. Essentially, it recommended that spatial planning considerations should identify suitable wind farm locations, informed by the availability of the resource and the strength of the electricity networks. The strategic plan-led approach would determine the market mechanism and grid infrastructure required. Given the timescale required for this plan-led approach to take full effect, a short- and medium-term strategy was recommended for each area in order to allow for targets to be met and a transition to the new approach.

In the short term, it was recommended that the strategy should promote those projects with, or well advanced within, the planning process—in the form of an early AER V[3] round—in order to promote the early delivery of additional capacity.

In the medium term, it was recommended that the suitable locations for projects be identified in a strategic way, and appropriate market mechanisms and grid upgrading be implemented in a timely and efficient manner, in order to stimulate wind-energy deployment to help meet Ireland's renewable energy and greenhouse gas emission targets.

PROGRESS IN DELIVERING 2000–2005 STRATEGY

RESG presented its report to the government in July 2000. The action plan from the report is reproduced in Appendices 1–3, tabulating the key recommendations of the strategy grouped into the three areas mentioned previously and differentiating between short-term and medium-term measures. Considerable progress has been made on the implementation of a number of key actions, and this is also shown in the action plan in Appendices 1–3. In many cases, however, the actions were delivered later than anticipated, and this is one of the key reasons why the delivery of the Green Paper target was not met. The target was set in order to achieve an additional 450 MW of wind capacity by 2005 (i.e., by the end of 2004) through a revised AER process, sales from merchant plant to green electricity suppliers, and EU 5th Framework ENERGIE-supported wind farms. IIn the period from 2000 to the end of 2004, wind capacity grew by 279 MW,[4] of which 74MW was delivered under the AER rounds (after 1999). By the end of 2006, the total installed capacity was 762

MW, and the 450-MW target was met by the end of March 2006, some 15 months later than projected.

Electricity Market—Appendix 6.1.

With this in mind, the short-term goal of operating a fixed REFIT based on AER III prices (see Table 6.1) was not advanced (following consultations with Brussels and anticipated delays in DG (Directorate Generale) Competition approving the scheme). This delayed AER V from becoming a further competitive tender initiative. Additionally, the mismatch between projects having market access but not planning permission was removed with the condition in AER V that all applicants secure planning permission before entering the competition. Competition was therefore very tight, and AER V results were announced in February 2002. The 2003 budget announced in December 2002 removed a tax incentive relating to capital allowances that were being used to finance a number of a number of AER V wind farms. This issue was addressed in two ways by AER VI. Firstly, AER V projects could resubmit; and secondly, they could accelerate up-front payments by stepping up the bid price by up to 35 per cent in the first 7.5 years and stepping it down in the second 7.5 years of the 15-year PPA. Consequently, wind farms with a combined capacity of 44 MW were installed under AER V by the end of 2005 (42 MW by the end of 2004—the original target was 240 MW by the end of 2004), and a further 275 MW under AER VI by the end of 2006 (32 MW by the end of 2004—the original target was 535 MW by the end of 2004, including AER V projects and 50 MW of offshore wind energy.)

Table 6.1 summarizes the success rates in reaching the AER targets for wind energy, distinguishing between how much was achieved on time and the eventual outputs achieved. As mentioned, the failure of AER III arose due to a misalignment between those wind farm projects that had planning permission and those with AER PPA contracts. This was somewhat addressed by the late success in securing planning permission, leading to an eventual 42 per cent success rate.

In AER V, the withdrawn tax incentive led to a low success rate of 18 per cent. In AER VI, there was a misalignment between projects with grid

Table 6.1   AER Wind Targets Set and Reached

MW	AER I	AER III	AER V	AER VI
Target	30	90	240	433
On Time	21	5	42	32
Eventual	46	38	44	275
Success	153%	42%	18%	64%

Source: Author generated.

connection agreements and those with AER PPA contracts. This misalignment was exacerbated by the moratorium on new grid connection agreements (Ó Gallachóir et al. 2007) that was introduced in December 2003 and effectively continued until May 2005.

Regarding merchant plant projects in the liberalized market, the fall-back eight-year PPA[5] to mitigate the risk for wind farms built—selling wind-generated electricity outside the AER scheme did not materialize. The idea was further developed, but there was little appetite for an eight-year PPA. Merchant plant wind farms (selling output to green electricity suppliers) with an installed capacity of 168 MW were built by the end of 2004 (including the first offshore wind farm of 25 MW) and a further 170 MW were built during the years 2005–2006.

Electricity Network—Appendix 6.2.

From Appendix 6.2., we note that the Steering Group on the Grid Upgrade Programme for Renewable Energy addressed the major issue that existed for developers, where they were forced to raise the entire capital expenditure for any upgrade, forming part of a potentially shared connection, with money subsequently remitted as others connected to the facility. They concluded (Department of Communications, Marine and Natural Resources 2003) that the €30 million available in the National Development Plan (NDP) (NDP 2000–2006) should be used to fund grid upgrades based on perceived demand for shared infrastructure (based on clusters with two or more projects with full planning permission intending to connect to the upgrade). Against this backdrop, the Steering Group identified five clusters that had at least two projects with full planning permission in each cluster (Sustainable Energy Ireland 2003). Overall, there were eighteen projects (totalling 272 MW) with full planning permission within the five clusters selected for inclusion in the initial programme. It was anticipated that the fund would be a revolving one (i.e., expenditure on the shared connection assets would be recovered from the connecting parties and be used to fund other connections) and that the Steering Group would continue its work to identify suitable sites for development as funding allowed. The Commission for Energy Regulation approved the scheme in April 2003 (Commission for Energy Regulation 2003) and decided that the programme be underwritten with transmission use of system charging.

The medium-term goal of identifying strategic sites on the transmission network to upgrade for wind energy using NDP funding does not appear to have progressed. One issue regarding this is the size of the funds earmarked in the NDP for infrastructure upgrading for renewables compared with the scale of investment required for a significant upgrade. A significant body of work was undertaken in order to address the uncertainties relating to the specific impacts of large-scale wind energy penetration on the Irish electricity network (Gardner et al. 2003; Garrad Hassan et al. 2003; Doherty et al. 2004; and Bazilian et al. 2004) but not within the twenty-four-month timeframe envisaged in the action plan. In addition, limited work has been completed on operating reserve requirements (Ilex et al. 2004), electricity storage technologies (Gonzalez et al. 2004), and short-term forecasting of wind-generated electricity (Jørgensen et al. 2005).

Spatial Planning—Appendix 6.3

In considering Appendix 6.3, progress in delivering the actions in the area of spatial planning have been rather slow, but this has not acted as a major barrier to projects securing planning permission. Wind farms with a combined installed capacity of over 2000 MW secured planning permission by November 2003 (Gonzalez et al. 2004). The revised DEHLG Wind farm Planning Guidelines were issued in August 2004, with final guidelines published in 2006 (Department of the Environment, Heritage and Local Government 2006), four years later than targeted by RESG. While some planning authorities have revised their development plans, taking into account the recommendations of the strategy, in the absence of clear direction in the form of guidelines (the letter from the DCMNR and DEHLG Ministers notwithstanding), movement can be seen to have been *ad hoc*. Since 2006, the key actions relating to changing attitudes towards wind energy and the wind energy map had been completed, although most actions have been between one and two years behind the planned strategy schedule.

WIND-ENERGY POLICY DEVELOPMENT 2005–2010

In reviewing this particular period, there appear to have been a number of lessons that were learned from the experiences in implementing the RESG-proposed policy instruments, which were developed to meet the 2005 targets. The REDG, established in 2004, drew on these targets to develop a strategy to 2010 and highlighted a number of issues related to setting targets beyond 2010. The lessons learned are summarized as follows:

- A clear and structured strategy can be developed in a short time-frame. The time frame given for RESG (six months) was equivalent to the time frame given to REDG.
- While delivery on the action plan checklist appears achievable (see Appendices 1–3), a number of key areas that were delayed resulted in failure to deliver the targets in a timely manner.
- The delays in establishing the market AER V and AER VI mechanisms are evident from the low level of AER-supported projects installed in the period of 2000–2003, as illustrated in Figure 6.1.
- The Department of Environment's Wind Energy Development Guidelines (Department of the Environment, Heritage and Local Government 2006) were not issued until June 2006 (four years late), and

local authorities have been slow to act (with notable exceptions) in the absence of these revised guidelines.

- Eirgrid (Ireland's TSO) did not allocate sufficient resources to prepare for a significant increase in wind farms and to carry out system modeling to assess the impact of wind farms. This, coupled with the lack of development of adequate models by wind-turbine manufacturers, prompted the TSO to secure a moratorium on new grid connection agreements in December 2003 that effectively lasted for an eighteen-month period.

An interesting feature of the Irish experience with wind-energy deployment is the extent of merchant plants that have been installed outside of the AER mechanism (see Figure 6.1 for details). This accounted for 60 per cent of installed wind in the period of 2000–2004, and 49 per cent of wind installed over the period of 2000–2006, respectively. The wind-generated electricity is sold competitively within the liberalized electricity market and does not fall within a green pricing system, where customers pay a premium for green electricity. Based on available evidence internationally, this would appear to be a uniquely Irish development. Furthermore, the Electricity Regulation Act 1999 (Government of Ireland 1999) provided third-party access to the electricity network to 'green' (wind and other renewable sources) electricity suppliers, in order to sell directly to all final customers, irrespective of their respective consumption. Under the Act, 'brown' (fossil fuel-based) electricity suppliers could initially sell only to large customers (> 4 GWh per annum). Green electricity suppliers thus had total market access before brown suppliers. The threshold for brown electricity customers reduced gradually until February 2005, when the whole market was opened up. This market opening for green suppliers was important, particularly for the sections of the market which pay the most for electricity (commercial and domestic customers). This provided wind farm developers with an alternative to the AER route to the market and has resulted in capacities of 168 MW by the end of 2004, and 338 MW by the end of 2006, respectively.

The success of the merchant plant, coupled with the high failure rates of the AER competitions, prompted a change in the market mechanism. The new market support mechanism for wind energy (introduced in May 2006) in Ireland is called a renewable energy feed-in tariff (REFIT) scheme. It is, however, seen as a REFIT with a difference, compared with those schemes in operation in Germany, France, or Spain. In order to be eligible, a wind farm developer (generator) must negotiate a fifteen-year PPA with a licensed electricity supplier before applying for a REFIT (Department of Communications, Marine and Natural Resources 2006a). If successful, the wind-farm developer will receive a REFIT letter of offer. This will confirm to the electricity supplier that, in return for entering into a PPA to purchase the output from the proposed wind energy-powered plant, the supplier will be entitled to receive a REFIT payment for fifteen years. The payment due to the supplier amounts to 15 per cent[6] of the reference price, which is €57/MWh for large-scale wind farms and

€59/MWh for small-scale wind farms (both adjusted annually in line with the consumer price index). In Germany, France, and Spain the REFIT represents the amount paid to the wind-farm developers. In this Irish context, the REFIT for large wind farms is €8.55/MWh (index linked) paid to electricity suppliers who enter into a PPA with wind-farm developers. It builds on the success of a merchant plant delivering wind energy by compensating the electricity supplier who purchases wind-generated electricity. In order to address previous misalignments between price supported projects and those with planning permission or grid connection agreements, the REFIT mechanism requires that projects have secured planning permission and a grid connection in order to be eligible for support mechanisms.

MEETING THE 2010 TARGET

Under Directive 2001/77/EC, the indicative target for Ireland is to achieve 13.2 per cent gross electricity consumption from renewable energy sources by 2010, and this national target was increased in 2006 to 15 per cent. Translating this into a target for renewable energy capacity depends on growth in future electricity demand; however, based on national forecasts of electricity demand and the contribution of other renewable resources, this requires that 1,195 MW of wind be installed by the end of 2009 to achieve the 15 per cent target.

In the context of the renewable resources available in Ireland and the current status of different technologies and their supply chains, it is to be expected that wind, hydro, and biomass will be the dominant technologies of the future. The most likely scenario of RE (Renewable Energy) deployment would be approximately 1,195 MW of wind energy (on-shore and offshore), 240 MW of hydro;[7] 92 MW of bioenergy, and 1 MW of ocean energy installed by the end of 2009, as shown in Table 6.2. The implication for wind energy is that installed wind capacity must increase by approximately 433 MW.

Table 6.2   Meeting National RES-E (Renewable Energy Sources—Electricity) 15% Target by 2010

	Wind	*Biomass*	*Hydro*	*Ocean*	*Total*
Generating (Jan. 2007)	762 MW	35 MW	240 MW	0 MW	1,037 MW
Requirement to Meet 15% RES-E Target for 2010	1,195 MW	92 MW	240 MW	1 MW	1,528 MW
Capacity Gap Required to Meet 2010 Target	433 MW	57 MW	<1 MW	1 MW	491 MW

Source: Author generated.

This requires 433 MW of wind capacity, or an annual deployment rate of less than 150 MW in the period of 2007–2009. Based on recent experience (178 MW in 2004, 163 MW in 2005, and 253 MW in 2006) these figures would seem readily achievable. In addition, there are currently 473 MW with grid connection agreements and 599 MW with REFIT contracts (Ó Gallachóir et al., 2007).

CHALLENGES BEYOND 2010

While the 2010 targets appear achievable, there are a number of technical, regulatory, and fiscal challenges involved in delivering the 2020 target of achieving 30 per cent of gross electricity consumption from renewable sources that was announced in the Green Paper published in October 2006 (Department of Communications, Marine and Natural Resources 2006). Using one published energy forecast scenario (Howley et al. 2006), this will require approximately of 2,900 MW installed wind capacity[8] or an increase of 170 MW per annum in the period of 2010–2019. Hence, by 2020, wind energy could account for 21 per cent of gross electricity consumption in the country. Further, to achieve such a high level of wind-energy penetration, a number of the key issues which were identified and discussed by the REDG in 2004 (Renewable Energy Development Group Short Term Analysis Group 2004), i.e.: grid code and modelling, constraints,[9] connections process, and support mechanisms require attention. These items are identified as embodying significant challenges to deployment and it is also acknowledged that the ability of projects to obtain suitable sources of financing is a critical issue, and this is further evidence of the challenges facing this industry, and as a consequence, these issues would greatly benefit from appropriate policy and regulatory reform.

Options recommended as strategic routes forward include:

- The prioritisation of delivering connection offers.
- Aligning support mechanism(s) with the TSO/DSO connection policies so that the grid connection status of projects is considered when awarding any future PPAs. Further, any viable projects with PPAs should be prioritized for progression through the grid connection process, and both processes should inform each other simultaneously.
- Ongoing monitoring of grid code compliance issues for wind generators (including modelling).
- Facilitation of optimal planning of the electricity infrastructure in the short term in order to facilitate the achievement of longer-term RE targets.
- The time frames for planning permissions should be aligned with infrastructure planning and construction, and should allow for a simplified extension process. This is particularly relevant where significant delays are encountered that appear beyond the control of developers.

- The level of constraint to be applied to wind-energy generators should be quantified and bounded with confidence. High-level rules should be developed to apportion the 'burden' of constraint, and these should be clear, transparent, and well aligned with the delivery of RE targets.
- The future operation of, and the portfolio of plants on, the power system should be aligned to deliver targets beyond 2010 in an integrated manner.
- Accurate forecasting of wind-power output in a–zero-to-forty-eight-hour time window would facilitate delivery of the 2010 target (and beyond) and should be developed as a priority.
- Consideration should be given to the scale of financial commitment required from RE project developers at the various stages of the connection process in order to ensure high percentage uptake and use of grid connection offers.

CONCLUSIONS

Wind-energy policy, planning, and strategic decision making are now the focus of attention of many theorists, governments, and practitioners, and as such, this chapter outlines some of the evolving issues associated within the context of the renewables market in Ireland. A combination of important factors, including recent historical and substantive rises in electricity prices, excellent wind resources, a likely upward pressure on natural gas prices, and downward pressure on wind development costs, should form a fertile backdrop for the implementation of wind policy in Ireland. To date, significant progress has been made to adapt wind-energy policy, and this appears to be based on experiential learning. These developments, however, have typically not occurred in sufficient time to meet targets set, and in some instances, the context has changed in a manner that reduces their respective independent and collective effectiveness.

In total, 762 MW of wind capacity had been delivered to the market by the end of 2006. Of this, 403 MW was delivered through the primary market support mechanism, namely, the AER programme. The remainder of capacity has been delivered through merchant plant delivering to green electricity customers (338 MW) and EU-supported demonstration projects (14 MW). Based on the success of the merchant plant in delivering wind power, the new market mechanism (REFIT 2006) encourages suppliers to enter into PPAs with wind-farm operators through a compensation payment of €8.33/MWh.

Looking ahead, a significant number of constraints have been identified and examined in detail, and options to address the barriers now exist. The targets for 2010 appear achievable (1,195 MW by the end of 2009), but it is important that the necessary groundwork be put in place to meet the 2,900 MW target by 2020, which is deemed achievable but ambitious, and will require a focussed and concerted effort by all stakeholders.

APPENDIX 6.1 RESG ACTION PLAN 2000—ELECTRICITY MARKET

Short-Term Strategy

Title	Recommendation	Time-scale	2007 Update
Promote large scale wind energy	Conduct a further AER competition (AER V), at prices linked to CPI based on AER III results, concentrating on projects with all necessary statutory permits up to a quantified limit. In AER V, signal a further round (AER VI) based on open competition. Remove the ownership and project size gaps.	Scheme open for 24 months (2000–2002)	*Based on communication with Brussels, AER V was a competition rather than REFIT. Results announced in February 2002 and 42 MW installed by 2005 (44 MW by end 2005)*
Promote small-scale wind energy schemes	Include a small-scale category in AER V but project size reduced to, say, 2.5 MW installed.	Scheme open for 24 months (2000–2002)	*Project size reduced to 3 MW for AER V and raised to 5 MW again for AER VI*
Support the liberalised green electricity market	Offer a fall-back eight-year PPA at a fixed price without indexation for a limited amount of wind-generated electricity plants entering the liberalised market.	Scheme open 24 months (2000–2002)	*Progressed further but ultimately not delivered. Some favourable conditions for wind emerged as liberalisation developed. 168 MW delivered by 2005 (338 MW by end 2006)*
Review of market mechanism	Light-handed review of the proposed mechanisms in the context of capacity delivered, emerging requirements relating to Kyoto compliance and binding EU law, and experience of wind energy developments within the liberalised market.	12 months from commencement of AER V (2001)	*AER VI rules revised based on experience with AER V. Full indexing, accelerated up-front payment; AER V projects could resubmit*
AER VI	Competition for wind farms based on price to follow AER V.	Commencing not later than month 12 (2001)	*AER VI launched in February 2003, 12 months after AER V results. 32 MW installed by 2005 (253 MW by end 2006)*

(continued)

APPENDIX 6.1   RESG ACTION PLAN 2000—ELECTRICITY MARKET (CONTINUED)

Medium-Term Strategy

Title	Recommendation	Time-scale	2007 Update
Review of market mechanisms	Detailed review of the proposed mechanisms in the context of capacity delivered, emerging requirements relating to Kyoto compliance and binding EU law, and experience of wind energy developments within the liberalised market.	Months 36–60 (2003–2005)	*Completed November 2004. REFIT announced as mechanism to deliver 2010 target in May 2006 (month 72).*

APPENDIX 6.2 RESG ACTION PLAN 2000—ELECTRICITY NETWORK

Short-Term Strategy

Title	Recommendation	Time-scale	2007 Update
Network upgrading	Commit some funds for renewable energy developments in the National Development Plan to upgrade the distribution and transmission networks to accommodate wind farms where a bottleneck exists or can be reasonably predicted. As the funding is remitted, it should be made available for further upgrades, so long as additional capacity requirements can be identified under reasonable assumptions.	24 months	*Steering Group for the Grid Upgrade Programme established November 2001 and reported September 2002. CER approved scheme in April 2003, funded by EU funds and transmission use of system*
Grid connection issues	Studies on the impact of wind energy in relation to connecting to the distribution network should be implemented	18 months	*Refer to DSO*
Impact of wind energy on the electricity network	Studies should be undertaken on the impact of wind-generated electricity on the network, with data collected from all existing wind farms. These studies should examine short-term impacts, forecasting, requirements for stability and frequency regulation, and additional dispatch costs. The effects of interconnection should be included.	24 months	*ESB NG involved in ongoing review of forecasting models; CER funded study on wind impacts on grid completed February 2003.*

(continued)

APPENDIX 6.2   RESG ACTION PLAN 2000—ELECTRICITY NETWORK (CONTINUED)

Medium-Term Strategy

Title	Recommendation	Time-scale	2007 Update
Network upgrading	Continuation of short-term recommendation, so long as additional capacity requirements can be identified under reasonable assumptions	Month 24–60	*Scheme utilisation poor to date*
Network upgrading	Strategic sites on the transmission network, where additional capacity requirements can be identified under reasonable assumptions, should be upgraded to allow increased wind penetration.	Month 24–60	*Refer to TSOs*
Impact of wind energy on the electricity network	The results of the studies carried out in the short-term strategy should be incorporated into the medium-term proposals.	Month 24–60	*SEI funded studies on operating reserve, storage, forecasting to be completed in 2004. ESB (Electronic Supply Board) NG (National Grid) developed Grid Code for Wind energy, finalised in July 2004.*

APPENDIX 6.3 RESG ACTION PLAN 2000—SPATIAL PLANNING

Short-Term Strategy

Title	Recommendation	Time-scale	2007 Update
Amend local authority development plans	Department of Environment and Local Government (DoELG and DPE invite local authorities to submit draft proposals identifying areas as 'preferred', 'open for consideration', 'strategic', and 'no-go' for wind energy development. The areas should then be modified based on information on the local electricity infrastructure and wind energy resources from the Renewable Energy Information Office (REIO) in consultation with others, and then incorporated into the development plan.	18 months for initial plans	*Invitation from Ministers issued March 2001. Slow, ad hoc progress. Recommended in draft DEHLG guidelines.*
Landscape assessment	In parallel with the characterisation of the landscape, it is recommended that local authorities determine the sensitivity of different landscape character types to different kinds of wind energy development. This will involve assessing landscape quality, sensitivity, robustness, and capacity.	24 months	*Ad hoc development. Recommended in draft guidelines. SEI commissioned study to assess How the Irish Public View Windfarms in the Landscape.*
Information campaign	The REIO of the Irish Energy Centre should research into attitudes toward wind farm developments to develop and implement an information campaign addressing public concerns regarding wind energy development.	24 months	*SEI published Attitudes Towards the Development of Windfarms in Ireland 2003 in December 2003 (28)*
Wind energy map	A map should be prepared digitally which contains information regarding the wind energy resource; the transmission and distribution networks; and the sites which have received, failed, or are passing through the planning system	12 months	*SEI published Irish National Onshore Wind Energy Resource Study and BOC prepared map of sites with planning permission for Steering Group on Grid Upgrade Programme*
Wind farm guidelines	DoELG should revise and update the 'Windfarm Development—Guidelines for Planning Authorities based on the recommendations in this document to assist planners in operating to a national standard and to increase certainty, to the extent possible, for developers.	24 months	*Revised Wind Energy Guidelines published June 2006, four years late*

(continued)

APPENDIX 6.3 RESG ACTION PLAN 2000—SPATIAL PLANNING (CONTINUED)

Medium-Term Strategy

Title	Recommendation	Time-scale	2007 Update
Amend local authority development plans	Local authorities should further develop their plans for wind energy based on experience, additional network infrastructure requirements, and the results of landscape assessment	Month 24–60	*Progress likely to increase with publication of draft guidelines*
Regional Planning Guidelines and National Spatial Strategy (NSS)	Areas which are deemed to be of regional (national) importance for the development of wind farms or protection from wind farm development, should be identified and incorporated into the Regional Planning Guidelines (and possibly the NSS)	Month 24–60	*Old bog sites in the midlands identified as suitable for wind energy in NSS. No mention in energy section. Referred to in some Regional Planning Guidelines.*

NOTES

*Most of the hydro capacity that will contribute to the target has already been commissioned.

1. AER II was specifically for a 30-MW biomass plant and did not include a target for wind energy.
2. Plus 3 MW of hydropower, 7 MW of biomass, and a pilot 5-MW wave power plant.
3. The AER IV competition focussed on Combined Heat and Power (CHP) only.
4. This includes 33 MW of AER III-supported projects, which were excluded from the 450-MW target.
5. This would be an optional eight-year PPA offered to generators selling to green electricity suppliers, to come into effect if the electricity supplier ceases to trade. The purpose of the proposed scheme was to reassure lenders. This mechanism was reassessed and formed the basis for the REFIT market mechanism introduced in 2006.
6. There are additional payments for non-wind and in cases where the reference price for wind generated electricity per MWh is higher than the Best New Entrant price (based on long run marginal cost of a new 400 MW plant).
7. Most of the hydro capacity that will contribute to the target has already been commissioned.
8. Assuming 414 MW of biomass, 41 MW of ocean energy, and 269 MW of hydropower.
9. Constraining the electrical output of the generating plant. Both technical and process (legal, fiscal, and policy) issues were examined.

ACKNOWLEDGEMENT

This work was funded in part under the Environmental RTDI (Research Training and Development Initiative Programme 2000–2006, through research contract 2001-EEP-MS-1, financed by the Irish Government under the National Development Plan, and administered on behalf of the Department of the Environment and Local Government by the Environmental Protection Agency.

REFERENCES

Bazilian, M., Denny, E. and O'Malley, M. (2004) 'Challenges of increased wind energy penetration in Ireland', *Wind Engineering*, 28(1): 43–56.
Commission for Energy Regulation. (2003) *Funding of Grid Upgrade Development Programme for Renewables.* Commission for Energy Regulation, Decision Paper (CER/03/090), 7th April 2003, (The CER is the regulator for the electricity and natural gas sectors in Ireland)
Council Regulation (EEC) No. 3301/86. (1986) 'Instituting a Community programme for the development of certain less-favoured regions of the Community by exploiting endogenous energy resources (Valoren programme)', 27 October. Report, Published by European Commission, Brussels.
Daly, D. (1999) *Zoning: Criteria for a Protected Area Approach,* Proceedings from Irish Energy Centre/Irish Planning Institute Workshop on Wind Energy Planning for 2000, 25–26 November 1999, Galway, Ireland.

138   Brian P. Ó Gallachóir, Morgan Bazilian, and Eamon J. McKeogh

Department of Communications, Marine and Natural Resources. (2003) *Options for Future Renewable Energy Policy, Targets and Programmes*, Consultation Document.
———. (2004) *Grid Upgrade Development Programme—Steering Group Report, Ireland*.
———. (2004) *Minister Establishes Group To Drive Renewable Energy Development*, Press release, 6 May.
———. (2005) *Alternative Energy Requirement Programme and Profile of AER I—VI Competitions*, Dublin: Stationery Office.
———. (2006) *New Renewable Capacity will treble "clean green electricity" from 5% to 15% by 2010*, Press release, 29 September 2006. Dublin: Stationary Office.
———. (2006b) *Renewable Energy Feed in Tariff (REFIT) Competition—List of Successful Applicants*, Ireland.
———. (2006c) *Green Paper—Towards a Sustainable Energy Future for Ireland*.
———. (2006) *Renewable Energy Feed in Tariff (RE-FIT 2006a)*, Ireland.
Department of the Environment. (1996) *Wind Farm Development—Guidelines for Planning Authorities*, Dublin: Stationery Office.
Department of the Environment and Local Government. (2000) *National Climate Change Strategy Ireland*, Ireland.
Department of the Environment, Heritage and Local Government. (2006) *Wind Energy Development Guidelines*.
Department of Public Enterprise. (1999) *Green Paper on Sustainable Energy*, Dublin: Stationery Office.
Department of Transport, Energy and Communications. (1996) *Renewable Energy—Strategy for the Future*, Ireland.
Doherty, R., Bryans, L., Gardner, P. and O'Malley, M. (2004) 'Wind penetration studies on the Island of Ireland', *Wind Engineering*, 28(1): 27–42.
Energie Cités, Irish Planning Institute, Garrad Hassan and Adème (1999) *Municipal Action and Wind Power Final Report*, THERMIE B project DIS/1558/97. Brussels: European Commission.
ESBI and ETSU. (1997) *Total renewable energy resource in Ireland*, European Commission ALTENER Report XVII/4.1030/T4/95/IRL. Brussels: European Commission.
European Union. (2001) *Directive 2001/77/EC of the European Parliament and of the Council on the Promotion of Electricity from Renewable Energy Sources in the Internal Electricity Market*. Brussels: European Commission.
Gardner, P., McGoldrick, S., Higgins, T. and Ó Gallachóir, B. P. (2003) *The effect of increasing wind penetration on the electricity systems in the Republic of Ireland and Northern Ireland*, proceedings from European Wind Energy Conference, 16–19 June, Madrid.
Garrad Hassan, ESBI and UCC. (2003) *The impacts of increased levels of wind penetration on the electricity networks of the Republic of Ireland and Northern Ireland*. Brussels: European Commission.
Gonzalez, A., Ó Gallachóir, B., McKeogh, E. and Lynch, K. (2004) *Study of electricity storage technologies and their potential to address wind energy intermittency*, report published by Sustainable Energy Ireland. Dublin, Ireland.
Government of Ireland. (1999) *Electricity Regulation Act*. Dublin: Stationery Office.
Howley M. and Ó Gallachóir B. P. (2005) *Energy in Ireland 19902003*, Sustainable Energy Ireland. Sustainable Energy Ireland, Glasnevin, Dublin 9, Ireland.
Howley, M., O' Leary, F. and Ó Gallachóir, B. P. (2006) *Energy in Ireland 1990–2005—Trends, Issues, Forecasts and Indicators*, Sustainable Energy Ireland.

International Energy Agency. (2004) *Renewable Energy—Market and Policy Trends in IEA Countries,* OECD/IEA. Paris: Organisation for Economic Cooperation and Development, CEDEX 16.

Ilex, UCD, QUB and UMIST. (2004) *Operating reserve requirements as wind power penetration increases in the Irish electricity system,* report published by Sustainable Energy Ireland. Dublin: Sustainable Energy Ireland.

Jørgensen, J., McKeogh, E., Ó Gallachóir, B. and Moehrlen, C. (2005) *Development of a short range ensemble prediction system for wind energy forecasting in Ireland,* interim report to SEI under Renewable Energy Research, Development and Demonstration Grant RE/W/03/006. Cork: Sustainable Energy Research Group, Department of Civil and Environmental Engineering, University College Cork, College Road.

Ó Gallachóir, B. P. (2000) *Market Mechanisms—future possible options,* proceedings from Energy Show 2000 Workshop, The Changing Market for Renewables, 18 May, Industries Hall, Dublin.

———. (2001) *Regional Wind Power Development—the Irish approach,* proceedings from Colloque National Éolien, 7–9 December, Narbonne.

———. (2007) *The future of wind energy in Ireland,* proceedings from Irish Sustainable Energy Summit, 9 March, Dublin.

Ó Gallachóir, B. P. and McKeogh, E. J. (2000) *Ireland's strategies for wind energy,* Proceedings from the Conference Wind Power for the 21st Century—The challenge of high wind power penetration for the new energy markets, 25–27 September, Kassel, Germany.

Ó Gallachóir, B. P., Gardner, P., Snodin, H. and McKeogh, E. J. (2007) *Wind Energy and System Security - The Grid Connection Moratorium in Ireland,* International Journal of Energy Technology and Policy (IJETP) Special issue on: Control and Protection of Distribution Systems with Distributed Generators 5, 633–647.

O'Leary, F., Ó Gallachóir, B., Howley, M. and Waugh, T. (2004) *Renewable energy in Ireland. Trends and issues 1991–2002,* report published by Sustainable Energy Ireland. Dublin: *Sustainable Energy Ireland, Glasnevin, Dublin 9.*

Renewable Energy Development Group Short Term Analysis Group. (2004) *Final Report on Policy Considerations for Renewable Electricity to 2010.* Department of Communications, Marine and Natural Resources.

Renewable Energy Strategy Group. (2000) *Strategy for Intensifying Wind Energy Deployment.* Dublin: Stationery Office.

Sustainable Energy Ireland. (2003) *Attitudes Towards the Development of Wind Farms in Ireland.* Dublin, Ireland. (Sustainable Energy Ireland, Glasnevin, Dublin 9, IRELAND), 28.

Van der Kamp, H. W. (1999) *National Spatial Planning and Wind Energy Infrastructure,* presentation at Wind Energy Planning for 2000 Conference, 25th–26th November 1999. Galway, Ireland.

7 Assessing the Performance of the UK Renewables Obligation
Cinderella or an Ugly Sister?

Afolabi Otitoju, Peter A. Strachan, and David Toke

INTRODUCTION

Energy production from renewable energies continues to be somewhat of a hot topic within United Kingdom (UK) policy debates. Indeed, there appear to be increasing concerns over security of supply, and combining this with the growing threats of climate change, these issues have fuelled demands for renewable energies to play a greater role in the UK energy mix.

The UK's commercial renewable energy programme began in 1990, with the inception of the renewables section of the Non-Fossil Fuel Obligation (NFFO). However, as we discuss later, this produced only small amounts of wind power. The election of the Labour Government in 1997 presaged a bigger focus on delivering large volumes of renewable energy, resulting in the Renewables Obligation (RO), which began operation in 2002. This development has paralleled other initiatives, such as the Climate Change Programme, and the 2003 and 2007 Energy White Papers. The RO was established with an obligation on electricity suppliers to supply 10 per cent of their electricity from renewables by 2010. This target was extended in December 2003, toward providing 15 per cent by 2015 (Toke 2005). The UK government has also committed itself to extending this target to 20 per cent by 2020. With this in mind, much of this capacity will come from wind power—with wind having an exalted position in UK energy-policy debates. Additionally, Scotland has played an increasingly important role in onshore wind-power deployment, as it possess a large part of not only the UK's, but also Europe's potential for exploiting wind power. Recognizing this natural advantage, the devolved Scottish government has stipulated a national target of providing 18 per cent of Scottish electricity generation from renewable sources by 2010, and 40 per cent by 2020.

Against this backdrop, however, the UK is not on course to meet its 10 per cent target. Indeed, by the end of 2006, 'new' (i.e., non-large hydro) renewable energy was supplying 4 per cent of electricity when, according to the escalating target, it ought to have been supplying 6 per cent.

An expanding literature has begun to emerge which attempts to explain the situation whereby, given the apparent governmental support for renewable energy and the technical and economic feasibility of wind, why are current deployment rates falling far short of those necessary to meet targets? As was noted in the introduction to this book, the UK remains a member of the second division of deployed wind-power capacity—behind Germany, Spain, the United States, and Denmark, and alongside countries like France, The Netherlands, Italy, and Portugal.

Reasons outlined to explain this phenomenon have revolved around the lack of widespread farmer- and community-owned wind power. However, the truth may be more prosaic in that, in the UK, energy activism at the grassroots level has been limited compared to some other countries on the European continental shelf (Germany and Denmark, in particular), a context which is associated with low levels of interest in developing locally owned wind-power schemes. As noted in Chapter 1, the vast majority of wind capacity is owned by the six major electricity companies, with reportedly limited direct community benefits having been realized as a result. Other reasons given include hostility from some very high-profile landscape protection campaigners and other campaigning organizations, restrictive planning practices (Warren et al. 2005; Cowell 2007), the weak transmission system in Scotland (Strachan and Lal. 2004), and the fact that there is little domestic manufacturing base to support the deployment of wind power in the UK (Strachan et al. 2006). Incentive systems, which have been adopted by the UK for wind-power deployment since the early 1990s, have also been criticized (Toke 2007; Elliott 2005; Grotz and Bischof 2005).

While we recognize the importance of these factors, as well as the fact that they are complexly intertwined, this chapter aims to critically evaluate the performance of the RO—since 2002, the main incentive scheme to be used to promote the expansion of renewable energies in the UK. Meyers (2007) and Grotz and Fouquet (2005) note that the success of achieving politically fixed renewable targets rapidly will not come about without reliable, long-term support schemes which secure investor confidence. Thus, the main research question this chapter aims to address is: To what extent is the RO an appropriate support scheme, and is the RO performing according to governmental and other stakeholder expectations?

Before presenting a critique of the RO, we begin by providing a contextual discussion of UK wind-energy policy and related developments. This will be followed by an overview of the theoretical framework supported by objective criteria, which have been formulated to evaluate the performance of the RO. The development of this framework was based on a comprehensive literature review of existing practitioner and academic frameworks, methods, and criteria, and piloted with a range of organizations operating in the European and UK wind sector. To ensure our framework is fit for purpose, it has also been used to evaluate the performance of support schemes in Germany and The Netherlands, though we do not discuss our research findings from these countries in the current chapter. Furthermore, it is noted that our analysis of the RO was facilitated by in-depth semi-structured interviews with eighteen senior representatives (see Appendix 7.1) drawn from the most important organizations involved in the design and management, operation, and regulation of the RO.

UK RENEWABLE ENERGY POLICY: 1970–2008

Plans to promote renewable energy in the UK can be traced back to the 1970s. At this time, renewable energy was based on research and development, with only very limited electricity produced from renewable energies. During the 1970s and 1980s, renewable energy was both marginalized and shackled by the technocratic corporatism of the then-country-centred nationalized energy industries.

During the 1980s, the UK government began to pursue a wholesale liberalization and privatization programme of the electricity market. Becoming the first European Union member state to open up its market for competition through the adoption of the Electricity Act in 1989 (Meyer 2003), the regulatory framework started to become geared toward promoting competition, promoting lower prices for consumers, and avoiding market distortions. However, electricity production from renewable energy continued to be confined to competitive-market conditions, which appeared to be rolled out to the institutions and rationalities of the then-dominant energy market. While the NFFO, which was introduced in 1990, did kick-start the wind energy sector in the UK, its failings have been well documented. As a consequence, although the NFFO served as an initial financial support mechanism to promote the take-off of renewable energy technologies (which were the most commercially viable), Connor and Mitchell (2004: 136) reveal, however, that the NFFO was set up as a means to subsidize nuclear generation, which had proved extremely difficult to privatize. At that particular time, it was clear that only limited support was provided to renewable energies, and this important issue is alluded to in depth by Szarka and Bluhdorn (2006).

The NFFO was arranged in rounds—as a form of tendering system—which allowed companies to compete for financial support for investing in renewables. In simple terms, the cheapest bid submitted won the contract and the company then received a subsidy. By the year 2000, a total of 1,500 MW of installed capacity of renewable energy sources was proposed, but after all of the rounds of the NFFO, it failed to deliver the required target. Hence, Brennand (2004: 89) noted that:

> the failure of the NFFO to achieve its 1500MW target of new renewable generating capacity in the UK by the year 2000 led the government

in the same year to declare a new target of 10%, therefore the NFFO was put on hold.

Much was said about the planning problems faced by wind-power schemes (Connor and Mitchell 2004), but perhaps a bigger factor contributing to a disappointing rate of installation of wind farms was the competitive bidding system itself. It encouraged low-cost schemes. Unfortunately, however, many seemed to be proposed on the basis of optimism and a desire to win a contract, rather than develop robust, appropriate, or sophisticated schemes, which in reality often proved to be rather more costly than the original bids suggested.

The change in UK government in 1997 brought a sea-change of thinking to the renewables debate and, consequently, the Labour Government's commitment to the ecological modernization of the UK economy brought about significant changes to energy policy. Valle Costa et al. (2007) indicated that the Utility Act, which was introduced in 2000, was intended to further strengthen these changes and to establish a new regulatory framework for gas and electricity markets; thus, the New Electricity Trading Agreement (NETA) came into operation in 2001. However, the uncertainty created by the formation of NETA effectively put a halt to renewable energy developments at that time. On this note, NETA was designed more or less like a community market, meant to bring down the price of bulk electricity. Further, in order to encourage a low-carbon economy and to reduce carbon dioxide emissions, the Carbon Trust was created in 2001. In the same year, the UK climate change programme was published by the government and Strachan and Lal (2004) reported that the climate change programme had pushed forward governmental policies that gave way for renewable energy to further strengthen the government's intention to reach the 10 per cent target by 2010.

In 2002, the RO was introduced to replace the NFFO, and this once again stimulated investor confidence in wind power (the best-developed technology) amongst, in particular, large and integrated utility companies. The RO is a form of renewable portfolio standard (RPS), mandating all utility companies to produce 10 per cent of their electricity mix from renewables by 2010, and 15 per cent by 2015. This was intended to increase annually, beginning with 3 per cent in 2002–2003, and the quotas were to be achieved through the issue of a green certificate for each unit of generation, and the RO will be in force up to 2025–2026. Here, renewable energy generators receive renewable obligation certificates (ROCs) for each megawatt-hour of renewable-energy electricity generated. The ROCs can either be obtained by buying from generators or from the ROC's market. Failure of suppliers or utilities to meet the required ROCs leads to the payment of a "buy-out price", and the funds from the buy-out price are recycled amongst generators that meet their quotas. To date, the RO has helped to deliver the surge in onshore wind-energy investment and installed capacity.

The Energy White Paper, published in 2003 (Department of Trade and Industry 2003), arose from the need to address a series of emerging energy challenges, i.e., meeting UK energy demand, dealing with the threat of climate change, and reducing dependency on fossil fuels, especially from other parts of the world. The 2003 Energy White Paper set out four principal goals which have continued to date:

(i) Putting the UK on a path to cut its carbon dioxide emissions by 60 per cent by 2050.
(ii) Maintaining reliability of energy supplies.
(iii) Promoting competitive markets in the UK and abroad.
(iv) Ensuring that every home is adequately and affordably heated.

Renewable energy—particularly wind power—is expected to play an important role in making this become a reality (Department of Trade and Industry 2003; Foxon and Pearson 2007).

Since being elected, the Labour Government has also sought to improve the planning environment for wind farms. This has featured the adoption of the Planning Policy Statement 22 (PPS22) guidelines for local authorities in England. These guidelines introduced 'criteria based' assessment of wind farms and undermined efforts by local authorities to declare 'no-go' areas for wind farms. However, the Westminster government no longer has control over wind-power planning in Wales (except for schemes over 50 MW) and Scotland (not at all). The Welsh and Scottish Executives have both maintained pro-wind-power planning policies, albeit, in the case of Wales under TAN-8, through limiting wind-power development mostly to a few small wind-power development zones.

Scotland is more important than England toward reaching the renewables target in onshore planning terms. However, the previously high proportion of wind-power planning approvals has been falling in Scotland. The most recent planning policy statement (SPP6) allows local authorities to earmark some areas for 'significant protection' (against wind farms). The emergence of an SNP Scottish Executive in May 2007 has further dampened the possibilities for high approval rates. Nevertheless, the Scottish Executive's attitude toward onshore wind farms, while more cautious than the Labour Party, is still moderately supportive. It is thus still likely that half or more of wind farms will be approved on top of the many that have already received planning consent, and the goal of achieving 50 per cent of Scottish electricity from renewable energy by 2020 is still realistic. There is no shortage of schemes in the planning pipeline. A large backlog of wind-farm schemes given planning approval but which are waiting for transmission upgrades before they can be constructed already exists. The 'Beauly-Denny line'

(North–South Scotland) transmission line has been subject to a lengthy planning enquiry and, while it seems likely to be approved, it will not be operational before 2010.

Other different sorts of delays have afflicted the offshore programme, although some of these can indeed be attributed to the operation of the RO. Because the RO favoured the cheapest projects, offshore schemes have sometimes been put on the 'back burner'. This problem has been exacerbated by the increase in wind-turbine prices since 2005, a consequence of the burgeoning global demand for wind turbines and increases in the cost of energy, steel, and concrete. In addition, the British government and its regulator, Office of the Gas and Electricity Market (OFGEM), have been relatively slow to organize an agreement that would allow the bulk of the charges for grid connection of offshore wind farms to be passed on to electricity consumers through the transmission change element of bills. Even so, it has to be said that Britain is now (end of 2007) roughly equal with Denmark, having around 400 MWe of offshore wind capacity, and is therefore the joint world leader in this particular subtechnology.

According to the first annual report on implementation of the Energy White Paper (Department of Trade and Industry 2004: 5), of the 112 key milestones set as a first step toward achieving the White Paper's long-term commitments, 56 of them had been completed by the end of March 2004. In the context of renewable energy sources, 1.6 GW was consented, with 2 GW capacities under way. While 2004 mainly set in place long-term strategies for achieving the targets set out in the 2003 White Paper (Department of Trade and Industry 2005), one important development were the changes made to the RO order 2004. This increased the level of the obligation to 15.4 per cent by 2015–2016, which was meant to "provide investors with additional confidence" (Department of Trade and Industry 2005: 5). During 2005, the UK became one of only eight countries to reach over 1,000 MW installed wind capacity (Department of Trade and Industry 2006).

Following the Energy Review, the 2007 Energy White Paper (2007) was published and a "banding" system was introduced to the RO.[1] This reform was introduced in response to criticisms that the RO was allowing development of only the cheapest technologies (including onshore wind), rather than more expensive renewables, such as offshore wind and wave power. The aim of the banding system is to allocate more or less than one ROC for each megawatt of electricity produced from renewable energy sources, depending on the stage of technological development and associated costs (Department of Trade and Industry 2007: 150). Therefore, enabling the increase of the deployment of emerging marine (wave, tidal, etc.) renewable technologies, and improve overall cost-effectiveness of the RO (Department of Trade and Industry 2007). Interestingly, this involved a reversal of policy that had been established earlier by the Department of Trade and

Table 7.1   An Overview of UK Renewable Energy Policies 1970–2008

Policies and Programmes	Period	Focus
Development initiatives	1970–1988	Research, Development and Demonstration (R&D&D) limited renewables
Liberalization and privatisation of electricity market	1989	Opening up market for competition
NFFO nuclear and renewables	1990–2002	Nuclear subsidy
Utility Act	2000	Gas and electricity market
NETA	2001	Reducing prices for bulk electricity
Carbon Trust	2001	Carbon dioxide emissions reduction 12.5% Kyoto target achievement
United Kingdom Climate Change Programme	2001	Kyoto target and renewable energy sources targets
Renewables Obligation	2002	Renewable energy sources
Energy White Paper	2003	Meeting energy demand and climate change, and reducing dependency on fossil fuels from other parts of the world.
Energy White Paper	2007	Meeting energy demand and climate change, and creating an enabling environment for all renewable energy sources to grow through the introduction of 'banding'

Source: Author generated.

Industry (DTI). This is an issue which we pick up later when discussing our research findings. The new Energy White Paper just came into operation in May 2007; therefore, it is too early to comment further on its progress and success.

Table 7.1 summarizes the development of UK renewable energy policies discussed in this section.

ASSESSING PERFORMANCE: AN EVALUATION FRAMEWORK

Having provided the background to UK renewable energy policy, this section presents our theoretical framework, supporting evaluation methods, and criteria developed from a review of the literature on international support schemes, and piloted with a range of EU and UK organizations. The section begins by providing an insight into EU framework conditions that support schemes should meet. The evaluation criteria and questions which guide our research are then outlined, and these are summarized in Table 7.2 before our theoretical and integrative framework is presented, which is used to assess the performance of the RO.

Framework Conditions

The available evidence clearly identifies that the implementation of support schemes are crucial to the delivery of renewable energies. As such, the EU Directive 2001/77/EC indicates that support schemes should satisfy the following strategic conditions:

- Contribute to achievement of national indicative targets.
- Be compatible with the principle of the internal electricity market.
- Take into account the characteristics of different sources of renewable energy, together with the different technologies and geographical differences.
- Promote the use of renewable energy sources in an effective way; be simple and, at the same time, as efficient as possible, particularly in terms of costs.
- Include sufficient transitional periods for national support systems of at least seven years and maintain investor confidence.

Morthorst et al. (2005: 8) reveal, however, that support schemes are not by themselves sufficient for the deployment of renewable sources; other issues need to be in place. It is clear that such schemes must be well designed, but electricity-producing companies should also have good access to the grid. Administrative barriers should be removed, application processes streamlined, and public participation and acceptance widely encouraged. Thus, support schemes should receive wide-ranging support from stakeholders and interest groups. Support schemes should further provide incentives for both small and large investors alike, such that a level playing field of competition is created without discrimination occurring in the market place; hence, support schemes need to be designed to conform to the legal and market regulations, especially the internal electricity market or electricity market liberalization pursued by the EU. Further, support schemes must be capable of reaching politically fixed targets within the time frame stipulated at minimum or least cost possible, with little or no risk of uncertainties to investors.

Evaluation Criteria

Various frameworks and approaches have been developed to evaluate the performance of support schemes. Drawing on the international wind-power literature—including, for example, del Rio and Gual (2007), Dinica (2006), Harmelink et al. (2006), Mitchell et al. (2006), Toke (2006), Connor (2005), Elliot (2005), van der Linde (2005), Lauber (2004), Sawin (2004), van Dijk et al. (2003), Menanteau et al. (2003), Sijm (2002), Wiser et al. (2002), Haas et al. (2004), Enzensberger et al. (2002), and Hvelplund 2001—we have identified the following criteria that seem to permeate existing debates. These criteria will be subsequently applied to assess the performance of the RO.

Administration

Any support scheme needs to reduce regulatory and nonregulatory barriers; streamline and expedite administrative procedures; ensure that guiding principles and rules are objective, transparent, and nondiscriminatory; and fully take into account the particularities of the various renewable energy technologies. Support schemes should also be cost-effective and simple to implement. Transparency is defined here as the ease of access to information on investment and financial data from governmental regulatory bodies. Under this criterion, questions we explored included:

- To what extent is the support scheme transparent and easy to understand?
- Is the support scheme flexible and practicle?
- Is the administrative and transactional cost low compared to other support schemes?

Stakeholder Support/Involvement

Stakeholders in this context are defined broadly to include parties or groups that are affected by policy choices and facilitating support schemes. Stakeholders can react differently—they can facilitate or, indeed, inhibit the deployment of wind power. The extent to which the support scheme encourages stakeholder groups to participate and be involved in wind-power deployment is crucial to successful implementation. Under this criterion, questions we explored included:

- Does the scheme involve stakeholder groups in the design and implementation of the support scheme?
- Do stakeholders largely favour the scheme?
- Ultimately, to what extent does the support scheme encourage corporate ownership and/or community ownership of wind power?

Certainty for Industry

The willingness of investors to enter the wind-power market is crucial to the expansion of wind-power capacity. A support scheme must be capable of attracting a wide range of new investors to the market, and it must be stable over the longer term, such that investor confidence can be guaranteed. Support schemes are high risk when they are not stable and are unpredictable, with investors usually being put off when this happens. Under this criterion, questions we explored included:

- Does the scheme possess characteristics that ensure investor confidence?
- To what extent is the RO scheme perceived by investors and stakeholders as stable or unstable both in the short-to-medium term and in the long term?
- To what extent does the support scheme mitigate investment risks?

Effectiveness

Effectiveness can be simply measured by the extent to which the support mechanism has performed in terms of how fast and in what quantity wind power has added to new installed capacity in meeting politically fixed targets. For renewable energy campaigners, this is the key measure of effectiveness. Under this criterion, questions we explored included:

- To what extent has the support scheme performed in achieving politically fixed targets?
- How much and in what quantity has the support scheme delivered over time?
- How does this compare with other support mechanisms?

Efficiency

One of the main means used to assess the performance of support schemes has been to focus on the cost of their operation. Efficiency can be measured in terms of the costs of operating the scheme to ensure a reasonable market and competitive price for investors when compared with other forms of energy. This concern has been prioritized by the regulators, OFGEM. Efficiency also needs to take into consideration the risk factor over time. For investors, assessing risk is essential in terms of price, volume, and for system balancing. Under this criterion, questions we explored included:

- Is the support scheme capable of delivering wind energy at a low cost to consumers?
- Is the support scheme efficient in reducing production risks and investment costs?

- Does the support scheme provide a reasonable market and competitive price for wind energy?

Market Conformity

Support schemes need to be designed in a way that they fit into the existing market and legal systems. Directive 2001/77/EC, Article Four, subsection 2(b) also states that support schemes implemented by member states should be compatible with the principles of the internal electricity market. Morthorst et al. (2005) advocates that, through the adoption of the EU Electricity Directive, the EU member states are in the process of liberalizing their power markets and new policies, such as emission trading, and other Kyoto instruments are being introduced in the EU. Some countries already have fully liberalized power markets, including power exchanges, while others are still in transition. Thus, it becomes increasingly important how well a support scheme fits into a liberalized power market. However, it is perhaps interesting to note that the electricity companies that are keenest on advocating the creation of green electricity certificate trading markets for renewable energy—especially utilities in Germany, such as E.On and RWE—are themselves trading in an electricity market that is only slowly moving toward electricity market liberalization. Market conformity aims to examine the extent to which support schemes are compatible with the legal and market system of the internal electricity market, hence, liberalization of the electricity market, international and crossboundary trade (Wiser et al. 2002; Sijm 2002). Under this criterion, questions we explored included:

- Is the support scheme compatible with the legal and market conditions of the internal electricity market?
- Does the scheme encourage competition among suppliers and generators of electricity?

Finance

Financial security examines the extent to which a support scheme is able to guarantee security and return on investment with low or no risk over a long period of time. Sawin (2004) argued that long-term certainty results from guaranteed prices that facilitate the willingness of investors to invest in wind-energy projects. A further dimension is also to assess the ease with which wind-energy projects are able to secure financing from banks and other lending institutions. Under this criterion, questions we explored included:

- Does the scheme guarantee a return on investment?
- Is it easy to obtain financing for investment in wind energy with the scheme?

Table 7.2 Evaluation Criteria and Questions Guiding the Research

Evaluation Criteria	Questions Guiding the Research
Administration	• To what extent is the support scheme transparent and easy to understand? • Is the support scheme flexible and practicle? • Is the administrative and transactional cost low compared to other support schemes?
Stakeholder Support/ involvement	• Does the scheme involve stakeholder groups in the design and implementation of the support scheme? • Do stakeholders largely favour the scheme? • Ultimately, to what extent does the support scheme encourage corporate ownership and/or community ownership of wind power?
Certainty for Industry	• Does the scheme possess characteristics that ensure investor confidence? • To what extent is the RO scheme perceived by investors and stakeholders as stable or unstable, both in the short-to-medium term and in the long term? • To what extent does the support scheme mitigate investment risks?
Effectiveness	• To what extent has the support scheme performed in achieving politically fixed targets? • How much and in what quantity has the support scheme delivered over time? • How does this compare with other support mechanisms?
Efficiency	• Is the support scheme capable of delivering wind energy at a low cost to consumers? • Is the support scheme efficient in reducing production risks and investment costs? • Does the support scheme provide a reasonable market and competitive price for wind energy?
Market Conformity	• Is the support scheme compatible with the legal and market conditions of the internal electricity market? • Does the scheme encourage competition among suppliers and generators of electricity?
Finance	• Does the scheme guarantee a return on investment? • Is it easy to obtain financing for investment in wind energy with the scheme? • Does the scheme possess a high or low risk to encourage or discourage support from financial institutions?
Impact on Economic Development	• Does the support scheme encourage local and economic development? • Does the support scheme contribute to environmental objectives, including the reduction of greenhouse gas emissions?

Source: Author generated.

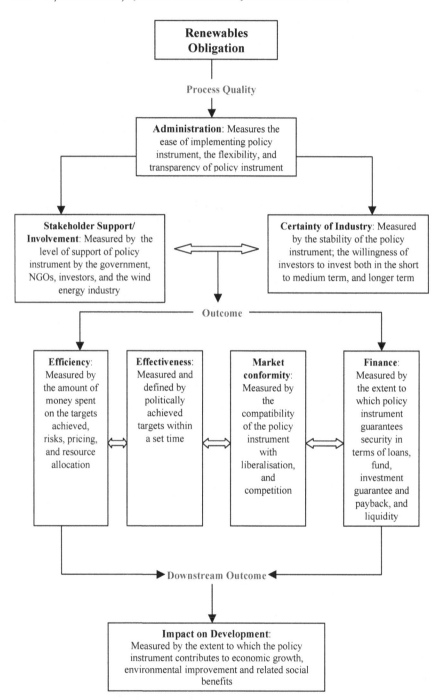

Figure 7.1   An integrative framework for evaluating wind-power policy instruments. Source: Author generated.

- Does the scheme possess a high or low risk to encourage or discourage support from financial institutions?

Impact on Economic Development and Environmental Responsibility

This aims to assess the impact of support schemes in contributing to economic development (e.g., employment) and environmental responsibility (e.g., reducations of greenhouse gasses). Morthorst et al. (2005) have also identified that positive local effects need to be considered, including enhanced public support for renewable energies. Under this criterion, questions we explored included:

- Does the support scheme encourage local and economic development?
- Does the support scheme contribute to environmental objectives, including the reduction of greenhouse gas emissions?

Integrating the Evaluation Criteria

To enable us to assess the performance of the RO, the criteria discussed previously were integrated to produce a theoretical but pragmatic framework. Figure 7.1 outlines the framework and identifies four possible dimensions of support scheme performance evaluation.

Dimension One describes the process conditions where the administration of the support scheme are examined. It is assumed that support schemes need to be transparent and flexible enough to understand and bring about a positive investment environment for investors.

Dimension Two describes the stakeholder interests and the certainty for industry. In this case, the support from stakeholder groups and the perception of the support scheme varies from one stakeholder to another. If conditions are favourable enough, stakeholder support is likely to be higher than when conditions are not favourable, or when the risk is high. This implies that a favourable scheme and conditions encourage investment in the wind-energy industry. As such risks and uncertainties are reduced and averted completely. The transparency and flexibility of the support scheme will have a strong impact on the commitment of the stakeholders and their support. Hence, a strong wind-energy industry should emerge.

Dimension Three describes the possible outcomes of the interaction of the process and the variables. Four key parameters are utilized in this stage to access the support schemes, namely effectiveness, efficiency, market conformity, and finance.

Dimension Four describes the downstream outcome of the implementation of the support scheme. The impact of the support scheme and its contribution to economic and environmental development is important. This might include the contribution of support schemes to the economy in terms of employment opportunities created, and the contribution to the overall reduction of greenhouse gas emissions.

THE RESEARCH FINDINGS AND DISCUSSION

Administration

When asked about transparency, practicability, and flexibility, fourteen of the eighteen respondents interviewed said that the RO is transparent in its design. However, it is very complex when it comes to administration. In addition, with the RO being relatively new—having been in operation for only four to five years—there have been a number of teething problems. This is consistent with the observations of van Dijk et al. (2003: 21) that:

> The targets of the RO themselves may be very transparent, the administrative rules of the Tradable Green Certificate (TGC) trading system are often a bit more complicated.

In terms of the flexibility, fifteen of the eighteen respondents said that the RO was not flexible in its operation. A senior manager from one well-known renewable energy company said that:

> I think the RO is transparent and practical but I am not sure about flexibility. It is a market based mechanism so in that sense I would say certainly on the first two issues it is good but again I am not so sure of its flexibility. (Interview, 13 December 2006)

This is also consistent with Sawin's (2004: 16) findings that the quota system is inflexible:

> Once targets and timetables are established, they are difficult to adjust. Even as markets change and technologies advance, experiencing major breakthroughs in efficiency and or cost, it is highly unlikely that targets or timetables can be altered. . . .

This inflexibility, however, is not seen to be a bad thing from the perspective of most respondents. The certainty of the RO makes it desirable to investors. A senior government official interviewed said that:

> We just want to know what exactly is going to happen and how that is set out in the law, so the RO cannot just be changed in a window of anyway, it is there and it is concrete, it is something we can make financial decisions on. But if it is made vague and flexible that would dilute market confidence and make it hard for stakeholders to be able to make financial decisions on the basis of it. (Interview, 14 June 2006)

One problem is that RO personnel at the DTI have changed on a regular basis, with some respondents saying that this has been detrimental to the scheme. Illustrating this, a senior manager of one utility company said that:

The personnel that manage it (the RO) have changed every 16–18 months, so there is inconsistency on the government side which is an issue. (Interview, 28 November 2006)

From the perspective of this respondent, the high turnover affected the performance and credibility of the scheme.

To summarize this discussion, the RO seems to be a transparent scheme, but one which is complex and inflexible in its operation. Once targets are fixed, it is usually not easy to reverse, though this was actually seen as a strength of the scheme by those interviewed in this study.

Stakeholder Support/Involvement

The DTI is the dominant player in the design of the RO, while OFGEM is charged with the administrative responsibilities. When asked about the role and the involvement of stakeholders in the operations of the RO, all the respondents said that they were involved—one way or the other—in the consultation process, design, and operation of the RO. A senior manager from one major utility company said that:

Stakeholders are involved; there are consultation processes. And personally I think the RO is working at the moment, and it is doing what it is set out to do, so I think at the moment, it is operating effectively. (Interview, 13 December 2006)

A director of a renewable company also said that:

Well the RO involves us and other bodies. There are plenty of opportunities to get involved in the consultation forum and I think the finance community gives a lot of support to the RO because it is an attractive mechanism. (Interview, 27 November 2006)

When asked about the extent to which the RO supports small-scale generating companies, it was clear that the scheme seemed to favour larger integrated utility companies. Respondents from the renewable energy associations interviewed said that the RO does not provide opportunities for small-scale generating companies. The nature of the scheme makes it difficult for small-scale investors to get money. One of the respondents from a popular renewable energy association said that: "the system is designed to attract a larger scale build and therefore it attracts large scale developers" (Interview, 14th August 2006). This is, perhaps, one of the key reasons that helps explain why so little community ownership has developed in the UK.

Certainty for Industry

When asked about certainty for the wind industry, fifteen of the eighteen respondents said that the RO had been surrounded by uncertainty, and this has had a detrimental effect on industry confidence. This was due partly to the early stages of RO implementation, but also to later changes made through consultations and amendments. This finding is consistent with van Dijk et al. (2003) and van der Linde et al. (2005), who reported that revisions to support schemes from annual renewals can easily lead to uncertainty amongst producers. The head of power in one popular renewable energy association said that:

> I think the RO is remarkably unstable. From the investors perspective it has changed every single year since it's been in existence and it is going to change very fundamentally in 2009/2010. So right from the beginning it is being subjected to a kind of political interference. And the fact that there have been a lot of investment going on doesn't matter, investments in renewable energy is probably because the value of the certificate is so high . . . that is why it has been attractive. . . . there is just a lot of money in it, so that is why it is attractive. (Interview, 14 June 2006)

However, ten of the eighteen respondents interviewed, particularly those from the utility companies, said that the recent energy review had created further uncertainty in the market place, especially with the banding that had been introduced into the RO by the 2007 Energy White Paper (Department of Trade and Industry 2007). Most of the utility companies would have preferred for the RO to have remained largely unchanged. Prior to the recent Energy White Paper, a senior manager of one utility company said that:

> The RO is rapidly moving to a phase of no confidence and no stability, and potentially could disintegrate into a heap with the review that is going on at the moment and the potential introduction of banding which fundamentally undermines the concept of the RO which was technology blind. Banding here means technology specific, fundamental change will just undermine the whole thing. (Interview, 15 December 2006)

The RO may introduce yet another element of uncertainty which may potentially hurt investors' confidence. It makes it difficult for investors to fully understand the fundamental components of the RO so they can manage and mitigate associated risks. A senior manager of one utility company confirmed this, and said that:

> If the mechanism (RO) keeps changing there is a premium that we need to factor in for unknown risk, and that is not the most efficient way of developing projects . . . (Interview, 28 November 2006)

When asked if the changes to the RO had affected investments in wind energy in the UK, almost all the respondents indicated that it had, and that it also had an impact on their decisions to invest further. Trade association respondents indicated that, from the interaction with investors, any changes on the RO affects project finance. Investors dislike change and prefer stable market conditions in the long term, which allows them to forecast a definite return on investment. A manager in one utility company said that:

> The change to the RO does affect investment absolutely, what it basically says is that the government will come and interfere as it wants and when it wants. . . . (Interview, 15 December 2006)

But on the government side, the changes are necessary to create an atmosphere for a convenient investment that is stable and attractive. A senior government official said that:

> There is no doubt at the moment that the ROC does not provide absolute certainty; I mean there is the rise of obligation up to 2015–2016 and platoon there up to 2027. So we need to think very correctly as to whether or not that should be extended to get guaranteed higher returns for a little longer period or whether or not the licence of the obligation in 2027 will or not need to be extended. We also do need to balance the desire to create a more stable and attractive scheme for investors against the cost the obligation imposes on all the consumers . . . (Interview, 5 June 2006)

Effectiveness

Foxon and Pearson (2007: 1541) reported that: "the RO has succeeded in creating a niche for renewable generation in the electricity supply market". However, when asked about the effectiveness of the RO in delivering the 10.4 per cent politically fixed target by 2010, all of the respondents indicated that the RO will not meet this target. The respondents, therefore, argued against the effectiveness of the RO. There is no doubt that the RO has been very successful in delivering much onshore capacity, yet there is a long way to go in reaching the 10.4 per cent target.

Eight out of the eighteen respondents claimed that the inability of the UK to reach its target is not the fault of the RO. A senior manager in charge of the RO in one utility company said that:

> The RO has made a viable and valuable contribution in moving the UK towards the 10% goal, but realistically, it is not going to hit the target. And you could argue actually that the RO is a market mechanism and it does not intend to achieve set target. But what it has helped to do is to stimulate onshore wind in particular. . . . (Interview, 29 November 2006)

Two main reasons seem to account for why the RO will not meet the 10.4 per cent target by 2010. The first is attached to a design flaw which means that the closer one gets to the target, the less value a ROC is worth. To keep the market moving and to attract new investments, ambitious rather than realistic targets have to be set. During one interview, a senior deputy head of renewable energy policy in a government organization said that:

. . . the closer you get to actually hitting that target, then the less valuable the ROCs become. And there is a kind of phenomenon known as 'CLIFF EDGE' which suggests that if the whole renewable criteria is actually met in a given year, ROC prices will plunge down . . . (Interview, 5 June 2006)

Second is the issue of planning permission and connection to the grid. In England and Wales, only around 60 per cent of planning applications have been approved (Toke 2005), and, as was discussed earlier, there are still a lot of projects in the queue waiting for connection to the grid, especially in Scotland. However, planning difficulties are not usually attributed to the RO. Sixteen of the eighteen respondents interviewed argued that the problem is not with the RO; the scheme has done exactly what it said it was going to do when it was set up. The failure of the UK to meet its target can be attributed to other factors, such as planning and consenting regimes. A senior manager of one utility company said that:

> The RO has performed exemplarily. . . . what has failed arguably are the delivery channels: the consenting regimes and other aspects. But as an economic instrument it has been a whole heartedly 100% success. We have just witnessed a number of planning applications and a number of grid applications; what has failed is the delivery channel. (Interview, 15 December 2006)

In summary, the effectiveness of the RO is still subject to a great deal of conjecture and debate, and it remains to be seen whether or not 2010 targets will be met, but this looks increasingly very unlikely.

Efficiency

The RO is often heralded as an efficient mechanism for supporting renewable energy sources. However, when asked about the efficiency of the RO, ten of the eighteen respondents disputed this. This is also consistent with Szarka and Bluhdorn (2006), who argued that the efficiency of the RO is lower than argued. The EU Paper (COM 2005) also reported that the RO offers higher levels of support when compared to other systems operating in other member states, including Germany. One senior policy officer in a renewable energy association said that:

> The RO is not very efficient as a means of bringing renewable energy generating capacity for the reason set out in the carbon trust report. One of the reasons is the fact that the RO always cost the consumers at large the same amount irrespective of the degree of success of the ROC recycling or buy-out mechanism. So that means that it isn't very

efficient. It's more of a problem when planning permission and grid access is holding back deployment. If those weren't there at all, then the efficiency of the RO would be improved but because of these factors are present and the cost being the same for all consumers, it becomes less efficient. I mean for example with NFFO contracts and with the FIT, consumers only pay for the actual renewable electricity generated whereas with the RO consumers pay a buy out price for the stuff that is not generated. (Interview, 14 June 2006)

Contrary to this view, the utility companies interviewed argued that the RO is not expensive, and that it is the operation and the perception of people that is voiced regularly that makes the RO look expensive. They also argue that the RO is a level of support that is valid to make projects compete in the market, and without it, projects are not economical. Therefore, the general consensus of the utilities is that the RO—if allowed to work—is very efficient because it becomes a self-correcting mechanism in terms of the money it pays out to the parties involved. One senior manager of a company further confirmed this, and said:

> The problem is that . . . the RO looks expensive because if you compare the cost of the RO to the MW been built, the RO is absolutely expensive compared to the FIT, but that again is not the fault of the RO, that is because there are less MW being built; this has nothing to do with the RO, it is the planning system. So if all the stuff that is currently in the planning system is allowed to come through and fed through the grid system, then the RO will be highly competitive and highly effective when compared to any FIT system. (Interview, 27 November 2006)

Looking at other available evidence, Szarka and Bluhdorn (2006: 13) have reported that:

> The outcome during 2002–2006 indicated not only that the RO is failing to provide a more cost-effective system than continental fit, but worse-the RO is making wind power progressively more expensive to the UK consumer at a time when digressive FIT rates are making it cheaper in Germany.

Market Conformity

When compared to feed-in tariffs, many commentators (e.g., Wiser et al. 2002; Sawin 2004) argue that the RO works better in an open and liberalized market. When asked about the compatibility of the RO with liberalization of the electricity market, fifteen of the eighteen respondents interviewed claimed that the RO is a market-based system and, in that sense, it is compatible.

Amongst other things, the aim of liberalization is to foster competition among suppliers and give consumers the opportunity to choose their own suppliers. It is argued that this is what the RO does for the renewable market because it does not, in theory, discriminate between small and large suppliers. A senior manager of a utility company said that:

> The RO is compatible because it affects all suppliers. All suppliers have the same obligation to meet a percentage of total demand via RES, so there is no discrimination between the suppliers, they work towards the same obligation, and they have been able to provide electricity to a great number of customers in absolute and percentage terms. Also, it is designed to be a market based mechanism to enable investors to make the most and efficient decisions. We do operate a liberalised market in the UK and customers have the right to change suppliers and so no one has a monopoly over a customer whatsoever, and we all compete within that market place . . . (Interview, 29 November 2006)

A senior manager in one of the organizations interviewed also confirmed this, and said:

> The RO is compatible with liberalisation because its fundamental principle is market based, and it is an economic incentive which leaves it up to the firm to decide how to meet its obligation. I mean you have the authorisation, you choose, you make the most rationale efficient economic decisions, and that is the heart of the RO, so it is wholly compatible with liberalisation. (Interview, 15 December 2006)

The main argument in support of this is twofold. The first is that the RO does create an incentive for renewable-generated electricity to trade in the British Electricity Trading and Transmission Agreement and compete with other forms of energy. Secondly, the RO is also a form of quota that provides financial benefits to both customers and suppliers, especially from the supplier perspective; it helps provide a way of recovering money from customers as a whole. It drives the development of the lowest-cost technologies and best resources captured by market mechanism.

On the contrary, one of the main arguments against the compatibility of the RO with market liberalization is that it does not allow market entry. A senior policy officer of a popular renewable association said that:

> . . . it does not allow or encourage new entrants in the market all action at the moment is tied up within the BIG 6. (Interview, 14 June 2006)

Another respondent from a nongovernmental organization said that:

> I personally think that the kind of competitive market we would like to see is the one that does allow new entrants but the government does not perceive it this way, therefore, clearly the RO is not good in terms of allowing new entrants. (Interview, 8 September 2006)

The other argument in support of this is that the RO has worked well as an obligation, and not in terms of competition. A senior policy officer of a renewable consultancy firm said that:

> The RO is there to speed up competition and does that without looking at the supply side or a large number of people who dominate the market . . . and in as much as it is an imposed market mechanism; it is not a sort of a role model of a perfect part of a liberalised electricity market. It is not completely compatible and the two are quite separate. Though it accepts that RES do receive the value of the base local electricity to which the ROC prices or value is added on, yet, I wouldn't agree they are completely compatible . . . (Interview, 19 October 2006)

Finance

As noted elsewhere, respondents highlighted that the RO is characterized by many uncertainties, which has had the effect, at times, of undermining project ownership and investments, especially for smaller players in the market. For larger players that do not need equity and finance from financial institutions, this is not such an issue. This perhaps explains why the RO generates windfall profits to large utility companies who take up the risk to invest in wind energy. A senior policy officer of a popular renewable energy association said that:

> The RO is very poor at guaranteeing investment certainty . . . therefore you cannot get finance unless you have your own corporate assets, and that is why there are so few new entrants because new entrants find it impossible to get finance based on the contract, based on the RO contract. (Interview, 8 September 2006)

Impact on Development

When asked about the contribution of the RO to the development of wind energy and the UK national economy, seventeen of the eighteen respondents said that that the RO has been important in pushing onshore wind energy since 2002. The UK wind sector now employs approximately 4,000 people. It has been further estimated that with Round 2 of offshore wind deployment, approximately 20,000 more jobs will be created. However, there remains no large indigenous wind-turbine manufacturing industry, except for smaller and microproducers with maximum production capacities of 20 kW, and this should be of concern.

Also, according to the British Wind Energy Association (2007),[2] wind energy contributes annually to the reduction of greenhouse gasses in the UK. Table 7.3 provides an overview of the amounts of carbon dioxide[3] (CO_2), sulphur dioxide[4] (SO_2), and nitrogen oxide[5] (NO_x) reduced with the current installed wind capacity of the UK.

Table 7.3   Greenhouse Gas Reductions

CO_2 reductions per annum	SO_2 reductions per annum	NO_x reductions per annum
4940275 Tonnes	57445 Tonnes	17234 Tonnes

Source: British Wind Energy Association. Online. (accessed 23 October 2007).

CONCLUSION

Renewable energy policies in the UK over the last two to three decades have addressed three key issues: cost reduction and competitiveness; security of energy supply; and, more recently, environmental responsibility, particularly climate change. Prior to the introduction of the RO, UK renewable energy policies had not been effective, with little installed capacity having been deployed; this has been well studied by other commentators. The RO has now been in place for a period of five years, but the scheme has changed each year, and this has dented investor confidence. Nevertheless, the RO has helped to deliver record levels of installed onshore wind power to date, with wind proving to be the cheapest renewable technology in the UK. From the analysis provided in this chapter, the RO appears to be an expensive system, and in looking beyond the UK, it appears more expensive when compared to other support schemes in the EU, including the German Feed-in Tariff (FIT) system. Until, at least, the reforms suggested in 2007, it also failed to offer sufficient financing to more expensive renewables, including offshore (as opposed to onshore) wind farms. In addition, it is opaque in its operation and, thus, is likely to be relatively unsuitable for encouraging local investments in renewable energy.

On the other hand, it is also the case that cultural reasons mean that the interest in locally owned wind farms in the UK is likely to be smaller than in other countries, such as Denmark, Germany, and The Netherlands. It is also possible to put too much blame on the RO for the failure to keep up with the RO targets. Other issues, including planning delays and delays in developing the necessary transmission infrastructure, have provided most of the reasons for the failure to meet the targets. However, it is certainly the case that the RO has been marked with significant government interference, and this has undermined the rhetoric of being a truly market-based scheme.

Overall, we must conclude that the RO has underperformed and still has a long way to go to before catching up with other EU support schemes, like the German FIT system, and the level of installed capacity in countries such as Spain, Germany, and Denmark. However, we must also add that this state of affairs cannot solely be blamed on the RO, which is certainly a lot better than having no renewable support scheme at all, and also better in promoting renewable volume than the previous 'NFFO-SRO' policy.

APPENDIX 7.1   INTERVIEWED ORGANIZATIONS

Type of Organization	Position Held	Date of Interview	Total Number of Interviews (18)
Department of Trade and Industry (DTI)	DTI Officer in Charge of the Review of the Renewable Obligation (RO) 2005/2006	14 June 2006	1
Office of Gas and Electricity Markets	Head of RO	15 August 2006	1
British Wind Energy Association	Director of Economics and Markets	14 June 2006	1
Association of Electricity Producers	Head of Renewables	15 June 2006	1
Greenpeace UK	Renewable Energy Policy and Environmental Campaigner	13 June 2006	1
Scottish Executive	Policy Officer, Renewables and Consenting; Deputy Branch Head, Renewables and Consent	5 June 2006	1
Scottish Renewable Forum	Chief Executive	5 June 2006	1
Renewable Energy Association	Head of Power	14 June 2006	1
Friends of the Earth UK	Environment and Policy Campaigner	14 June 2006	1
British Institute of Energy Economics	Fellow British Institute of Energy Economics, and Renewable Energy Policy Academic Expert	8 September 2006	1
DM Energy Consultants, UK	Director and Renewable Energy Policy Consultant	19 October 2006	1
Ecofys UK	Renewable Energy Policy Consultant	24 November 2006	1
Npower Renewables UK	Head Strategy and Regulation	12 December 2006	1
E.ON (Powergen) UK	Commercial Manager, Development and Construction	29 November 2006	1

(continued)

APPENDIX 7.1　INTERVIEWED ORGANIZATIONS *(continued)*

Type of Organization	Position Held	Date of Interview	Total Number of Interviews (18)
Scottish Power	Managing Director, Renewables and Major Projects	27 November 2006	1
Scottish and Southern Energy	Head of Projects Development	15 December 2006	1
EDF UK	Carbon Policy Market Manager	28 November 2006	1
Good Energy	Commercial and Renewable Energy Policy Management Staff	13 December 2006	1

Source: Author generated.

NOTES

1. The breakdown of the proposed banding regime is further found in p. 151 of the Energy White Paper (2007).
2. Accessed 22 October 2007, Online at http://www.bwea.com.
3. Created by the combustion of fossil fuel.
4. Sulphur oxide is released when coal and petroleum are burnt, thus causing acid rain.
5. Mono Nitrogen oxides are produced during combustion of fossil fuel at high temperatures.

REFERENCES

Brennand, P. T. (2004) 'Renewable energy in the United Kingdom: policies and prospects', *Energy for Sustainable Development*, 8(1): 82–92.
British Wind Energy Association (BWEA) (2007) *Currently Operational—at a Glance* [Online] Available at http://www.bwea.com [Accessed 23 October 2007]
Connor, P. M. (2005) 'The UK Renewable Obligation'. In V. Lauber (ed.) *Switching to Renewable Power: A Framework for the 21st Century*. London: Earthscan Publications, 159–186.
Connor, P. M. and Mitchell, C. (2004) 'Renewable energy policy in the UK 1990–2003', *Energy Policy*, 32(17): 1935–47.

Cowell, R. (2007) 'Wind power and the 'planning problem': the experience of Wales', *European Environment,* 17(5): 291–306.

Cowell, R. and Strachan, P. A. (2007) 'Managing wind power deployment in Europe', *European Environment,* 17(5): 285–90.

Del Rio, P. and Gual, M. A. (2007a) 'The promotion of green electricity in Europe: present and future', *European Environment,* 14(4): 219–34.

Department of Trade and Industry. (2003) *Our Energy Future: Creating a Low Carbon Economy, Energy White Paper,* February. London: DTI.

———. (2004) *Creating a Low Carbon Economy—First Annual Report on the Implementation of the Energy White Paper,* April. London: DTI.

———. (2005) *Energy White Paper: Commitment and Milestones Completed Between April 2004 and May 2005,* July, London: DTI.

———. (2006) *The Government Report on "the Energy Challenge,"* July. London: DTI.

———. (2007) *Meeting the Energy Challenge: A Energy White Paper on Energy,* May. London: DTI.

Dinica, V. (2006) 'Support systems for the diffusion of renewable energy technologies—an investor perspective', *Energy Policy,* 34(4): 461–80.

Directive 2001/77/EC of the European Parliament and the Council of 27 September 2001, on the promotion of electricity produced from renewable energy sources in the internal electricity market. *Official Journal of the European Communities,* 27 October 2001.

Elliot, D. (2005) 'Feed-in or quota? Is REFIT better than the RO?' *Refocus,* 6(6): 53–4.

Elliott, D. (2005) 'Comparing support for renewable energy power'. In V. Lauber (ed.) *Switching to Renewable Power: A Framework for the 21st Century.* London: Earthscan Publications, 219–227.

Enzensberger, N., Wietschel, M. and Rentz, O. (2002) 'Policy instruments fostering wind energy projects—a multi-perspective evaluation approach', *Energy Policy,* 30(9): 793–801.

European Union (EU) (2005) *The Support of Electricity from Renewable Energy Sources. Communication from the Commission,* COM(2005) 627 Finals, Brussels, December.

Foxon, T. J. and Pearson, P. J. G. (2007) 'Towards improved policy processes for promoting innovation in renewable electricity technologies in the UK', *Energy Policy,* 35(3): 1539–1550.

Grotz, C. and Bischof, R. (2005) 'Minimum price systems compared with the quota model—which system is more efficient?'. Berlin: German Wind Energy Association (BWE).

Grotz, C. and Fouquet, D. (2005) 'Fixed prices works better', *New Energy,* 2: 18–21.

Haas, R., Eichhammer, W., Huber, C., Langniss, O., Lorenzoni, A., Madlener, R., Mentanteau, P., Morthorst, P. E., Martins, A., Oniszk, A., Schleich, J., Smith, A., Vass, Z., Verbruggen, A. (2004) 'How to promote renewable energy systems successfully and effectively', *Energy Policy,* 32(6): 833–9.

Hvelplund, F. (2001) 'Political prices or political quantities? A comparison of renewable energy support systems', *New Energy,* 5: 18–23.

———. (2005) 'Tradable Certificate Systems and Feed-in Tariff: Expectations Versus Performance'. In V. Lauber (ed.) *Switching to Renewable Power: A Framework for the 21st Century.* London: Earthscan Publications, 203–216.

Menanteau, P., Finon, D. and Lamy, M. (2003) 'Prices versus quantities: choosing policies for promoting the development of renewable energy', *Energy Policy,* 31(8): 799–812.

Meyer, N. I. (2003) 'European schemes for promoting renewable in liberalised market', *Energy Policy*, 31(7): 665–76.

Meyers, N. (2007) 'Learning from wind energy policy in the EU: lessons from Denmark, Sweden and Spain', *European Environment,* 17(5): 347–362.

Mitchell, C. (1995) 'The renewables NFFO', *Energy Policy*, 32(12): 1077–91.

———. (2000) 'The England and Wales non-fossil fuel obligation: History and lessons', *Annual Review Energy Environment,* 25: 285–312.

Morthorst, E. P., Jergensen, H. B., Chandler, H. and Kjaer, E. (2005) 'Support schemes for renewable energy: a comparative analysis of payments mechanism in the EU-RE-Xpansion Project'. May, Brussels: European Wind Energy Association (EWEA).

Sawin, J. (2004) *National policy instruments—policy lessons for the advancement and diffusion of renewable energy technologies around the world,* June 1–4, report of the International Conference for Renewable Energies, Bonn.

Sijm, J. P. M. (2002) *The Performance of Feed-In Tariff to Promote Renewable Electricity in European Countries,* ECN-C—02–083, Petten, the Netherlands: Energy Research Centre of the Netherlands (ECN).

Strachan, P. A. and Lal, D. (2004) 'Wind energy policy, planning and management practice in the UK: hot air or gathering storm?', *Regional Studies,* 38(5): 551–71.

Strachan, P. A., Lal, D. and von Malmborg, F. (2006) 'The evolving UK wind energy industry: critical policy and management aspects of the energy research agenda', *European Environment,* 16(1): 1–18.

Szarka, J. and Bluhdorn, I. (2006) *Wind power in Britain and Germany: explaining contrasting development paths.* Anglo-German Foundation for the Study of Industry Society.

Toke, D. (2005) 'Explaining wind power planning outcomes: some findings from a study in England and Wales', *Energy Policy*, 33(12): 1527–1539.

———. (2006) 'Are green electricity the way forward for renewable energy? An evaluation of the UK's Renewable Obligation in the context of international comparisons', *Environment and Planning C: Government and Policy,* 23(3): 361–74.

———. (2007) 'Renewable financial support systems and cost-effectiveness', *Journal of Cleaner Production,* 15(3): 280–7.

Toke, D., Breukers, S. and Wolsink, M. (2008) 'Wind power deployment outcomes: How can we account for the differences?', *Renewable and Sustainable Energy Reviews* 12(4): 1129–1147.

Valle Costa, do C., Rovere, La E. and Assmann, D. (2008) 'Technological innovation policies to promote renewable energies: Lesson from the European experience for the Brazilian case', *Renewable and Sustainable Energy Reviews,* 12(1): 65–90.

van Dijk, A. L., et al. (2003) *Renewable Energy Policies and Market Development,* Energy Research Centre of the Netherlands (ECN): Petten ECN-C—30–029, The Netherlands.

van Dijk, A.L., Beuskens, L.W.M., Boots, M.G., Kaal, M.B.T., de Lange, T.J., van Sambeek, E.J.W., and Uyterlinde, M.A. (2003) *Renewable Energy Policies and Market Development,* ECN-C—30–029. A publication of the Energy Research Centre, Petten, the Netherlands.

van der Linde, N. H., et al. (2005) *Review of International experience with Renewable Energy Obligation support mechanisms,* ECN-C–05–025, The Netherlands.

Warren, C. R., Lumsden, C., O'Dowd, S. and Birnie, R. V. (2005) '"Green on green": Public perceptions of wind power in Scotland and Ireland', *Journal of Environmental Planning and Management*, 48(6): 851–73.

Wiser, R., Hamrin, J. and Wingate, M. (2002) *Renewable Energy Policy Option for China: A Comparison of Renewable Portfolio Standards, Feed-in Tariffs, and Tendering Policies*, a report of the Center for Renewable Energy Solutions, Chicago: Centre for Renewable Energy Solutions.

8 Gone With the Wind?

Prospects of Community-Owned Wind Energy in the United States

Dennis Tänzler

INTRODUCTION

Wind energy is on the rise in the United States. Wind power generating increased by more than 50 per cent in 2007 and was expected to increase at nearly the same rate in 2008. This is a surprising development, since the promotion of renewable energies in the United States is hardly an example of active government intervention (see Tänzler 2006; Calvert and Hock 2001). The national energy strategy of 2001, for example, remains more or less silent about the potential of renewable energies to contribute to the future energy supply of the country. The legislative proposals that were introduced in the Congress have, so far, been rejected. Hence, at the national level, the instrument of production tax credits (PTC) is perceived as the only driver behind the recent increase of wind-power installations. In addition, renewable portfolio standards (RPSs) exist in more than twenty states. As a policy tool, RPSs mandate electricity suppliers to provide a certain proportion of their electricity through renewable energy sources by a stated date.

Against the background that little wind-power development takes place either outside states where there is an RPS or, for that matter, during periods when the PTC has not been available, there is some reason to believe that these two instruments are the most important factors contributing to the wind energy boom in the United States. In fact, such a perspective would fail to address the fact that there are some remarkable developments at the local and regional level for the expansion of renewable energies. These entrepreneurs are not only important drivers of bottom-up processes to expand the use of alternative energies: they are also an important source for economic development in rural areas which face enormous difficulties entering the twenty-first century, namely the challenges of globalization. The principal focus of this chapter is to examine the role of corporate and community wind-power players in the United States. We will show that, in sum, the current regulatory framework is mainly aimed at the expansion of renewable energies by large companies in order to achieve major steps toward a greater energy independency of the nation and the states, respectively. Whereas this is a positive policy objective from a national security, as well as climate change, standpoint, it is not necessarily the appropriate way to proceed to meet the social aspects of an overall sustainable development. However, examples at the local level in Minnesota show that there is an active cooperative movement at the local level to generate renewable energies. In order to learn from some of the country and market leaders in wind, there is a distinct requirement for a greater degree of economic involvement of the local population, and furthermore, this need should be encouraged and supported by the national and regional government, as well as by regional enterprise networks. Against this background, this chapter critically evaluates the development of policy and instruments (e.g., PTCs, RPSs) in the United States supporting wind power. The main opportunities and constraints facing its development in the near and medium-term future are discussed, especially regarding the contribution to promote activities at the local level.

FRAMEWORK CONDITIONS FOR WIND ENERGY IN THE UNITED STATES

According to the American Wind Energy Association (AWEA), the wind resources of Kansas, North Dakota, and Texas alone are, in principle, sufficient to provide all the electricity the United States currently uses (AWEA 2006). Hence, prospects for wind-energy expansion in the United States are enormous. If appropriate supportive and consistent policies are implemented, wind power's contribution to the US electricity supply could grow rapidly, according to the Department of Energy, which announced in June 2006 the development of an action plan aimed at providing up to 20 per cent of US electricity with wind power. However, wind power presently provides less than 1 per cent of US electricity, although the respective technology has advanced steadily over the past two decades. Starting with average turbine size below 100 kW in the beginnings of the 1980s, today, the average size is about 1,200 kW. Due to technological improvements, costs have been reduced to a level where wind farms on appropriate sites are able to generate electricity for 3–5 cents/kWh (wind energy is competitive when the price of competing electricity exceeds 5.5 cents/kWh). In addition, sharp increases of fuel prices have contributed to more favourable framework conditions for the expansion of wind energy in many regions of the United States.

As a result, in 2006, there were 11,600 MW installed capacity of wind energy in the United States. As Figure 8.1 illustrates, there have been significant increases since 2001 that were interrupted in 2002 and 2004, when only minor additional capacities were installed due to pending legislations regarding the extension of the promotion of wind energy by Congress.

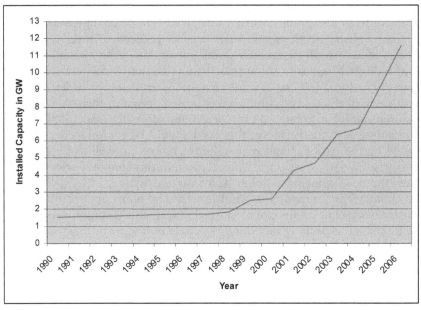

Figure 8.1   US wind-power capacity installed from 1990–2006.
Source: AWEA 2007.

The installed capacity of the entire country concentrates on a limited number of states—mainly those where political support is known to be strong. Thus, it might come as a surprise that Texas passed California at the end of 2006 as the state with the highest level of development. However, Texas has actively promoted the installation of wind turbines through the instrument of binding quotas for the expansion of renewable energy generation. Texas and California alone are responsible for nearly half of the overall wind energy generated throughout the United States. The top five states listed in Table 8.1 accounted for two-thirds of the US capacity in 2006.

A number of states with good wind resources and huge growth potential are lagging behind due to a lack of state-level support. According to an assessment of the Battelle Pacific Northwest Laboratory, states like North Dakota and Kansas show an enormous potential for wind-energy generation. So far, however, states like Washington, Oregon, or California, which hold far less promising wind-energy potential, show significantly more progress in extending the generation of wind energy. One reason for this lack of progress in some states might be that the overall framework for promotion of renewable energy in the United States is—compared to countries like Denmark or Germany—still in its early stages, and has merely been attractive for big companies. The US wind market is dominated by

Table 8.1 Installed Capacity of Wind Power in the United States (as of 31 December 2006)

Rank	State	Installed Capacity as of 31 December 2006	% of US Total Installed Wind Energy Capacity	Potential in Billions of kWhs
1	Texas	2,768 MW	23.9%	1,190
2	California	2,361 MW	20.4%	59
3	Iowa	963 MW	8.3%	551
4	Minnesota	895 MW	7.7%	657
5	Washington	818 MW	7.1%	< 50
6	Oklahoma	535 MW	4.6%	725
7	New Mexico	497 MW	4.3%	435
8	Oregon	439 MW	3.8%	< 50
9	New York	370 MW	3.2%	62
10	Kansas	364 MW	3.1%	1,070
11	Colorado	291 MW	2.5%	481
12	Wyoming	288 MW	2.5%	747

Sources: AWEA 2007; Battelle Pacific Northwest Laboratory 1991.

a few big players. By mid-2006, FPL Energy owned around 35 per cent of the United State's total installed capacity (3,192 MW). Following are PPM Energy (518 MW), MidAmerican Energy (360.5 MW), Edison Mission Group (316 MW), and Shell Wind Energy (315 MW) (AWEA 2006). Hence, in early 2006, these companies accounted for about 4,700 MW of installed capacities of wind energy, which means—for that point in time— that nearly 50 per cent of wind-energy capacity was in the hands of only five companies. In addition, with General Electric and Vestas, two international players dominate the turbine supply market, followed by Suzlon that entered the US market in 2005 (Ernst & Young 2006: 7). In the project-development sector, the scene is dominated by Florida Power and Light (a large, diversified power company), which develops and owns wind farms throughout the country.

Nevertheless, progress in recent years, and the prospects for the years to come, is promising for the United States. This is not only true with respect to an increased energy security and an environmentally sound supply, but also in terms of new income opportunities, especially in rural areas. Already in 2004, the Renewable Energy Policy Project (REPP) published a study pointing out that increasing wind energy from 6,000 MW to 50,000 MW can create 150,000 jobs in the manufacturing sector (REPP 2004). According to a study by the New York State Energy Research and

Development Authority, wind energy produces 27 per cent more jobs per kilowatt-hour than coal plants, and 66 per cent more jobs than natural gas plants. However, it is important to note that, in order to tap the whole potential of wind resources throughout the country, the adoption of further policies is required. Given that the greatest potential could be found in the Great Plains, an expansion of transmission capacity is needed to connect this region to areas with high energy demands, e.g., the West Coast of the United States. Offshore wind projects which have been proposed off the coast of Texas or Massachusetts will also require appropriate transmission infrastructure. As the current dispute in Massachusetts indicates, offshore project proposals are still facing concerns by consumers as well as decision makers. Part of the reason is that environmental impacts of such large-scale projects are not yet fully understood (*New York Times*, 31 March 2007).

Whereas these problems are part of the process to diffuse large wind-energy infrastructure throughout the United States more generally, the remainder of this chapter will focus more intensively on the overall conditions of locally owned wind installations. Therefore, the two main pillars to promote wind energy in the United States—the PTC at a national level and RPS at the state level—will be discussed. Subsequently, examples of community-based approaches are illustrated and finally the regulatory developments which might help exploit the potential of wind energy for rural development are presented.

INITIATIVES TO PROMOTE WIND ENERGY AT THE NATIONAL LEVEL

The development of a national energy strategy under the auspices of Vice President Dick Cheney in the summer of 2001 clearly demonstrated that, even from a perspective of securing the energy supply of the United States, there is no emphasis on the expansion of the use of renewable energies (US National Energy Policy Development Group 2001). Instead, an increasing energy supply is to be provided through a diversification of global energy supply, the increased use of nuclear energy, and the contested plans to drill for oil in protected areas in Alaska. The Energy Policy Act adopted by Congress in July 2005 is also an example of a lost opportunity to significantly change the direction of the US's energy policy for the years to come. Nearly two-thirds of the overall funding was allocated to support conventional energies represented by oil, natural gas, coal, and nuclear industries. Yet, the long-lasting negotiations of Congress to adopt a national energy bill underscored an increasing willingness in the Senate to support legislation for a binding target to increase the share of renewable energies. The revised Senate proposal from June 2005 contained a provision for a nationwide RPS aiming at a 10 per cent share in 2020. However, when the law finally passed

Congress in July, the House successfully had abandoned the RPS (see *New York Times*, 28 July 2005). The performance of the Senate with respect to the promotion of renewable energy sources has, in sum, not been very encouraging. There have been a few examples of legislative proposals as that of senator Jim Jeffords (I-VT) in April 2003. The proposals, that did not turn out to be successful, aimed at increasing the proportion of renewable energy to 20 per cent of the national energy supply. This lack of political support is further intensified by discriminatory transmission rules and inefficient transmission capacity which makes it difficult to explore the full potential of wind energy throughout the United States. Here, the overall problem seems to be fragmented regulatory rules and procedures for access to the US transmission network. This leads to different conditions for new market entrants and inhibits the development of a fair-market competition (AWEA 2005). In addition, more investment is needed to upgrade existing transmission lines, as well as to finance new ones.

At a national level, mainly the instrument of PTC has turned out to be crucial for the extended use of wind energy. As part of the national energy law of 1992, the PTC had been established to support electricity generated from wind and certain bioenergy resources. It provides a 1.5-cent/kWh benefit for the first 10 years of a facility's operation. The credit is adjusted for inflation; accordingly, it is currently 1.9 cents/kWh. Actually, this measure was supposed to expire in 1999, but was extended a couple of times. The national energy law mentioned above extended in July 2005 the PTC again until 2008. According to the analysis of the Union of Concerned Scientists (UCS) in 2004, the PTC is crucial for the further expansion of wind-energy use throughout the country since, for companies active in the wind business, it provides security of investment.

A look at the actual growth rate of wind energy in the United States during the early years of this new century illustrates very clearly the need to provide for stable framework conditions. The stop-and-go policies of expiring and extending the instrument have caused tremendous swings in new installations and discouraged the industry from making long-term investments. Whereas the industry invested to set up nearly 1,700 MW in 2001 and 2003, it reduced their activities to 400 MW due to the pending decision of Congress in 2002 and 2004.

This situation also has enormous consequences for the manufacturing of wind turbines. Companies are forced to reduce turbine production in times when they could not know whether there will be continuity within the regulatory framework. In addition, this situation resulted in limited availability of wind turbines and other equipment for wind-energy installations, when the PTC was extended again and investors restarted their activities in the sector. As a consequence, prices for the wind-energy equipment were increasing. In order to invest in the most expensive wind-energy facilities— offshore wind farms—more certainty in the market is needed. In light of these regulatory shortcomings, Earl Pomeroy, a member of Congress for the state North Dakota, introduced H.R. 197, a bill aimed at extending the PTC for an additional five years, until 2014.

> The Production Tax Credit is vital for the further development of the wind industry in North Dakota. We have seen how critical this credit has been during the three periods in which the credit was allowed to expire. Local jobs were furloughed, economic activity was halted, and, of course, less energy was produced in-state .[. . .] a long-term extension of this tax credit will put North Dakota much farther down the road toward energy independence.

The example of North Dakota illustrates how important the instrument of PTC is for the further development of wind-energy capacities in the United States. As the sixth-largest energy producing and exporting state, it currently has a capacity of 128 MW of wind production. With this capacity, the state is lagging far behind the frontrunners in the United States (see Table 8.1, above). However, North Dakota has the potential for 138,400 MW of production, ranking it first in the nation. The state is only using less than one-tenth of 1 per cent of its wind-power potential. When the wind energy credit expired at the end of 2003, it cost thousands of jobs and millions of dollars in states across the country.

Apart from this incoherent policy signal for investors, there are further aspects of the PTC that are influential in the structure of the overall wind market, as well as locally owned schemes. The nature of the incentive means that companies or individuals with large tax liabilities have to be the main investors. Hence, typically, small developers cannot take full advantage of the PTC. In other words, the instrument prevents small- and medium-sized investors from being the owners of wind energy installations during the first ten years of the project. However, the question of getting capital does not seem to be the only problem: the nature of the PTC can also create specific difficulties for locally owned schemes (see Toke 2007). According to Mark Willers, the prime mover behind a 3.8-MW project in Buffalo Ridge, Minnesota:

> [T]he most difficult step in these projects was not finding capital for the hardware, consultants and legal fees because farmers were enthusiastic about investing from the very beginning.[. . .] The biggest obstacle, rather, was negotiating a power purchase agreement, a crucial step to moving any wind project forward. (Windustry 2002).

One way to use the PTC for small- and medium-sized investors, despite these difficult framework conditions, is through tax syndication. Through the building of partnerships, the syndication strategy creates opportunities for project developers to retain ownership and management control of the wind-power facility. In case a partner in need of the tax credit could be found, there is no need for the developer to sell the entire project. According to the federal tax law, such a partnering strategy is possible because more than one owner of a wind-power plant is allowed. The partners can share the PTC benefits in proportion to their ownership interest in the plant's gross sales. Such examples can provide some insights into how players at the local level can be enabled to make use of the benefits of this national instrument to build up local capacities.

WIND ENERGY AS A SUBJECT OF STATE REGULATION

A number of studies on existing promotional activities for the expansion of renewable energies and wind energy demonstrate that manifold approaches are currently used at a state level. Public benefit funds (PBF), for example, aim to assure continued support for renewable energy resources and energy efficiency initiatives, and are often set up in the course of electric utility restructuring processes. More than a dozen states have established renewable energy funds, totalling around $3.5 billion set aside for renewables. In 2003, these states united into Clean Energy States Alliance (CESA), a non-profit programme that fosters a multistate approach for promoting renewables development.

However, there are calculations that more than half of the new wind-energy investments are the result of state mandates to produce clean wind energy. Twenty-three states and the District of Columbia have so-called RPS—also known as renewable electricity standard (RES)—to ensure that provides a certain amount of the electricity to the market (Union of Concerned Scientists 2004). When the utility fails to meet the target, it needs to purchase RPS attributes equal in quantity to the shortfall or pay penalties. These payments could be channelled into public funds to finance renewable energy projects. Against the background of the successful history of trading emission certificates (see, e.g., Aulisi et al. 2000), the RPS is sometimes accompanied by a respective market system. The market approach is based on the rationale that utilities that over-fulfil their prescribed targets in the proportion of renewable energies can sell their credits to companies that have not been able to achieve their targets. It is worth noting that the instrument of feed-in tariffs that has become widely accepted in Europe (cf. Bechberger and Reiche 2006) has not been applied in the United States. This is especially surprising, since the establishment of this instrument in California in the 1980s significantly influenced the increased use of renewable energies. One reason for the reluctance to adopt feed-in tariffs today is the fact that it is difficult to adjust the level of payments to current market developments due to a lack of flexibility (Center for Resource Solution 2002: 4–5).

The proponents of an RPS argue that the main advantages of this instrument are twofold: First, this approach offers a sound basis for companies to make long-term investment decisions. Second, the fulfilment of targets to increase the envisaged proportion of renewable energies could be ensured by an effective compliance system. Of course, the functioning of the systems depends *inter alia* on the amount of penalties to be paid when the target is not achieved. As it has already turned out in some states, the implementation of the system can cause processes of policy learning. This could result in step-by-step improvements of the effectiveness of the instrument.

An analysis of the diffusion process of RPS within the United States demonstrates that, since 2000, the number of states that have adopted an RPS has reduplicated (Tänzler 2006). In 2004 alone, five states established an RPS. Regarding the regional distribution of RPS adoptions, four centres of innovations could be identified within the United States. Six southwestern states adopted portfolio standards between 1999 and 2004. It is worth noting that it is not—as might be expected—California that acted as an early mover, but Texas. Three midwestern states adopted an RPS. Among these states, Iowa—the first state to establish an RPS, in 1991—is the frontrunner. Finally, there are nine states in the northeast of the United States with an RPS. Three of four states in New England established the instrument during the 1990s. The remaining five Mid-Atlantic states, including Washington, D.C., mainly adopted their RPS in 2004. It is interesting to note that eight states introduced an RPS in the course of processes to deregulate their energy sectors. This context might facilitate the establishment of measures to promote renewable energies because, during negotiations of an overall policy package, it is easier for proponents of a certain energy source to articulate their interests and arguments, and to achieve that, specific provisions find their way into final legislation.

For the example of wind energy, the outstanding position of Texas is especially interesting. At the end of the nineties *Texas*—being among the early movers—developed initiatives to promote wind energy and other renewable sources in order to retain its status as "energy state". This status was in danger due the high level of energy consumption—the state even became a net importer of energy. It was then-Governor George W. Bush who introduced an RPS, combined with the set up of a trading system for renewable energy credits in 1999. Since the state has an enormous potential for wind energy, this instrument was implemented to accelerate the installation of wind-energy facilities. The introduction and further expansion of the RPS has been justified with the need to secure the state's energy supply and hence improve energy security. Moreover, decision makers pointed out the positive effects on the job market, emphasizing the social dimension of renewable energy promotion. In order to build awareness for the necessity of this political decision among the population of Texas the introduction of the RPS was accompanied by a broad dialogue process (Rabe 2002: 12–14). The interim results have exceeded all expectations. In 2004, capacities of renewable energy in the form of wind energy were installed equalling 1,100 MW (up from an initial capacity of 400 MW in 2002). That means that Texas was already well beyond the interim target for 2005 (850 MW). At the end of 2006, Texas passed California as the state with the greatest amount of wind energy installed (2,768 MW).

How relevant is the diffusion of RPS for an ecological transformation, and to what extent can the activities at the state level compensate for the lack of action at the national level regarding the support for activities at the local level? According to the information provided by the Union of Concerned Scientists, the targets of the RPS will support the generation of renewable energy amounting to 25,550 MW until 2017 (Union of Concerned Scientists 2005). This represents enough clean power to meet the electricity needs of 16.9 million typical US homes, and an increase of 192 per cent compared to the 1997 total production in the United States (excluding hydropower). In addition, these measures will help to reduce greenhouse gas emissions by 64.3 million metric tons every year. The expansion of renewable energy use is therefore also an important instrument of US climate policy that, at present, is mainly driven by policies and measures adopted at the state level (cf. Tänzler and Carius 2004). The increasing influence of RPS on the US energy mix could also be derived from the fact that two-thirds of the wind power installed between 1998 and 2003 was generated in states with such a standard (Union of Concerned Scientists 2005: 2). However, the RPS, as such, is only a minor trigger of locally owned wind-power installations. So far, the RPS instrument as public policy tool has tended to focus primarily on achieving the quantitative target of expanding renewable energy production. New, more qualitative-related objectives, such as promoting rural economic development through the promotion of renewable energy, have largely been overlooked (Morris 2007).

LOCAL OWNERSHIP OF WIND ENERGY

The discussion of dominating instruments for promotion of renewable energies, and wind energy as a specific case at the national as well state level, indicated that they are not necessarily in favour of locally owned wind-power installations. This is especially true in regard to PTCs. RPS might, at least to a certain extent, empower local owners, depending on how ambitious the targets for utilities are set and if the RPS is accompanied by specific provisions reflecting the challenge of rural development. However, political priorities so far have been focused on the establishment of the wind-energy sector as a whole. These results meet the expectation one might have given the US's reputation as a country dominated by corporate interests. However, such a perspective neglects the importance of local entrepreneurship as an economic, social, and cultural force during

American history. In the following sections, we illustrate this vital role of local ownership for the future development of wind energy.

Benefits of Community Wind Projects

There are a number of benefits to community wind projects (cf. Morris 2007; Pahl 2007: chap. 3). First of all, the benefits for the rural economy and the local community are the most important reason to promote community wind projects. At the end of the day, local ownership means that more financial resources will remain in the rural community where they are urgently needed. There are numerous examples for projects by cities, municipalities, school districts, farmers, and even tribes. In addition, partnerships and networks are built in order to reduce costs and to gain a stronger position, e.g., to negotiate power purchase agreements.

Because of the smaller project size, wind farms can be connected to the transmission grid, where larger wind facilities cannot. This is important for regions in the United States like the Midwest where, so far, transmission has turned out to be difficult and, thus, states could not explore their great potential for wind energy. Small-scale wind farms can be integrated into the existing grid to serve the energy needs of local communities. Because the impact of the projects on the landscape is small, the overall permission process could be limited, thus saving both time and money. Reducing costs is a key issue because small-scale projects cannot gain the financial returns like large-scale ones can. Therefore, the establishment of liability corporations or other forms of partnership are useful to drive down costs and increase profits. It is important to note that landowners can earn significantly more money in case they own wind turbines than to lease land to large investors to build up the installations (Morris 2007).

Local Ownership in Minnesota

Minnesota is the leader in terms of local ownership of wind power. By the middle of 2006, there was around 150 MW of locally owned wind power installed, around half of that being farmer-owned and the rest being a mixture of individuals, schools, and municipally owned schemes. Farmers tend to establish schemes which are owned by what, in effect, amounts to farmer cooperatives. Key to this successful example is that Minnesota has a cooperative tradition which is also illustrated by the recent experience of forming cooperatives to produce ethanol from corn (Toke 2007). Farmers try to pool their investments to mobilise the production tax incentive and provide equity finance for the wind projects. Examples are the set up of two limited liability companies, Minwind I and Minwind II, which tried to maximize their ability to use tax credits. Key aspects of both "companies" comprising more than sixty investors have been voluntary and open membership, as well as democratic member control. Doing so, they explore the potential of a programme by the state of Minnesota to expand community wind power. In the late 1990s, Minnesota created a producer payment for locally owned wind turbines—a ten-year producer payment to facilities under a certain size. According to members of Minwind I and II, the negotiation of the purchase agreement was the most difficult part of the project. Barriers to overcome have been *inter alia* interconnection requirements, as well as the overall costs. Minwind I and II Whereas discussions with their rural electric cooperative were not successful, instead they entered into a fifteen-year contract with Alliant Energy, which was in need to satisfy the renewable energy standards in other states like Iowa or Wisconsin.

The utility tariff established by the state of Minnesota in 2005 further encourages locally owned wind enterprises. This community wind-power scheme offers around 3 cents/kWh to locally owned schemes, in addition to the PTC incentive. Owners receive the same amount of money over the life of the contract; however, they receive a higher payment in the early years in order to increase the cash flow at the beginning of the project. With this policy, state governor Tim Pawenty intends to achieve a target of installing 1,000 MW of community wind power by the year 2010.

This specific objective for local wind power is accompanied by Minnesota's RPS. In 1993, the state had enacted an agreement with the energy utility Xcel to ensure that the share of renewable energies increased, and this subsequently became legally binding in 2003. The standard has been tightened step by step and was expanded to other suppliers as well. Today, the provisions are aimed at an overall 19 per cent target for 2015. The specific targets for Xcel are the installation of capacities amounting to 125 MW generated through biomass and 1,125 MW through wind energy by 2011. Ironically, these provisions are part of a package deal, which, in turn, enables Xcel to store its nuclear waste close to the power plant (National Renewable Energy Laboratory 2003: 17; Minnesota Department of Commerce 2004: 8). Based on this policy mix to trigger the expansion of wind energy, basically through community wind power, but also with the help of utilities like Xcel, future increases are more than likely. Analysis of Minnesota's existing distribution and subtransmission capacity indicates that as much as 6,000 MW of additional capacity might be built without the need for new high-voltage transmission lines. That is about seven times the current wind-electricity output in Minnesota. Given Minnesota's cooperative tradition, further progress in this direction is more than likely.

Community Wind Power as a Means of Empowerment

There is a growing number of encouraging examples that indicate an increasing role of community wind power throughout the United States. Activities in Kansas and Colorado by "jwpw"(JW Prairie Wind Power) show that local entrepreneurs are very well aware of the success stories of ownership approaches, for example, in Germany. They are eager to learn from the experiences gained abroad and to try and trigger policy transfer, thus compensating for the lack of promotional government activities, like a nationwide feed-in tariff. Such developments can also be important factors of local democracy, as the example of the Lakota reservation in South Dakota shows (LaDuke 2007). In order to explore the enormous potential for wind energy in this region, the Rosebud Tribal Utility Authority was established, and the first wind project was developed in 2003. The 750-kW turbine is a prototype for a larger, 30-MW project currently planned and, at the same time, an encouraging symbol for the ongoing struggle of the tribal communities for local control through energy sovereignty. In order to use the wind potentials on the Indian reservations, a number of groups like the Native American Foundation try to organize trainings for the tribal communities to build capacities needed to increase renewable power production. Seen in this light, community wind power is also a way of local empowerment addressing, not only the ecological and economic potential of the sustainable energy supply, but also the social and cultural ones.

CONCLUSIONS

The example of local activities in the area of local wind power in Minnesota illustrates significant opportunities for developing rural areas by expanding the use of renewable energies. By providing new sources for income and environmentally sound energy, local communities can gain the chance of self-empowerment vis-à-vis big companies that established a dominant position within the US wind-energy market. Minnesota has the largest community wind-power programme in the United States, and the example shows clearly how important the support of the decision makers is in assisting the local communities. There are some incidents of growing support at the national level. Senator Ken Salazar (D-CO), for example, introduced an investment tax credit bill (S. 673 "Rural Wind Energy Development Act") that would provide $1,500 per 0.5 kW of capacity for small wind systems. There is also some state governmental support for local wind power in states like Iowa, Montana, or Oregon. However, despite this progress, no more than around 2 per cent of the more than 10,000 MW of wind power installed in the United States by summer 2006 is community-owned (Toke 2007).

The discussion of the existing regulatory framework outlined some of the reasons responsible for these limits. The analysis of the regulation to promote the expansion of wind energy throughout the United States indicates that, so far, the framework conditions have not been favourable for local wind-energy ownership. As a result, the "wind boom" of the past has merely generated business opportunities for big companies. The PTC as the major national incentive is a good example since, normally, project developers will not have enough tax liability to take full advantage of this instrument. However, there might also be strategies for local communities to use the incentives of tax credits. In order to retain control and owner-ship of the wind-power facility, a "partnering strategy" is needed. Since the PTC, or Federal Tax Law, does not prescribe single ownership, project partners can share both risks and benefits in proportion to the specific con-tribution to the plant in operation.

A further deficit of the PTC to support local ownership structures is that it excludes wind energy consumed on-site, although it has the same impact as energy exported to the grid. One might even argue that there is, in fact, more reason to support the wind facilities that serve on-site demand, since they give no reason to adjust the grid system to the fluctua-tions produced by the feed-in of wind energy. In the course of a revision of the PTC by Congress, the regulation should allow these facilities to be eligible for tax incentives. Finally, further empowerment of local owner-ship structures could be achieved by setting limits for the installed capac-ity that receive payments each year. However, such a provision would mean a strong intervention into the booming wind-energy market and is thus more than unlikely.

Regarding the RPS as a dominating instrument of promoting the expan-sion of renewable energies like wind power at the state level, the overall conditions can be more favourable for local players when the targets are ambitious. Utilities will then depend on additional capacities of wind energy to be installed in order to comply with its renewable energy standard. In this case, local communities can gain a more powerful position within the wind-energy market. In addition, as part of the RPS, a provision can be introduced that a certain amount of the energy produced should come from the state itself. This means that energy utilities would not be allowed to buy the complete amount of renewable energy needed for compliance from installations outside the state, but would promote local ownership struc-tures and, hence, promote rural development.

REFERENCES

Aulisi, A., et al. (2000) *From Obstacle to Opportunity: How Acid Rain Emissions Trading is Delivering Cleaner Air*, New York: Environmental Defense.

AWEA. (2007) 'Wind energy projects throughout the United States (as of 31st December 2006)'. Available at <www.awea.org>.

———. (2006) 'Wind energy: an untapped resource'. Available at <www.awea .org>.

———. (2005) 'Wind power outlook 2005: burgeoning wind energy market gener-ate new investment jobs'. Available at <www.awea.org>.

Battelle Pacific Northwest Laboratory. (1991) An Assessment of the available Windy Land Area and Wind Energy Potential in Contiguous United States, PNL.

Bechberger, M. and Reiche, D. (2006) 'Diffusion von Einspeisevergütungen in der EU-25 als instrumenteller Beitrag zur Verbreitung erneuerbarer Ener-gien', in M. Bechberger und D. Reiche (eds.) *Ökologische Transformation der Energiewirtschaft, Erfolgsbedingungen und Restriktionen*, Berlin: Erich Schmidt Verlag, 199–217.

Calvert, S. D. and Hock, S. M. (2001) 'United States wind energy growth and policy framework', paper presented at the European Wind Energy Conference, Copenhagen, 2–6 July.

Center for Resource Solutions. (2002) 'Project development and public policies: feed-in tariffs, green pricing, PBF, RPS'. Available at <www.resource-solutions.org>.

Ernst & Young. (2006) *Renewable Energy Country Attractiveness Indices*. London: Ernst & Young.

LaDuke, W. (2007) 'Local energy, local power', *Yes Magazine*, , Special issue, winter issue.

Minnesota Department of Commerce. (2004) 'Minnesota's leadership in renewable energy'. Available at <www.state.mn.us>.

Morris, D. (2007) *Energizing Rural America. Local Ownership of Renewable Energy Production is the Key*. Institute for Local Self-Reliance, Center for American Progress.

National Renewable Energy Laboratory (NREL). (2003) 'Policies and market factors driving wind power development in the United States', (NREL/TP-620–34599). Available at <www.nrel.gov>.

New York Times. (2005) 28th July 2005.

Pahl, G. (2007) *The Citizen-Powered Energy Handbook*, Vermont: Chelsea Green Publishing.

Rabe, B. G. (2002) 'Greenhouse & statehouse: the evolving state government role in climate change', prepared for the Pew Center on Global Climate Change, Washington, D.C.

REPP. (2004) 'Wind turbine development—location of manufacturing activity: technical report'. Available at <http://www.repp.org/articles/static/1/binaries/WindLocator.pdf>.

Tänzler, D. (2006) 'Die Förderung erneuerbarer Energien im Strommarkt der USA: Der Ansatz des Renewable Energy Portfolio Standard', in M. Bechberger und D. Reiche (eds.) *Ökologische Transformation der Energiewirtschaft, Erfolgsbedingungen und Restriktionen*, Berlin: Erich Schmidt Verlag, 219–38.

Tänzler, D. and Carius, A. (2004) 'Prospects for a transatlantic climate policy', *Journal of Transatlantic Studies*, 2(2): 209–26.

Toke, D. (2007) 'Supporting renewables: local ownership, wind power and sustainable finance', in D. Elliott, *Sustainable Energy, Opportunities and Limitations*. Palgrave Macmilan (forthcoming).

Union of Concerned Scientists USA. (2004) 'Clean energy: renewable energy'. Available at <www.ucsusa.org>.

———. (2005) 'Fact sheet: renewable electricity standards at work in the States', Cambridge: Union of Concerned Scientists.

US National Energy Policy Development Group. (2001) 'National energy policy, reliable, affordable, and environmentally sound energy for America's future', Washington, D.C: US Government Printing Office.

Windustry. (2002) 'Minwind I & II: innovative farmer-owned wind projects', *Windustry Newsletter*, Fall. Available at <http://www.windustry.com/newsletter/2002FallNews.pdf>.

9 The Development of Wind Power in the Netherlands and Denmark

The Impact of Different Innovation Strategies and Policies

Linda M. Kamp

INTRODUCTION

Several Western countries started to develop renewable energy in the 1970s. The reasons for this development were the oil crisis and the Club of Rome report, which warned of imminent shortages of traditional energy sources like oil and gas. The renewable energy source that people had the highest expectations of was wind energy. Two of the countries that were involved in the development of wind energy were The Netherlands and Denmark. Both governments gave active support to this development. Furthermore, both countries have a comparable wind regime. However, the result of the development of wind energy in each country is very different. In the year 2000, Denmark had a flourishing wind-turbine industry, which produced wind turbines for the world market. Furthermore, at the end of the year 2000, the cumulative installed capacity of wind turbines in Denmark was 2,340 MW, and wind turbines produced 15 per cent of the electricity demand. In The Netherlands, the situation was far less rosy. Although ten to fifteen wind-turbine manufacturers were active on the Dutch market at the beginning of the 1980s, only one remained by the year 2000. Furthermore, at the end of the year 2000, only 442 MW of wind turbines had been installed in The Netherlands, the target for that year having been 2,000 MW.

What are the reasons for this difference in performance? Often, siting problems are mentioned as the reason why The Netherlands is lagging behind in the realization of wind-turbine capacity. However, this research reveals that The Netherlands was already lagging behind in the 1980s, when the siting problems were not as prominent. Therefore, other reasons were examined in order to explain the difference in performance.

The aim of this chapter is to investigate the reasons why The Netherlands was far less successful in developing wind power than the Danes in the period of 1970–2000. We look for the answer to this question by comparing the innovation strategies that were followed by the governments of both countries in order to set up this new technology.

The research methodology used is that of comparative case study research.[1] To achieve validity in a case study, it is important to use multiple sources of information. For this reason, a wide array of data sources were utilized: interviews, scientific and technical articles, conference proceedings, press releases, policy documents, technical reports, statistics, articles in popular magazines on renewable energy, and promotion material from manufacturers. The people interviewed were from various professions, including academic researchers, manufacturers, and wind turbine owners. For validity purposes, the triangulation method was adopted: testing and cross-checking the information gathered from various sources. Actors' statements were tested against statements by other actors and against written material. Furthermore, the method of 'participatory observation' was employed, by way of a three-month stay at the Dutch ECN[2] Research Centre and a three-month stay at the Danish Copenhagen Business School.

In this chapter, the results of the research will be presented. In the following section, the theoretical approach will be outlined by explaining the concept of 'innovation system' and the different strategies that can be followed to set up an innovation system. This will be followed by an overview of the Dutch case study before presenting the Danish case study. Both cases will be described in two parts: part one will focus on the large-scale innovation subsystem, and part two will focus on the small-scale innovation subsystem. The discussion that follows will explain why this distinction was made. The chapter concludes by offering ideas for further research.

THEORY: THE INNOVATION SYSTEM AND INNOVATION STRATEGIES

The Innovation System

The concept of an 'innovation system' was developed at the end of the 1980s and the beginning of the 1990s by Freeman (1987), Freeman and Lundvall (1988), Lundvall (1988, 1992), and Nelson (1993, 1994). It starts from the idea that innovations are often developed within systems formed by actors and organizations. Companies, governments, universities, banks, consumers, and other organizations all contribute in different and interactive ways to the innovation process. These actors and organizations, the relationships between them, and the institutions influencing them, together form the innovation system (Carlsson et al. 2002).

Because 'innovation system' is such a broad concept, authors can define it differently and stress the element(s) they consider the most important. However, there is a set of characteristics upon which all researchers agree. In a study of a specific innovation system, these characteristics can be used as guidelines to build the theoretical framework. Lundvall summarizes them as follows (1992):

- The central focus is on technological innovation, but organizational and institutional changes are considered important as well.
- Innovation systems in various countries are claimed to be different, and it is important to study these differences.
- The viewpoint is holistic; in other words, many determinants and their relationships are included in the analysis.
- A historical perspective is used. Innovation is seen as an evolutionary and path-dependent process. Therefore, innovation can be understood best when the historical development is taken into consideration.
- Because innovation is path-dependent and open-ended, it is not possible to define an optimal innovation system. Since the system keeps changing, it is possible that, at one moment, one system is better suited for stimulating certain technological developments, whereas later on, another system performs better.
- Innovation is regarded as an interactive process. Firms do not innovate in isolation, but in interaction with other actors. Innovation is influenced not only by the structures and the actors in the system, but also by the interaction between them.
- The importance of learning, and especially of interactive learning, is stressed. The accumulation of knowledge and skills is considered to be crucial. The focus is on the interactivity between the structures and the actors in the system, and on the learning processes between them.
- Innovation systems consist of organizations and institutions on the one hand, and interacting actors on the other hand. Therefore, a structural view is combined with an actor-oriented view.

In short, an innovation system consists of four main components:

- the technological innovation, in this case wind turbines;
- the actors involved;
- the organizations and institutions involved; and
- the learning processes between the actors.

Developing a completely new technology implies developing a whole new innovation system. Apart from the technological innovation that needs to be initiated, developed, and fostered, actors need to be involved, organizations and institutions need to be set up, and learning processes between the actors need to be facilitated. These learning processes are especially important to 'glue the components of the innovation system together', to get the actors involved, and to make them develop a shared vision regarding the future of the technology developed. Learning processes help the network of actors involved become tighter.

Innovation strategies

Setting up an innovation system can be done in various ways, using different strategies. For instance, a top-down strategy or a bottom-up strategy can be used. A top-down strategy entails an active involvement from the initiating actor—in this case, the national government—in setting up the innovation system, while a bottom-up strategy leaves much more to the initiatives of the actors involved. Other examples of innovation strategies are science-push innovation strategies and demand-pull innovation strategies. Science-push strategies put a large emphasis on the development of new knowledge which is believed to result in the development of new technology. Such strategies are characterised by large expenditures on research and development (R&D). Demand-pull innovation strategies, on the other hand, start with the market. These strategies involve the stimulation of market formation. Demand from such a market is believed to stimulate the innovation process. Demand-pull innovation strategies are characterized by market or investment subsidies and other stimulation measures to develop a market.

In the remainder of this chapter, the cases of setting up a wind-power innovation system in The Netherlands and Denmark will be compared. It will be investigated to what extent the innovation systems and the innovation strategies differed in these two countries.

WIND-TURBINE DEVELOPMENT IN THE NETHERLANDS

The Large-Scale Wind-Turbine Innovation Subsystem

The Dutch NOW (Nationaal Onderzoeksprogramma Windenergie) programme, the National Research Programme on Wind Energy, started in 1976. Within this programme, subsidies were provided for R&D into the potential of wind energy in The Netherlands, and into wind-turbine building. The goal of this programme was to develop a significant wind-turbine capacity in The Netherlands, consisting of a large number of large wind turbines (Pelser 1981; BEOP 1981). As a result of this research programme, two innovation subsystems developed: the large-scale wind-turbine innovation subsystem and the small-scale wind-turbine innovation subsystem.

In the Dutch large-scale wind-turbine innovation subsystem, the paradigm was, from the 1970s, directed toward building many large wind turbines in The Netherlands. In this subsystem, a large amount of theoretical knowledge on wind turbines was gained during research projects at the Delft and Eindhoven Universities of Technology and at the ECN research centre. This knowledge was merely based on aerodynamic knowledge from the aerospace industry. Design models for wind turbines were developed, and more applied research was performed on for instance structural dynamics and aerodynamics of wind turbines. Slowly, it became clear that wind turbines had their own characteristics, and that models and theories from the aerospace industry could not be used without significant adjustment. Furthermore, in the late 1970s and the early 1980s, research into tipvanes was performed by the Delft University of Technology. Theoretical research had shown that small vanes on the tips of wind-turbine blades could lead to a 60–70 per cent higher energy yield (Van Holten 1978; BEOP 1981). Researchers at the Delft University of Technology attempted to build tipvanes that would produce this effect in practice. Disappointingly, they did not succeed. The major part of the knowledge within this subsystem was based on R&D.

The knowledge gained was applied to three wind turbine prototypes and two commercial wind turbines. The turbine prototypes that were built were two vertical-axis turbines, or VATs, and one horizontal-axis turbines, or HATs. Test results were to prove which turbine type was the best in terms of energy yields and efficiency (Pelser 1981).[3] In 1981, a HAT-turbine, the HAT-25, was built by Stork, Fokker, Holec, and Rademakers. It had a capacity of 300 kW and a rotor diameter of 25 m. As with the VAT prototypes, the main goal of the HAT-25 project was to obtain measurement results and operational experience (Sens 1981). The prototype was equipped with two blades and a very advanced regulation system. It could be operated with four regulating procedures (Dekker 2000; Pelser 1981). In this way, which regulating procedure functioned best could be tested. Measurement results of the turbine were satisfactory, and Stork decided to develop a commercial turbine on the basis of the HAT-25 prototype. Three of these commercial turbines, called the Newecs-25, were sold to utilities in The Netherlands and Curaçao.

Within this subsystem, the actors in the manufacturing companies Fokker and Stork, and the actors in the research institute and the universities of technology were completely in line with each other: they shared the goal of building a large number of large wind turbines that, together would make a significant contribution to the national energy provision (Dekker 2000; Van Holten 2000; Pelser 1981). This made cooperation and knowledge exchange between them very fruitful.

The intended turbine buyers within this subsystem were electricity production companies. The aim was to build large wind-power stations, which would deliver electricity to the electricity grid, analogous to other electricity production units, which were also owned by electricity production companies. However, in the design and manufacturing of the wind turbines, the aimed buyers were not involved. The design and manufacturing of the wind turbines was an ultimate science-push process: the turbines were developed by large companies and research institutes, and were based on scientific knowledge.

The electricity production companies, although they were the intended buyers, were not very enthusiastic about wind energy. They were of the opinion that only a maximum capacity of 650 MWe of wind turbines could be fitted into the electricity grid and not the thousands of MWe that ECN and other research institutes mentioned. Some electricity production companies, like those in Zeeland, Schiedam and Curaçao, were willing to try operating a wind turbine. They each bought a Newecs-25 turbine produced by Stork. However, because these turbines were not tested satisfactorily, they had a lot of operational problems (Verbruggen 2000). These problems were not good for the electricity sector's opinion of wind energy. Stork also built a HAT with a capacity of 1 MW and a rotor diameter of 45 m, the Newecs-45 (Hensing and Overbeek 1985). This turbine was meant as an in-between step toward a 3-MW turbine, which had been calculated to be the most cost-effective turbine (Van Holten 2000).[4] Only one Newecs-45 turbine was sold. Like the Newecs-25, it suffered many operational problems (Verbruggen 2000). Because only a limited number of turbines was built, only limited knowledge was gained.

In 1982, at the insistence of the Ministry of Economic Affairs, the SEP[5] (the Co-operation of Electricity Production Companies) became involved in the large-scale wind-energy subsystem. The SEP agreed to be involved in the development of a pilot wind-power station: the Sexbierum wind-power station. This time, the SEP was very much involved in the design and manufacturing of the wind turbines. Therefore, in this project, the subsystem was complete. The turbines of the wind-power station were produced by Holec. The design and building of the wind turbines, however, had a number of problems, resulting in a significant delay of the project and in even less enthusiasm about wind energy in the electricity sector (Hutting 2000; Toussaint 2000; Verbruggen 2000).

Because of the many problems, the great financial risks, and the small home market, the large companies in the large-scale wind-turbine innovation subsystem—Fokker, Stork, and Holec—stopped producing wind turbines in the mid-1980s. After the mid-1980s, the aim of the Dutch wind-energy policy makers was to make the knowledge developed in the large-scale wind-turbine innovation subsystem applicable to the small turbine manufacturers. In this way, in the eyes of the policy makers, the goal of developing a significant wind-turbine capacity in The Netherlands could still be reached (NEOM 1986).

The Small-Scale Wind-Turbine Innovation Subsystem

In the period of 1976–1980, about ten small companies in The Netherlands started to manufacture wind turbines. They became interested in wind turbines because R&D subsidies into wind energy and wind turbines had been made available by the National Research Programme on Wind Energy. The small companies all had different manufacturing histories, such as making steel constructions or polyester yachts and manufacturing farming equipment (Stam 2000; Dutch manufacturers, a.n.).

In the small-scale wind-turbine innovation subsystem, the knowledge developed was, in contrast with the large-scale wind-energy innovation subsystem, based on learning-by-doing instead of R&D. By way of trial and error, small wind turbines were built at first. These turbines were gradually improved and scaled up. Because the turbines were sold in the vicinity of the manufacturing companies, problems were observed and solved quickly in interaction with the users, enabling the manufacturer to learn from these problems (Boersma 2001).

In the beginning, the turbine manufacturers encountered many difficulties in building reliable wind turbines. Therefore, ECN set up a test field in 1981. On this test field, the turbines were tested and the manufacturers received indications on what was to be improved in their turbine (Stam et al. 1983). Because of the danger of competition distortion, ECN was not allowed to give specific indications on how to improve the wind turbines (Stam 2000). And the turbine manufacturers received no help at all from each other: they considered each other as competitors and were not willing to share any knowledge on how they built wind turbines (Stam 2000).

Another problem that the Dutch wind-turbine manufacturers encountered was the small size of the domestic market. The Dutch market was, and remained, small because, in The Netherlands, no investment subsidies were available for wind-turbine buyers. Therefore, payback times for wind turbines were large (Werkgroep Duurzaam Energieplan 1984). Furthermore, wind-turbine owners received only small buyback tariffs for the electricity they delivered to the grid. These two factors made buying wind turbines financially unattractive (Langenbach 2000; Blok, K. Personal communication, Professor at Department of Science, Technology and Society at Utrecht University, 2000). The main turbine buyers were renewable energy advocates and farmers (CEA 1993).

Gradually, the wind turbines became better and larger. However, this process went slower in The Netherlands than in Denmark. This caused the inability of Dutch manufacturers to compete with the Danes on the large California market.[6] This factor, together with the small size of the Dutch market, caused financial problems for the manufacturers in the mid-1980s.

From the mid-1980s, wind-energy policy started to get actively involved in the activities of the small turbine builders. Because the wind-turbine producers in the large-scale wind-turbine innovation subsystem had ceased their activities, the small turbine builders were to be responsible for the production of efficient wind turbines that could produce a significant part of the Dutch electricity supply. Therefore, from the mid-1980s onward, the research institutes and universities of technology could only receive R&D subsidies if they made their research results applicable for the small turbine builders (NEOM 1986). Furthermore, investment subsidies were introduced. This increased the Dutch home market because utilities started to show an interest in buying wind turbines (IEA 1987).

From then on, there were many attempts to incorporate the results of R&D in the design and manufacturing process of the small wind-turbine builders. Researchers from research institutes and Stork worked together with small wind-turbine builders in improving and scaling up their wind turbines. However, this cooperation was sometimes difficult, since the paradigms and approaches were completely different. This severely limited knowledge exchange. The researchers were academic-trained, science-based thinkers, whereas the manufacturers were 'builders' (Boersma 2001; Verbruggen 2000).

One manufacturer, Lagerweij, had a different approach. This manufacturer did not accept direct interference from researchers in his design process, but he did use knowledge obtained by R&D by way of picking up of the ideas of personal contacts in Delft. This resulted in gradual improvements in his small 75-kW/80-kW turbines, for which he used, for instance, ideas on flexible components developed at Delft University of Technology (Van Holten 2000; Boersma 2001).

In the 1990s, the Dutch manufacturers had severe difficulties. There were three main reasons. The first one was the drive towards rapid up-scaling and the problems involved with incorporating advanced concepts and components in the wind turbines. The second reason was the small Dutch home market. And the third reason was the competition from the Danish manufacturers, who offered better products. In the year 2000, only one Dutch turbine builder, Lagerweij, remained.

Now, let us reflect on the above discussion. What were the characteristics of the wind-turbine innovation system, in terms of the actors involved and the learning processes, and what were the characteristics of the innovation strategy in The Netherlands? To answer this question, we will distinguish between the large-scale wind-turbine innovation subsystem and the small-scale wind-turbine innovation subsystem.

In the development of large wind turbines, the focus was on the fast development of a high number of large wind turbines, based on advanced scientific concepts. Large amounts of R&D subsidies were available. This was clearly a science-push strategy. The main actors involved were the Dutch universities of technology; the research centre, ECN; and the large turbine manufacturing companies, Fokker and Stork. The users of the turbines were utilities. Interactive learning between the companies and the researchers went very well because they shared the same paradigm of research-driven technology development. However, hardly any interactive learning with the turbine users—the utilities—occurred. First, because the market was very small (only four turbines sold); and second, because the utilities had a very negative opinion of wind energy. They preferred large-scale power plants fired by gas or nuclear energy and had little trust in wind turbines. After the many operational problems occurred, they became more and more reluctant to cooperate in knowledge exchange. This resulted in the development of scientific articles and models, but not in the development of wind turbines that worked well. It turned out that the fast up-scaling of wind turbines was more difficult than foreseen. The science-push approach was clearly not sufficient for the development of wind turbines.

In the development of small wind turbines, the focus was on the gradual up-scaling of small wind turbines, based on learning-by-doing and trial and error. Also, here, the main innovation strategy was the science-push approach. The market was not stimulated at all until 1986, and the only subsidies available were R&D subsidies. Furthermore, after 1986 it was explicitly attempted to incorporate the insights of science in the wind-turbine innovation process. The main actors were small manufacturing companies and the owners of the wind turbines. Also, ECN was involved via the test field. Interactive learning occurred between turbine manufacturers and owners, which resulted in fast problem solving and the gradual improvement and scaling up of the wind turbines. Also, with ECN, interactive learning occurred on the test field. However, this remained limited to the transfer of general knowledge. The interactive learning process between researchers and turbine developers after 1986 went very badly. Because of their very different backgrounds and the different paradigms and concepts they used, these different actors did not succeed in transforming scientific knowledge into well-developed wind turbines.

As to top-down versus bottom-up innovation strategies, in The Netherlands, clearly a top-down strategy was followed. The government and the Ministry of Economic Affairs steered the developments to a great extent, and they were even heavily involved in technical choices made by the companies. This active steering did not yield great results.

WIND-TURBINE DEVELOPMENT IN DENMARK

The Large-Scale Wind-Turbine Innovation Subsystem

In Denmark, as in The Netherlands, a development programme for wind energy was set up in the late 1970s. The main objective was to determine under what circumstances and to what degree wind energy could make a contribution to the Danish electricity supply systems (IEA 1985). The programme was called the Wind Power Programme. Within the programme, the research centre Risø and the Technical University of Denmark were to develop the knowledge needed to build large wind turbines. It was envisaged that large wind-turbine parks owned and operated by utilities would be built by a consortium of large Danish firms. The first measurement programme carried out was on the Gedser turbine. This wind turbine had been built in the 1950s by the Danish technician Johannes Juul and had proved to work. It had a capacity of 200 kW, a horizontal axis, and three blades (Karnøe 1991). The Danes did not have an aerospace industry, so they could not use knowledge gained in that sector.

In 1977, it was decided to build two 630-kW turbines on the basis of the specifications of the Gedser turbine, one with a pitch control system—as the Dutch HAT-25 prototype had—and one with a stall control system, as the Gedser turbine had. These two turbines were called the Nibe turbines (Karnøe 1991). No Danish company was interested in building the Nibe turbines. Therefore, the turbines were procured on a multicontract basis. Other actors involved were Risø, the Technical University of Denmark, and the SEAS utility, which partly financed the wind turbines (Van Est 1999). So, unlike in The Netherlands, the turbine owners in Denmark were involved from the beginning. As with the Dutch large wind turbines, there were many problems with the Nibe turbines, e.g., fatigue problems in the blades and problems with the gearbox (IEA 1985).

In the early 1980s, eight more large wind turbines were built. All these turbines had a pitch control system because the Nibe turbine with pitch control functioned better than that with stall control (IEA 1985). Here also, the utilities were involved from the beginning. All but one of these eight turbines were built by the company, Danish Wind Technology. This company was established in 1981 by the Danish Ministry of Energy and the SEAS utility (Van Est 1999).

All wind turbines suffered problems with the blades and the gearboxes (IEA 1990; Heymann 1998). Building wind turbines proved to be more expensive and risky than expected. Furthermore, no large Danish company appeared to be interested in building large turbines. In the early 1990s, the Danish state sold its shares in Danish Wind Technology (Karnøe 1991). By that time, the Danish small-scale wind-turbine innovation subsystem had demonstrated its ability to manufacture reliable, well-working wind turbines that were far cheaper than the wind turbines developed by the large-scale wind-turbine innovation subsystem.

In the Danish large-scale wind-turbine innovation subsystem, as in the Dutch system, the emphasis was on R&D, by way of research and measurement programmes. Knowledge exchange was more successful in the Danish large-scale wind-turbine innovation subsystem than in the Dutch because, in Denmark, the turbine buyers were involved from the beginning and shared paradigms of the research institutes and the turbine producers: building large turbines that could make a significant contribution to the Danish energy supply.

The Small-Scale Wind-Turbine Innovation Subsystem

In Denmark, as in The Netherlands, a small-scale wind-turbine innovation subsystem developed in the late 1970s, which was relatively independent of the wind-energy R&D programme set up by the Danish state. The first wind-turbine producers in this subsystem were small entrepreneurs who were adherents of the grassroots movement. These actors rediscovered the Gedser wind turbine and started developing wind turbines based on this example.

The adherents of the grassroots movement were attracted to the idea of small, locally owned and locally governed power production units, instead of large power production units that were centrally owned and centrally governed by the utilities. Furthermore, they saw renewable energy as an absolutely essential substitute for environment-polluting fossil fuels and for the nuclear power plants that were planned by the Danish utilities (Jørgensen and Karnøe 1995). A famous turbine developed by left-wing-oriented people was the Tvind turbine. It was developed by teachers and students of the Tvind school with the help of people with different educational backgrounds. The design, blade profile, and calculations were performed with the help of engineers (Karnøe 1991).

By 1978, about ten small wind-turbine companies had developed. Many of these had previously manufactured agricultural equipment. Their knowledge was based on the manufacturing of machines, and they learned slowly, by way of trial and error, how to manufacture and improve wind turbines (Karnøe and Garud 2001). They obtained their knowledge from previous wind turbines, like the Gedser and the Tvind turbine, from their own trial-and-error experience in the design and production of wind turbines, and from the turbine users—either individually or collectively—during the so-called Wind Meetings.[8] The turbine companies' design philosophy was to build wind turbines that worked reliably and safely (Karnøe 1995). They were under pressure to improve their turbines, especially because the performance of their turbines was made public in the magazine *Naturlig Energi*. This magazine was set up by the Danish Windmill Owners Association. In the magazine, the performance of the several types of turbines was disclosed. Because they were organized, the users created a strong selection environment for the first Danish turbine builders (Karnøe and Garud 2001; Heymann 1998).

All kinds of problems with, for instance, rotor speeds, gearboxes, burned out generators, and broken yaw systems were handled. Design and construction were based upon trial and error and simple rules of thumb (Karnøe 1995). The manufacturers were used to this way of working and they refrained from taking risks. Gradually, practical and hands-on knowledge about the poorly understood technology accumulated. On the basis of this knowledge, the design rules gradually improved. Design and development problems stemmed from turbine failures or from construction problems. The failures were often solved by making the turbines more solid, or, in other words, by 'throwing metal on the problem'. This method increased the lifetimes of the Danish wind turbines by limiting aerodynamic loads and preventing dynamic vibrations (Karnøe 1995).

In 1978, a wind-energy department was created at the Risø research centre. Because the research centre had only received financing for three years,

their strategy was to be of immediate service to the wind-turbine manufacturers. If the manufacturers could be convinced of the usefulness of the
research centre, it could, in the future, get its financing through orders from
the manufacturers (Dannemand Andersen 1993). Therefore, the goal of the
members of the research centre was not to develop the technically best wind
turbine, but to develop a wind-turbine industry. In this way, a tight network between wind-turbine producers, owners, and the Risø research centre developed within the small-scale wind-turbine innovation subsystem.
Because most turbine producers chose to follow the technology guidepost
formed by the Gedser turbine, they produced the same turbine type, i.e.,
a three-bladed, stall-regulated wind turbine (Karnøe 1991). This made the
exchange of knowledge very efficient. Therefore, knowledge exchange went
very well within the subsystem.

Another favourable circumstance was the size of the Danish home market. In 1979, investment subsidies were introduced (Van Est 1999). This
made buying a wind turbine far more attractive than in The Netherlands.
The relatively large home market gave the Danish turbine manufacturers
the opportunity to produce a relatively large number of wind turbines and
learn by doing during the process. Furthermore, the relatively large user
group, which had organized itself as the Windmill Owners Association,
was able to act as a strong party during negotiations on buy-back tariffs
with the utilities.

In the early 1980s, the size of the Danish home market decreased. However, at the same time, a very large market arose in California because
large investment subsidies for wind-turbine buyers were introduced
there (Van Est, 1999). Because the Danes produced relatively good wind
turbines, and were able to prove this with the statistics in the *Naturlig
Energi* magazine, they were able to capture a large part of the California
market. In 1985, they sold 2,000 wind turbines to California (Karnøe
and Garud 2001). This favoured knowledge development a great deal.
However, the demand in California was different from that in Denmark.
In California, the buyers wanted larger and more cost-effective wind
turbines (Van Est 1999). This forced the Danes to speed up technology
development and to sell turbines that had not yet been thoroughly tested
(Karnøe 1991). This resulted in severe technical problems for the Danish
manufacturers.

In 1986, the Californian investment subsidies expired. Exports declined
and came to a halt in 1988 (Gipe 1996). However, the Danish market
had started to grow after 1985. In that year, the utilities had signed a
100-MW agreement, which meant that they had to install 100 MW of
wind turbines within the next five years (Van Est 1999). This enabled
the Danish turbine manufacturers to make a new start. The Wind Turbine Guarantee Company was set up to guarantee the long-term financing
of large export projects (Van Est 1999). One of the conditions that the
manufacturers had to meet in order to qualify for the guarantees was that

their turbines had to be approved according to a new, harsher approval system (Hvidtfelt Nielsen 2001). The manufacturers were required to lay down their knowledge in a more formalized way (Dannemand Andersen 1993). Furthermore, they had to scale up and improve their turbines further because the utilities' demand was for relatively large and cost-effective wind turbines. Turbine design, therefore, gradually changed from a trial-and-error process to a more R&D-based, formalized process (Dannemand Andersen 1993). With the help of Risø, the Danish manufacturers succeeded in meeting the utilities' demand and building up a strong position on the world market.

Now, let us again reflect on the previous discussion. What were the characteristics of the wind-turbine innovation system in terms of the actors involved and the learning processes, and what were the characteristics of the innovation strategy in The Netherlands? To answer this question, it is helpful to distinguish between the large-scale wind-turbine innovation subsystem and the small-scale wind-turbine innovation subsystem.

In the development of large wind turbines, as in The Netherlands, the focus in Denmark was on large, science-based technology development: a clear science-push strategy. This subsystem was further characterised by a top-down innovation strategy because of significant government involvement. The network of actors involved in Denmark was more complete, which resulted in more knowledge exchange between turbine users and producers than in The Netherlands. However, the large costs and technical problems made this development come to a halt in the mid-1980s.

However, the development of small wind turbines was very successful in Denmark. The innovation system was complete and functioning well. Because of market subsidies, a large group of users developed. Therefore, many turbines could be produced, and a lot of knowledge was transferred between the turbine producers and users. Furthermore, the paradigm at the Risø research centre was more hands-on than science-based, especially in the 1980s. This made knowledge transfer between Risø and the other actors very effective. Gradually, this tight network of actors succeeded in building up a strong knowledge base and industry—one of the leading wind industries in the world. In terms of innovation strategy, we see that, in this subsystem, a bottom-up strategy was much more prevalent. Much more was left to the initiatives of the actors themselves: companies, turbine owners, and researchers. As to science-push versus market-pull, we see a gradual shift in time. Until the 1990s, the focus was clearly on market-pull: stimulation of market development, little attention for development of science, and input of science into the innovation process. However, this gradually changed, because, in time, the wind turbines became larger and larger and more and more complex machines. Therefore, the input of science became more and more important. Cooperation between turbine-producing companies and scientific researchers developed and professionalized in time.

CONCLUSIONS

The goal of this research was to investigate the reasons why The Netherlands was far less successful in developing wind power than Denmark in the period of 1970–2000. In answering this question, the innovation strategies that were followed by the governments of both countries to set up this new technology were compared. Which conclusions can be drawn from this historic case study for the future, especially for policies on renewable energy sources? The main conclusions on innovation strategies and innovation systems are summarized in Table 9.1.

Based on the case material, some very distinct conclusions about innovation strategies and innovation systems can be drawn. As to top-down versus bottom-up, it can be noted that the only case where the bottom-up strategy was followed was successful in developing a wind-turbine industry

Table 9.1 Main Conclusions on the Innovation Strategies and Innovation Systems in the Four Wind-Turbine Innovation Subsystems

	Top-down or bottom-up strategy	Science-push or demand-pull strategy	Completeness of innovation system	Main learning processes
Large-scale wind-turbine innovation subsystem in The Netherlands	Top-down	Science-push	Intended buyers not involved	R&D-based learning
Small-scale wind-turbine innovation subsystem in The Netherlands	Top-down	Mainly science-push	Small group of buyers; researchers marginally involved	Learning-by-interacting between companies and turbine owners
Large-scale wind-turbine innovation subsystem in Denmark	Top-down	Science-push	Intended buyers only marginally involved	R&D-based learning
Large-scale wind-turbine innovation subsystem in Denmark	Bottom-up	Mainly demand-pull, later on more and more science-push	Complete and well functioning	Learning-by-interacting between all actors involved

Source: Author generated.

with a strong position on the world market. An explanation for this is that a bottom-up strategy will make actors more involved and less passive when awaiting government actions. This will stimulate knowledge exchange between the actors involved.

As to science-push versus demand-pull, it can be identified that in the only successful subsystem, a mainly demand-pull strategy was used, especially in the beginning. The explanations for this are:

- Because wind turbines are very complex machines and need to function in rapidly changing wind conditions, building up a large experience with them 'in the field' is very important. Therefore, it is important to build up a large market at an early stage.
- This large market can, if it is well organized, have a large input in the innovation process, which will result in better and more market-adjusted products.

On the subject of innovation systems, it can be concluded that a complete and well-functioning innovation system is a prerequisite for successful innovation. This means that all major actors (technology producers, technology owners [or foreseen owners], researchers, and policy makers) have to be actively involved from an early stage. This will facilitate learning-by-interacting between all actors involved, which is another prerequisite for successful innovation.

Furthermore, based on the case material, other conclusions which can be drawn from the research include:

- Building up a strong home market is very important. So, setting up policies to stimulate the development of renewable energy sources should at least include the stimulation of market development. The best way to do this is subsidize per kilowatt-hour produced. This will stimulate technology developers to develop cost-effective technology. The existence of a strong home market is important for two reasons. First, it will enable technology producers to sell more. Second, it will promote knowledge exchange between owners and producers. This knowledge exchange will be more successful if the owners are organized, as in the case of the Danish small wind turbines.
- Often, technology is developed without taking into consideration the wishes of (future) owners. This was the case in the development of the Dutch and Danish large wind turbines. These turbines were developed based on scientific theories and models, without looking at who the owners were going to be and what they wanted. In The Netherlands, the foreseen owners of the large turbines were the utilities, who were not enthusiastic about wind energy at all. The technology was more or less forced upon them. This hindered knowledge exchange to a great extent. Another example is the

development of photovoltaic solar panels, which is also very much science-based. The wishes of actors, such as designers of buildings and future owners, are not taken into consideration at all. Changing this would result, in our view, in a larger market.

- The case of the large wind-turbine development shows that developing large machines in a constantly changing environment (different wind speeds) is difficult and risky. Therefore, thorough testing and taking small technological steps is important. The way the Dutch manufacturing company Stork underestimated the jump from a 300-kW to a 1-MW wind turbine was the reason for a lot of the problems with the 1-MW turbine. Therefore, designing offshore wind turbines with a lot of new science-based concepts for deep water is very risky. However, this is just what the Dutch development programme on offshore wind energy is striving for. Taking smaller steps from shallow to deep water and from proven technology to new concepts would reduce the risks significantly. And, since wind energy is not popular in the eyes of the general public it is important that the Dutch development programme succeeds in developing good, reliable turbines, and does not turn into a failure.

- The case of the Danish development of small wind turbines shows that building up a strong network and involving several kinds of actors is important. Because, in Denmark, the wind turbines were often owned by a whole village or large parts of a village, the siting problems were less severe than in The Netherlands. The villagers had both the advantages and the disadvantages of the wind turbines. The same is true for siting policy. It is important to involve policy makers at all levels—local, regional, and national. In The Netherlands, local policy makers were not involved in the wind turbine siting programme of 1991, which resulted in a lot of opposition from the municipal councils.

- Setting up long-term, consistent policy is important. Since, as it appeared from the cases, developing wind turbines is expensive and risky, it is important that financers can be sure of the subsidising schemes remaining in place for the coming years. Recently, we saw that both in Denmark and in The Netherlands subsidising schemes were stopped. This poses a great threat for the further development of wind turbines.

To what extent are the results of this research applicable to other cases? In summary, the general conclusions that can be drawn on setting up a wind-turbine innovation system in The Netherlands and Denmark are applicable to setting up such an innovation system in other countries as well. Furthermore, these conclusions, except for the third bullet, which is specifically about wind turbines, are applicable to other kinds of innovation systems as well. Not only those systems concerning other energy technologies, but also other kinds of technologies in general as well. This would be an interesting starting point for further research: applying this theoretical research method to other innovation systems, e.g., the innovation system for solar cells or some other nonenergy technology and comparing the set-up of such a system in two countries.

NOTES

1. Most of the case study research was done as part of a PhD research program, published in Kamp (2002).
2. ECN means in *Energie Onderzoekscentrum Nederland* Dutch, and Energy Research Centre Netherlands in English:.
3. Only two VAT turbines were built in The Netherlands. For more information on these turbines, see Kamp (2002) and Kamp et al. (2004).
4. A 3-MW turbine was never built in The Netherlands. Only a predesign study was performed (Kuijs 1983). Because of the problems with the Newecs-25 and the Newecs-45, the risk of building a 3-MW turbine was considered too high (IEA 1987).
5. SEP means *Samenwerkende Electriciteits Productiebedrijven* in Dutch, and Co-operation Electricity Producing Companies in English.
6. This market appeared in the early 1980s because large investment subsidies were made available for wind turbine buyers in California.
7. As from the 1990s, the small size of the Dutch market was also caused by siting problems.
8. During the Wind Meetings, knowledge and experience on wind turbines were shared between wind turbine manufacturers, owners, and researchers.

REFERENCES

BEOP. (1981) *Perspectieven voor windenergie, Nationaal Onderzoekprogramma voor Windenergie in Nederland 1976–1981, resultaten en aanbevelingen*, ECN, Petten.

Boersma. (2001) Personal communication. Lagerwey employee.

Carlsson, B. and Jacobsson, S. (1997) 'Diversity creation and technological systems: a technology policy perspective', in C. Edquist (ed.) *Systems of Innovation—Technologies, Institutions and Organizations*, London: Pinter Publishers. 266–294.

CEA. (1993) *CEA Database on the Wind Turbines in the Netherlands*, Rotterdam: CEA.

Dannemand Andersen, P. (1993) *En analyse af den teknologiske innovation i Dansk vindmølleindustri—Herunder prøvestationen for vindmøllers dobbeltrolle som forskningsinstitution og godkendende myndighed*, Copenhagen: Samfundslitte-ratur.

Dekker, J. W. M. (2000) Personal communication. Employee of ECN research centre, Petten.

Dutch manufacturers (a.n.) Leaflets from several Dutch manufacturers.

Freeman, C. and Lundvall, B. A. (1988) *Small Countries Facing the Technology Revolution* (eds.) London: Pinter Publishers.

Gipe, P. (1995) *Wind energy comes of age*. Wiley, New York.

Hensing, P. C. and. Overbeek, H. H. (1985) 'Nederlands grootste turbine operationeel in Wieringermeer', *Energiespectrum*, December: 254–60.

Heymann, M. (1998) 'Signs of hubris: the shaping of wind technology styles in Germany, Denmark and the United States, 1940–1990', *Technology and Culture*, 39: 641–670.

Hvidtfelt Nielsen, K. (2001) *Tilting at Windmills*, Academic Thesis, Århus University. PhD.

IEA. (1985) *Wind energy annual report 1984*, Paris: IEA.

———. (1987) *Wind energy annual report 1986*, Paris: IEA.

———. (1990) *Wind energy annual report 1989*, Paris: IEA.

Jørgensen, U. and Karnøe, P. (1995) 'The Danish wind-turbine story: technical solutions to political visions?', in A. Rip, T. Misa and J. Schot (eds.) *Managing Technology in Society: The Approach of Constructive Technology Assessment*, London: Pinter Publishers. 57–82.

Kamp, L. M., Smits, R. E. H. M. and Andriesse, C. D. (2004). 'Notions on learning applied to wind turbine development in the Netherlands and Denmark', *Energy Policy*, 32(14): 1625–37.

Kamp, L. M. (2002) *Learning in wind turbine development: A comparison between The Netherlands and Denmark*. Ph.D. Utrecht University.

Karnøe, P. (1991) *Dansk vindmølleindustri: En overraskende international succes; Om innovationer, industriudvikling og teknologipolitik*, Copenhagen: Samfundslitteratur.

Karnøe, P. (1995) 'Institutional interpretations and explanations of differences in American and Danish approaches to innovation', in W.R. Scott and S. Christensen (eds.) *The institutional construction of organizations*, Thousand Oaks: Sage Publications: 243–276.

Karnøe, P. and Garud, R. (2001), 'Path dependence and creation in the Danish wind turbine field', in J. Porac and M. Ventresca (eds.) *Social construction of markets and industries*, Oxford: Pergamon Press.

Kuijs A.C.M. (1983). Ontwikkeling van een megawatt-molen. *Energiespectrum* Oct/Nov 1983.

Langenbach, J. (2000) E-mail.

Lundvall, B. A. (1988) 'Innovations as an interactive process—from user-producer interaction to the national system of innovation', in G. Dosi et al. (eds.) *Technical Change and Economic Theory*, London: Pinter Publishers. 349–369.

Lundvall, B. A. (1992) *National Systems of Innovation—Towards a Theory of Innovation and Interactive Learning*, London: Pinter Publishers.

Nelson, R. R. (1993) *National Innovation Systems—A Comparative Analysis*, New York: Oxford University Press.

NEOM. (1986) *Integraal Programma Windenergie (IPW) 1986–1990*, Utrecht: NEOM.

Pelser, J. (1981) 'Evaluatie resultaten Nationaal Onderzoekprogramma Windenergie', *Energiespectrum*, June 1981.

Sens, P. F. (1981) 'Het Nationaal Onderzoekprogramma Windenergie', *Energiespectrum*, July/August: 172–7.

Stam W. J. (2000) Personal communication. Petten, ECN.

Stam, W. J., Beurskens, H. J. M. and Dragt, J. B. (1983) 'Het ECN windturbinetestveld: algemene ervaringen en werkwijze', *Energiespectrum*, October/November: 274–81.

Van Est, R. (1999) *Winds of Change: A Comparative Study of the Politics of Wind Energy Innovation in California and Denmark*, Utrecht: International Books.

Van Holten, T. (1978). 'Energiedichtheid van wind vergroten: het tipvane-systeem', *Nederlands tijdschrift voor natuurkunde*, March 1978 : 44.

——. (2000) Personal communication. Professor at Flight Mechanics & Propulsion Department at Delft University of Technology.

Verbruggen, T. (2000) Personal communication. Stork, Amsterdam.

Werkgroep Duurzaam Energieplan. (1984) *Teruglevertarieven voor windelektriciteit*, Delft: Werkgroep Duurzaam Energieplan.

Contributors

Susanne Agterbosch has presented her work at a number of international conferences and has published articles in journals such as *Energy Policy* and *Renewable and Sustainable Energy Reviews*. Currently, she works at Landschapsbeheer Gelderland, which is a nongovernmental organization involved in countryside management.

Morgan Bazilian is a special advisor on Energy and Climate to the Minister for Energy in Ireland. He has worked as a research scientist, policy analyst, and consultant in the commercial, academic, and government sectors.

Sylvia Breukers has worked at the Department of Innovation and Environmental Sciences. Since August 2008, she has been doing research at the Energy Research Centre Netherlands. She has presented her work at a number of international conferences, as well as in various top academic journals.

Valentina Dinica is a senior research fellow at the Center for Clean Technology and Environmental Policy, University of Twente, The Netherlands. She joined the institute in 1998. In recent years, she has conducted research on policy implementation processes under new modes of governance.

Brian Ó Gallachóir is a lecturer in Energy Engineering and Director of the Sustainable Energy Research Group in University College Cork, Ireland. He provides strategic advice to Sustainable Energy Ireland's Energy Policy Statistical Support Unit, represents Ireland on DGTREN's Energy Economists' Working Group, and is a member of the Irish Energy Research Council.

Linda M. Kamp is an assistant professor at Delft University of Technology, The Netherlands. She has published several book chapters and had several articles published in top academic journals.

David Lal is professor and dean at the Kazakh-British Technical University (Almaty, Kazakhstan) and his Chair is sponsored by HSBC Bank Kazakhstan. He is visiting Professor at the Robert Gordon University (Aberdeen, Scotland) and graduated with his BA, MBA and PhD Degrees from the University of Strathclyde (Glasgow Scotland). He has spent almost fourteen years in the electronics industry with several multinational organisations and he is heavily involved in teaching, training, consultancy and research within the finance and energy sectors.

Eamon McKeogh is a statutory lecturer in University College Cork's Department of Civil and Environmental Engineering and Director (Wind Energy) of the Sustainable Energy Research Group. He is the former Director of Sustainable Energy Ireland's Renewable Energy Information Office.

Afolabi Otitoju is a doctoral candidate at the Aberdeen Business School, Robert Gordon University, Scotland. His research is centred on the implementation of European Union renewable energy policy in Germany, The Netherlands, and the United Kingdom.

Peter A. Strachan is a professor in Corporate Environmental Management at the Aberdeen Business School, Scotland. He has published one book, many articles in top academic journals, and is the joint founding editor of the journal, *Progress in Industrial Ecology: An International Journal*.

Dennis Tänzler is a research fellow at Adelphi Research in Berlin, Germany. His research focuses on climate and energy policies. In 2007 and 2008 he worked with the Policy Planning of the German Foreign Office. He holds degrees in political science, as well as in North American studies and cultural sciences.

David Toke is a senior lecturer in Environmental Policy at the University of Birmingham, Birmingham, England. He has published four books, over thirty journal articles, and many chapters, reports, and journalistic articles published on environmental—especially energy-related—issues. His work is widely cited and influential in both academic and public policy circles.

Index

Printed in the United States
by Baker & Taylor Publisher Services